REMEMBER THE PRISONERS

HE CAME TO SET THE CAPTIVES FREE

REVEREND JOAQUIN R. LARRIBA

WESTBOW
PRESS®
A DIVISION OF THOMAS NELSON
& ZONDERVAN

This book is a work of non-fiction. Unless otherwise noted, the author and the publisher make no explicit guarantees as to the accuracy of the information contained in this book and in some cases, names of people and places have been altered to protect their privacy.

WestBow Press books may be ordered through booksellers or by contacting:

WestBow Press
A Division of Thomas Nelson & Zondervan
1663 Liberty Drive
Bloomington, IN 47403
www.westbowpress.com
1 (866) 928-1240

Because of the dynamic nature of the Internet, any web addresses or links contained in this book may have changed since publication and may no longer be valid. The views expressed in this work are solely those of the author and do not necessarily reflect the views of the publisher, and the publisher hereby disclaims any responsibility for them.

Any people depicted in stock imagery provided by Thinkstock are models, and such images are being used for illustrative purposes only.
Certain stock imagery © Thinkstock.

ISBN: 978-1-5127-4343-2 (sc)
ISBN: 978-1-5127-4344-9 (hc)
ISBN: 978-1-5127-4345-6 (e)

Library of Congress Control Number: 2016908212

Print information available on the last page.

WestBow Press rev. date: 05/23/2016

CONTENTS

DEDICATION

This book is dedicated to the Lord Jesus Christ and the Holy Spirit, without whom my life would still be in ruin. Lord Jesus, thank You for staying the course, even unto the cross, where You poured Yourself out on my behalf and that of all humanity. You alone are the true King who is worthy of all praise. No words can equate Your worth, and I fall miserably short in my attempt. I tremble at the knowledge of my sin in the light of Your holiness and am unworthy to even utter Your name. Nonetheless, You called me forth to proclaim Your goodness. Please accept, Lord Jesus, this book as a testimony to Your power and willingness to deliver one out of darkness and into the light. I love You, Lord.

Thank You, Holy Spirit, for never giving up on me, even though I made You chase me into every dark corner and filthy place. Thank You for revealing Jesus to me and making God's Word come alive to me. Thank You for bringing to remembrance the Word that saves, transforms, and comforts. Thank You for guiding, instructing, and leading me in a victorious life over sin and shame. Thank You for empowering and emboldening me to preach and magnify the name of Jesus Most High. Without You I would never have known the depths of revelation awaiting the hungry and thirsty. Without You I wouldn't know how to act or speak or love. Thank You, Lord.

This book is also dedicated to my wife and dearly departed mother. To Jennifer, my beloved wife, who has supported my ideas and put up with my many hours of writing and researching. Not only that, but she too sacrificed much time in the editing and typing of this work. Her contributions of time, effort, and money have all been pivotal in the accomplished efforts to get this book published. Thank you for loving me so completely, hon. I love you.

And to my mother who gave me life, who also never gave up on me though she, through many tears, prayed for the Lord to take me and end my suffering. How ironic that is, for I too fell to my knees and prayed the very same words when she was dying of cancer. Mom, I hope I have finally made you proud of me. You're the best mom ever. Please tell Jesus I said, "Hi." I love you.

The Spirit of the Lord G<small>OD</small> is upon me; because the L<small>ORD</small> hath anointed me to preach good tidings unto the meek; he hath sent me to bind up the brokenhearted, to proclaim liberty to the captives, and the opening of the prison to them that are bound;

(Isaiah 61:1 KJV)

FOREWORD

It is no accident that you are reading this book at this time in your life.

Joaquin wrote this book on behalf of those of you who may be, or have been, incarcerated.

Tears flowed down my cheeks as I read this book, as it is so much more than an encouraging book to the prisoner. For every one of us has had a prison experience, whether inside a state-run correctional facility or in a mental, emotional, or situational prison, and we have no clue as to how we arrived there, let alone how we get out.

For myself, I just couldn't get away from alcohol and all life had to offer. One night while riding home on my motorcycle, so drunk I couldn't see straight, I fell off it. Lying in the barrow pit, everything spinning, I looked up to the sky and declared, "There has to be more to this life than this." I began from that moment to experience God, even though I didn't know Him personally. I had no idea what changes lay just ahead. Reading this book caused me to remember my own prison and to be so thankful of how Jesus got ahold of my life and delivered me from my prison.

This book is written to bring the reader into a real-life encounter with the Lord Jesus Christ. I mean, consider this. Where else are you going to turn?

More drugs? More of the same lifestyle? You will most certainly end up in the same place you are in today. But as the book unfolds, it takes the reader into a "how-to" in having a real and loving relationship with Jesus, and the result will be life changing.

When you say, as the book describes, "Jesus, come into my heart," something happens from that moment forward forever. It may not seem like it at first, but just you watch and see what begins from there. The supernatural protection, the divine love, the changes, the wisdom—really, you will never be the same again.

Dear friend, please read this book with an open heart and an open mind. Allow Joaquin to share his story, one I'm sure you'll relate to. Let this be your guide on a journey of healing, deliverance, health, wholeness, right living, and love for your fellow man.

Enjoy, but remember, grab some tissues, for you will need them.

I love you, and I will be praying for you.

Blessings in Jesus's name,
Bishop Martin Pangburn

PREFACE

This book ultimately seeks to glorify and magnify the Lord Jesus Christ. It's not the author's intention to sway the reader one way or the other on any mainline doctrinal or denominational views. The theology of this book is born out of one man's deliverance from drugs and alcohol, and from the lifestyle that goes with them. It is *my story* of how God rescued *me* and revealed Himself to *me*. The teaching or preaching elements that follow circumstantial experiences are *my* interpretations of the mysteries of God and His willingness to deliver me out of those circumstances.

It *is* the author's intention to draw readers into their own dynamic and living relationship with Jesus Christ by identifying his current situation with their past experiences. You don't need to be a prisoner to glean eternal truths from this book, but the truths I received were learned while in prison and ultimately transferred to the outside world, where I maintain a victorious life.

Though there will be obvious differences on certain doctrinal issues, we can all agree on these truths: A life was transformed from death to life. Jesus cared enough to die, even for the likes of me. There is only one God as revealed in the Scriptures as three distinct persons: Father, Son, and Holy Spirit. Unregenerate man is separated from God by sin, and the penalty for sin is death. God has made a way back to Him through the propitiatory sacrifice of His Son, Jesus, the Christ, through whom we have the forgiveness of sins. Jesus *is* God incarnate. He suffered, died, was buried, rose again, and is now seated at the right hand of power, making intercession for us even now. And He is coming back soon!

It is the return of the King and the coming judgment that most greatly concern the author. We know, based on the brevity of life, that every moment counts and that the next moment isn't promised. Time as we know and understand it is winding down, soon to disappear altogether as we step into eternity.

Eternity: the expanse of existence beyond time and space. It is infinite, without beginning or end, outside the constraints of this paradigm we call our universe. Since the possibility exists (and according to the Scriptures it does) that both souls and physical bodies will ultimately enter into eternity, it is of the utmost importance to the author to announce the imminent return of the judge of all the earth. There will either be an eternity with God in His glory or one that is destitute, void of His presence, in a place called hell that was designed for the Devil and his angels. Either way, eternity awaits us all.

For the unsaved, this subject is too dire to be suppressed; to the saved it's a timeless message of hope. To the author, my discovery of this truth led to the relentless pursuit to tell all who would hear.

Rev. Joaquin R. Larriba

ACKNOWLEDGMENTS

I would like to thank all the folks who made this book possible by their monetary contributions to publishing costs: friends, family, the body of Christ in denominations outside of and including my own, local businesses, and of course, my darling Jen.

I would also like to acknowledge Brita Hammit, who gave me helpful insights and brought balance to certain elements. She was full of encouragement and energy from the first moment we spoke. God bless you in your endeavors.

I would like to make special mention of Pastor Kirk Anderson, whose generosity and willingness to cross denominational borders and extend to me the right hand of fellowship encouraged me beyond measure.

And for my final but most important acknowledgment, I want to thank Mr. Doyle Wayne Williams, my father in Christ who has begotten me by the gospel of our Lord. No other human being save the Lord Himself has contributed more to this book by way of direct influence than Mr. Williams. It was his fierce dedication to resurrecting the image of Christ in me and his tireless effort in ministry that have played such a crucial role in the fruition of this work. This book is a testimony to one man's love for his fellow man and his deep understanding of the calling on his life as a minister of Jesus Christ. No other minister I have ever met bar none has a more profound sense of duty in awakening the spirit of man within him. Christ called, and he answered. Once a bond like this is formed, it cannot be broken, for Jesus is at the core. You, Doyle, are my father, and I am proud to be your son. Amen.

INTRODUCTION

If you or a loved one is suffering from the consequences of a broken life due to drugs and alcohol, resulting in jail or prison time, then this book is for you. If you find yourself unable to escape the wreckage of your past and want to be freed from the chains that bind you, then this book is for you.

Inside the chapters of this book you will laugh and cry. You will discover things about yourself that will give you the advantage in life for years to come. The knowledge that you learn here will be life changing and permanent, catapulting you forward into victory over drugs and alcohol, and over the lifestyle that goes with them. Shame, guilt, and self-destructive behaviors will be obliterated with this new knowledge.

- Chapter one reveals the importance and freedom that come from being brutally honest with yourself.
- Chapter two explores identities and how they are forged.
- Chapter three delves fearlessly into humanity's greatest need.
- Real-life stories uncover the raw truth about broken hearts and God's great desire and willingness to heal and restore.

Rock-solid doctrine and revelatory insight bring fresh interpretation to the Holy Scriptures, granting you, the reader, a profound look at age-old questions. A scholarly approach mixed with good old-fashion storytelling affords you the best of both worlds.

I wrote this book because people are hurting and looking for help and a word of encouragement from someone who has been there. I wrote this book for you, the inmate, and you, the loved one, to give you hope and direction.

Sample excerpt from Chapter 1:

> It is my fervent prayer that this book helps you to rediscover yourself—and more importantly, that it helps you to step into your greatness. I promise you that if you read this book from cover to cover and apply what you've learned to your life, your heart will be touched, your mind will be opened, miracles will happen, and lives will be restored.
>
> In some cases, restoration will come seemingly overnight. Some will be restored twofold; some, a hundredfold. Much depends on your willingness to participate. Remember when I said, "Right about now you would say or do just about anything to get out of jail and out of trouble, but would you do what it takes?"

CHAPTER 1

LET'S BE HONEST

If you are reading this, it's because you're unsure and scared. Your freedom has been taken away from you, and you have no idea what the future holds. For some of you, it's your first time in jail. For others, you could be facing prison time—time away from your family and friends, girlfriends, boyfriends, husbands, or wives. This is time you can never get back. For the rest of the world, things go on and continue day in and day out. But for you, time stands still. Some of you are lucky enough to make phone calls and receive mail. Others aren't so lucky. Their people won't accept the phone calls or are so fed up with them that they won't write, cutting them off altogether.

Those of you who are lucky enough to make phone calls and get mail get a boost of hope by connecting to the outside, but the end result is always the same—and that hope nevertheless fades as doubt and fear come creeping back into your mind. *Is he or she really being faithful to me? Who is taking my place as mom or dad? Who is with my girlfriend or boyfriend, or husband or wife, while I'm stuck rotting in here?*

Yes, fears and doubts always come creeping back in because you know friends and family have asked you time and again to stop drinking, drugging, doing crime, and cheating on them. Oh yes, doubt and fear will certainly return because, quite honestly, that is what you deserve— and you know it.

So why are you still reading this? I'll tell you why: because you're looking for hope, searching for something to give you peace and assurance in your time of need and separation. You're looking for something that can change your circumstances and grant you favor—something to plug that ever-widening hole of despair. Good, then. There is hope for you after all. Keep reading.

Everyone who ends up in jail says to himself or herself, "How did I end up here?" Some of you will cast the blame on everyone and everything else around you. "It's the cops' fault. The judge has it out for me. My probation officer doesn't really care what happens to me. The system set me up to fail. If my lady wouldn't have called the cops … Blah-blah-blah." Yeah, I know; it's everyone else's fault but yours, right? So ask yourself these questions and be honest with yourself. After all, it's just you reading this. No one else knows what you're thinking but you.

Questions: Who is the most important person in your life? Who means the most to you? Whose feelings, wants, and desires take first place in your life? We'll get back to these questions shortly.

So you have to admit that right about now you would do or say just about anything to get out of jail and out of trouble, but would you do what it takes?

Right now you are heartbroken and hurting. Everyone around you is too. Happiness is far from you, and the hope of a normal life seems unreachable—a distant, blurry vision that seems to get further and further away the harder you try. You need and are searching for someone to speak hope and encouragement into your circumstances and give you something to hold on to.

That is why I'm sharing my journey of hope and deliverance. There *is* a way out. There is hope. You can make it. What if I told you that you could put that drink down? What if I told you that you could be strong enough to resist the needle and spoon? What if I told you that crack or heroin would no longer have power over you? What if I told you that you could find peace? Wouldn't it be worth it just to hear me out? After all, if an alcoholic and a junkie with twenty-seven years of hard-core drug abuse and the lifestyle that goes with it can make it, so can you.

But first, you have to be honest. You have to truly want to stop. Let me ask you this: Right now, where you are, look over in the corner. See that steel toilet and sink combo? How about that really nice mattress they gave you? Do you like sitting on that toilet? Do you like sleeping on that mattress? Oh! How about the food? Do you find the food and how they dictate when you eat a particularly pleasant experience? And let's not forget that ever-present, sinking feeling of despair, fear, and uncertainty—yeah, that one you just got.

Sorry that I have to keep doing that to you, but I want you to realize how totally messed up your situation is and that what you're feeling right now is necessary to bring you to your next level—and one step closer to freedom.

You see, when you are out there on the street, running and gunning, all high or drunk, you act and feel invincible. "Come and get me, copper!" Right? You know how it is. You start getting a reputation; your friends are impressed with your ability to score the kinder dope. You pull off some crazy stuff, throw down on somebody, get away from the cops in a chase, and they can't ID you; or you leave the scene before they arrive. Pretty soon you start getting a big ol' head. The whole time you're doing dirt to support your habit, and you're either high or coming down. And coming down just isn't an option, is it?

So let's revisit that question: Who is the most important person in your life? Do you feel invincible and on top of the world right now? Did you lose all hope, and did reality set in when the cold steel of those handcuffs tightened around your wrists and the cops tossed your whining self in the back of their cruiser? Whose feelings, wants, and desires mean the most to you? Who would you do anything for?

Is it your mother or father? Nope, not them. They've asked you to slow down and get straight countless times. Is it your boyfriend or girlfriend, wife or husband? Nope. Despite all his or her pleading, he or she let you back in, hoping things would get better. You can definitely take advantage of his or her love. Nope, not him or her either. Is it your baby or child? Hmm ... Let's see ... diapers or dope, rent or drugs, food or fiend? Nope, not him or her either. You traded your food stamps for a quarter gram of bunk and got burned, but you'll do it again tomorrow—so nope, not him or her. We know for sure that it isn't the feelings of the judges, parole or probation officers, counselors, or law enforcement agents you're trying to put first, so we can scratch them off the list.

That doesn't leave a whole lot of choices, does it? See where I'm going with this? If you're totally, brutally honest with yourself, you'll come to only one logical conclusion. The most important person— whose feelings, wants, and desires you have put above all others—is *you*. Nothing or nobody really matters except you and what you want, or else you wouldn't be sitting where you are, wondering what everyone else is doing and who he or she is doing it with.

The thing about being selfish is that it leaves you empty. You connive, scheme, and manipulate to get what you want, and anybody in your way is the enemy. That includes parents, spouses, children, and the rest of the world. So, pretty much the only person who really likes your scandalous, lying self is you. Everyone else around you is either scared of you or puts up with you so he or she can get what he or she wants—because that person is selfish too, or he or she is in love with the idea of being in love with you.

All those you know who matter have put their hope and trust in you so you would step up and be the person they need, but you fall short every time. Sure, for a while you do well and catch a break, get a good job, or get out of trouble. But then you get in the way of success … No, you sabotage your own success because success means responsibility, responsibility means sacrifice, and sacrifice means no more drugs, alcohol, crime, and all that. So being selfish leaves you empty, alone, scared, uncertain, and locked up.

So where are all the hope and peace I was talking about? We'll get to that, but first we need to break it down so it's all raw and open; we need to clean out the wound before we dress it, if you catch my drift. But whatever you do, give yourself a real shot at freedom and keep reading.

I didn't have the benefit of someone to guide me through some pretty rough times and some even tougher questions. And for a long time, I felt like if I actually pointed the way, something would be lost in translation or that you wouldn't really get it because you didn't learn it like I did, but I have since reconsidered this position, since I knew I was called on to guide and teach.

It is my fervent prayer that this book helps you to rediscover yourself—and more importantly, that it helps you to step into your greatness. I promise you that if you read this book from cover to cover and apply what you've learned to your life, your heart will be touched, your mind will be opened, miracles will happen, and lives will be restored.

In some cases, restoration will come seemingly overnight. Some will be restored twofold; some, a hundredfold. Much depends on your willingness to participate. Remember when I said, "Right about now you would say or do just about anything to get out of jail and out of trouble, but would you do what it takes?"

I want you to think about that for a minute. If you're reading this, it's because you can't make bail or are currently serving out your sentence. Would you do what it takes? You've already begged, threatened, and tried to guilt everyone you know into putting up something for collateral to make 10 percent or the full amount of a cash-only bond. But everything you've tried has failed. That's because everyone who knows you knows you'll skip out and leave him or her hanging, losing whatever he or she has put up.

Some of you can't make bail because, quite frankly, they are scared of you and are glad you're in jail. You sure find out who your friends are; but more importantly, if you're honest with yourself, you know what people really think of you. Would you do what it takes? You can't tell me that you haven't at least one time said, "Please, God. Get me outta this, and I'll do better from now on. I promise."

You can't tell me that you're not sick and tired of sitting in there and wondering what you could do to make it all go away—somehow turn your life around and put it all behind you. Hold your head up high instead of looking over your shoulder or running when you hear a siren. You know what I mean: that feeling of terror that grips your heart when you see a cop and know you've got a warrant. This all stems from the choices you make when you're being the most selfish, when only your feelings, wants, and desires matter.

Stop throwing your life away, friend. The good news is that all this has led you somewhere where you can't hurt anybody anymore. Others are safe from you, and you can finally slow down and listen to the beat of your own heart. Every human has a greatest desire and need. We'll cover the desire first.

Men's (and women's) greatest desire is to love and to be loved, to belong to something greater than themselves. We seek out the fulfillment of this desire from the moment we leave the womb, desperately seeking to satisfy the hunger of a bond. To our great detriment, self is seeking out a way to satisfy its own hunger: lust. And we lose the image and virtue of love and replace it with the corrupted counterfeit of lust.

Our relationships, no matter how much we want to believe they are real, lasting, meaningful, and pure, are unstable at best because they are born out of selfish ambition. Not that they don't have value—every human heart seeks its bond of love—but until love is revealed, we are led by lust. Let me illustrate: If the love you have is true and the bond you claim to have is born out of love, then how can you be the most important person in that relationship? True love *always* prefers the other person over self. The other's wants, wishes, desires, and needs *always* are met above your own.

This doesn't mean you always give your boyfriend or girlfriend the first pull of a whiskey bottle or last cigarette or the last bump of dope. If you're thinking like that, you are *way* sideways. If you truly love someone, you don't *ever* turn him or her out just so he or she wants or needs to get high just so you don't have to feel guilty about your own fiend.

Now that we've established that our view of love is clouded, we can see that self has hijacked our greatest desire and replaced it with a counterfeit named "lust." So we owe it to ourselves to uncover and expose this imposter for what it is: a destroyer, a thief, a murderer. It has destroyed our lives, stolen our freedom and happiness, and killed our relationships.

Your circumstances may seem bleak and uncertain. You may even be nearing the end of your sentence, but deep down you're scared of what the future holds. All these temptations and thoughts of revenge or unfinished business fill your head, and every thought is consumed with what you'll do and how you'll do it. You know this for sure: if you don't make some serious changes, you'll be right back where you are right now.

At this time, I want to shift gears for a moment and introduce myself and the intent of this book. I'm the author of this book, and the reason I can identify with you is because I've been where you've been … more times than I care to count. I've done time in three different states and in five different counties; I've been to prison three times (twice in one state and once in another). So I think you would agree that I'm not just some self-help writer but a uniquely qualified expert on the subject.

I was born in a small town in Arizona in the late sixties. My father is Mexican, and my mother is white. Back then you didn't cross racial boundaries. So right off the bat, I was neither race. The Mexicans considered me a coconut, brown on the outside and white on the inside. The whites considered me a half-breed. Don't get me wrong: I had friends, some white and some brown. What I'm alluding to is identity.

Which leads me to the purpose of this book: to guide you to the knowledge of who you really are, the greatness that dwells within you, and the tremendous power that is waiting to be unleashed in you and through you: the power to be set free. Each of you reading this book is desperately seeking these things, and some of you are ready to do what it takes. Welcome to your future. This book will chronicle the main events in my life that shaped, transformed, and ultimately delivered me from the power of drugs, alcohol, and prison; and set me free.

Let's take a trip down memory lane to a time when gas was thirty-six cents a gallon and the Vietnam War was winding down. In the year 1972, I was five years old, and we had just moved from our thin-walled cabin at the base of the mountain on the outskirts of town. The snowstorm of 1967, the year of my birth, had left six feet of snow and an indelible impact on the residents of that area. My parents had decided that for safety sake, they would move closer to town and look for a house that was better built and more suited for winter conditions. By 1972, they both had their foot in the door with the VA and had saved enough money to put a down payment on a thirty-year mortgage.

In a sense, I was very fortunate to have both parents working. This situation provided enough income to afford food and clothing and a decent middle-income home. But since both parents worked, I had to go somewhere during the days, so they left me with my father's side of the family, the Mexican side. This too had its benefits, as I was in the constant care of family members, and I consequently grew up speaking two languages, a fact that would prove invaluable later in life.

In stark contrast to the new home my parents had bought stood the even thinner- walled shack my grandmother lived in. They used newspaper for insulation in the walls and floor. She heated the house and cooked on an old wood-burning stove or oven she had brought from Mexico. We didn't have any indoor plumbing as far as sewer went, but we did have running water at the tap. She would do laundry in a steel tub with one of the washboards you rake the clothes across and her own homemade lye soap.

So though while I was at home with my parents, I enjoyed all the amenities of middle-class America; at my grandmother's I knew what it meant to be poor, very poor. And you know what? I loved it there. Even though my grandmother, aunt, and uncle shared the raising duties and loved and cared for me very much, there was something missing in my life, something I desperately needed.

CHAPTER 2

WHO AM I?

As we discussed before, we exit the womb desiring to love and to be loved. It's the way we were designed to immediately seek out where we came from and connect to it. For boys and girls, it's different in how we seek it and the impact it has on our lives when those desires are or aren't met. Both sexes form special bonds with either parent. Both seek and receive their identity from the love and affection they get from either parent.

In most cases, young boys learn that mom is where we go when we get hurt, where a comforting word and embrace can be given. We also learn through time that a mother's love can be manipulated to our benefit. Moms usually let you get away with all kinds of stuff, and they are quick to forgive and always accept you back into her good graces, which teaches us that being selfish is not only okay but also an entitlement.

Fathers, on the other hand, are not so soft, comforting, or forgiving. But for boys, this is where we seek and get our identity. A boy looks to his father to instruct him and teach him who he is and how he should act. Whether good or bad, the propensity for a boy to emulate his father's every action is present and could manifest adversely. For example, if a boy sees his father abuse his mother, he may in turn abuse his own mother or wife. He may have little or no value for women and expect women to serve him. Of course, this isn't always the case, but the possibility is there. A girl looks to her mother for her identity, although a father's presence and influence will shape her self-worth.

So take care how you conduct yourself in front of your children, for they are watching and learning, looking to you for direction, whether good or bad.

I will share with you my personal example. As I've stated before, I'm half white and half Mexican. For my father, I think the impact of racial prejudice he experienced as a child growing up left a residue on his marriage and in how he treated me. When he attended school, there was still segregation: whites in one classroom and Mexicans and people of color in another. They weren't allowed to speak Spanish at school, or swift penalties were incurred, namely a good crack of a ruler across the mouth or any exposed area. So perhaps this contempt he endured promoted a root of bitterness he may have fostered, maybe unconsciously, maybe consciously. I'm not sure, but it definitely affected how he looked at me.

Since I was his firstborn, I should have received a focused commitment—you know, a proud father's special attention to his mini me. But that wasn't the case. He distanced himself from me and starved me of the one thing I needed most: love. Not that he didn't love me in some remote definition of the word, but the close, secure connection that I belonged to him and the sense that he would always protect me from whatever wasn't there. Lies and ridicule replaced promise and praise. I could never do anything right, and his words were sharp and cut deep. He drank continually and was a mean drunk. To his credit, he worked every day with all the overtime he could get, so in that sense he was a very good provider. But monetary provision meets only the basic physical needs of humanity. So I don't know what's worse: not having a father at all or having one that isn't really there.

So I began to build a wall brick by brick: insecurity, resentment, vain conceit, fear, doubt, mistrust, unbelief, selfishness, pride. I built this wall up until I couldn't see out and no one could see in. No one would be able to see the scared little boy crouching in the corner and crying, longing for his father to come find him, hold out his hand, and lead him back home where it was safe. So left alone behind my wall of shame, I built my own false identity, taking broken pieces of my heart to build a new one no one could hurt.

When my father should have been teaching me wisdom, honor, and how to be a man, I was taught instead that drinking was okay, lying was okay, cussing was okay, and mistreating everyone around you was okay. Worst of all, I think, rather than having that father-son talk about the birds and bees, he just left a stack of *Playboy* magazines under the bathroom counter. I guess this was his way of avoiding teaching me about sex. Big mistake. I don't think I need to go into any detail, save that I was exposed to something I shouldn't have been exposed to at such a young age, and that gift that should have been reserved for my wife was awakened and thrown to the swine. Yes, folks, be very careful indeed what you set before your children.

On the other side of the coin were my grandmother, aunt, and uncle, who basically raised me because my parents worked. They (my aunt and uncle) had no children of their own and lavished all their love on me, giving me pretty much whatever I wanted. This was a bad combination because the love I wanted, really needed, was my father's, so all that love was really being given to that little boy behind the wall. All that did was produce a conflicted and insecure fraud with a bad case of entitlement and a misguided sense of morality.

Since my aunt and uncle had no children, they were the family babysitters, not just for me but for all the family kids. My grandmother bore ten children, so there were other children in their care at the same time I was there. As you all may know, kids can be cruel, and it was no different for me. Being the youngest and the only child of my parents afforded me plenty of opportunities to suffer at the hands of older family members. Of course, kids will be kids, but that doesn't make the fear of ridicule and rejection, even a good dusting up, any less valid in the heart of a child. One would hope that children could find refuge in the arms of a parent, but when that refuge isn't found, they become mixed up and alone. Whenever I would come crying from the back room, where our parents made us play, my father would blame me, then yell at me and send me right back in there, where the other children were waiting. Needless to say, I found no reprieve in my father's arms, so I concluded that I was on my own in life. I would have to forge my own identity.

When I turned sixteen, I got in trouble with the law for the umpteenth time, and the court made me leave Arizona to live with my other grandfather on my mother's side. While there I continued my drug use and stole my step-grandmother's pain meds from the medicine chest, to my great shame. You see, she had cancer and needed those meds. But when you are addicted, rather when you have given yourself over to the spirit of addiction, you will lie, cheat, steal, deny, and make any and all excuses to get what you want.

I wasn't there long, though, before I was racing my grandfather's car, which he'd entrusted to me. It was a Ford Ranchero GT400, and it could scoot. I was racing my friend after work, showing off on a road I had never been on. It was dusk, and I thought I saw a hill coming up as the yellow line ascended up, so I punched it to gain speed for the climb. But to my horror, as I hit the brights, I realized it wasn't the yellow line in the center of an oncoming hill at all but a huge power line pole—and I mean big. I hit the brakes and immediately went into a skid. I pumped the brakes to try to control the skid as best I could and managed to wedge the car between the pole and an equally large oak tree. The crash completely folded one side of the bumper under the tire. The battery was on fire. I stood back from the wreckage in disbelief, wondering how in the world I had survived. It wasn't my driving skills; I'll tell you that. There was something, someone else, guiding that car. We'll talk more about that later.

So my grandparents promptly sent me back to Arizona, where I was not only unwelcome but still on probation. I had been on probation since the seventh grade.   I wasn't back very long before I fell in with a local guy my age who lived on his own with his girlfriend and kid. My girlfriend had a car, and she would let me run around in it while she was at work. We started to do all kinds of crime to support our drug habits, and I discovered this canned propellant used for airbrushing; if you inhaled it, it would give you one giant rush complete with hallucinations and everything. It was pure chlorofluorocarbons—you know, the stuff that ate a hole in the ozone layer? Yeah, that stuff. It eventually caused a severe respiratory infection that almost killed me, but do you think I stopped ingesting dangerous drugs or chemicals? Nope, I sure didn't.

One day our crime spree came to an end, and the law caught up with us while we were waiting for our court hearing and still on probation. My girlfriend and I went up to this one place on the edge of town to smoke some really good weed I had. Well, we both passed out dead asleep. I was rudely woken up by a very bright light in my eyes, followed by a voice: "What are you two doing up here?"

I blinked and said, "Nothing."

The cop asked, "Getting high?"

And I answered, "No."

Then he said, "Oh yeah? Well, what's this?" And reached over to the bag of weed I had sticking right out of my shirt breast pocket. Yep, I was so stoned that I had put the bag right there in my pocket where you could see it plain as day, and I'd forgotten it was there when I passed out.

Needless to say, that was the last straw. They handcuffed me and took me directly to juvy again, but this time there was no getting out. They sentenced me to Adobe Mountain Correctional Facility for juveniles. I was to stay there until I was eighteen, but I managed to spend only three and a half months there. But at that age, it was long enough.

While I was there, I began reading books on spiritualism and the like. I was still searching for my identity. I was looking for some special knowledge and power to deliver me out of my circumstances. I started reading about Transcendental Meditation, out of body experiences (called OBEs), and Eckankar (soul travel, the third eye, and the like). I was convinced that I was onto something. I remember always saying, "Something is coming for me." Some special knowledge, I believed. It would be another twenty-three years of heartache, failure, and pain before that special knowledge would find me—and find me and come for me it did. While there at Adobe Mountain, I played football and was involved in as many activities as I could to help make the time pass by. It seemed to drag on forever.

One day a church group came, and they had a revival tent set up; anybody who wanted to go could. Well, I would do anything to get out of my room for a while, so I went. They started talking about how God loved each and every one of us more than our own parents could, that God cared about what was happening to us. A lot of what they said made some kind of sense to me—not that I fully understood what they were saying, but somehow I knew that what they were saying was true.

I had been raised in a church environment, but all I knew about God was that He was up there somewhere and that His Son was hanging on a cross above the altar at my church. That was it. But these people were teaching something else altogether. They said that God was close to us and that we were close to Him. I didn't, couldn't, understand how, but that special knowledge I was seeking seemed to be more real in that meeting, more present, more tangible. They made an altar call and asked people whether they wanted to accept Jesus as Lord and Savior. So, trying to connect with that special knowledge somehow, I said the words.

After going back to my room, I went right back to the other books, thinking I could do more on my own, learn more, tap into this universal power and become somehow supernatural. I guess that in my young and immature mind, somehow it all fit together. It was all part of the same thing. I was grossly mistaken.

One thing I surely didn't understand or count on was that when I said those words regarding Jesus, in the spiritual state of readiness and hunger I was in, I was heard, and from that moment on I belonged to Him, and He would continue to chase me for the rest of my life.

You see, we were created in His image specifically for Him, and He reserves the right to call on us, and He is in constant effort to contact us and bring us back into that special relationship where we know we belong to something greater than ourselves. We were made to bear His image and carry His power, and I mean *power*, the same power that created the universe, the power to set you free … forever.

But I'm getting ahead of myself. Let's continue. I got out of Adobe Mountain, and I fell right back into the same old group of friends, doing the same old thing, getting high or drunk or both. I sought out a friend I had prior to Adobe, and he had a girlfriend. She looked my way, and my misguided sense of love (lust) prevailed and overrode any honor I might have had.

Needless to say, I hurt my friend, and I was now entangled in a doomed relationship. I was only seventeen at the time. I woke up one morning, wanting to do something to save what was left of the relationship and also prove to me, my father, and all others that I was a man capable of doing great and brave things. I would shut the mouths of all who had ever picked on me. I would join the service, not just any branch but the army, and I could fix my eyes on the Eighty-Second Airborne Division to do it.

The relationship wouldn't endure the hardships of military life and subsequently came to an end, leaving me devastated and unsure about my future. All I knew was that I didn't want to be alone.

The rest of my relationships would follow the same pattern until I finally came to Christ, and love was revealed to me. So what I'm trying to tell you in that story is that what I thought was love was really the cheap and dangerous counterfeit: lust. I know this because love would never have stolen the object of its desire from another. We can identify lust because it always acts like this; it sees, it wants, and it acts. If it is rejected, it becomes angry and vengeful. If it is fed, it is never satisfied and always seeks its own way and will above all else and all others.

Love, on the other hand, would never initiate a relationship by intruding on an already existing one. It would *never* cheat to get what it wants because what it truly wants is to give unconditionally, intentionally, unequivocally, and eternally. And since we are imperfect mortals with a beginning and an ending, we can never love this way. We *need* something, someone, the source of true love to love through us. We were made to carry this love, but we cannot generate or duplicate this love of our own volition.

It has to come from the source, and that source is almighty God through His Son, Jesus, the Christ. This leads us to man's (and woman's) greatest need … salvation.

CHAPTER 3

OUR GREATEST NEED

Salvation is the all-inclusive word that describes man's current condition both spiritually and physically as a result of his fall from grace, as described in the Bible, and the plan God set forth to bring man back into relationship and restore his rightful place in the universal order. (We will cover this topic shortly). You may want to take a few moments to reflect on your current situation. How did you get here? What is the condition of your heart? What did your eyes see that you thought you had to have, and what were your actions that led you here?

If you're honest with yourself, you'll agree that your own selfish ambition, fueled by lust, has been your guiding influence most of your life. You've tried it your way, and it's not working. That is to say that in our present condition, the self-centered choices we make, no matter how noble the intention, always lead to destruction. For example, "I'll just gamble one last time, one last paycheck. I'll hit big, come back home with all the lost earnings and more, and my family will be proud of me. Then I'll stop."

Or consider this: "I dropped out of school, I have a record. No one will hire me, I can never get a really good job. Just one more robbery, just one more heist, and I'll have enough that my family and I will be okay."

How about this one? "I've been breaking my back all day long for the man; my boss is so ungrateful. I have to do all the dirty work while he or she kicks back and reaps all the benefits. I deserve a drink, a puff, a bump." You know very well that you've convinced yourself of this many times, and the end result is always the same: getting drunk, acting like a fool no one likes, high or coming down; feeling ashamed, empty, and alone. Why do we do those things aside from the obvious entitlements and addictions? How did you become addicted, and how did you get to feel that the whole world owes you something?

What I'm about to tell you is life-changing knowledge. Remember that supernatural knowledge I told you about earlier, that special knowledge I was looking for in those books and trying to connect to? Well, here it is for real. What I'm about to reveal to you took me forty years to learn, and it is the absolute truth. From here on out, you will begin to learn the true secrets and mysteries of mankind: his origin, his purpose, and his destiny—*your* destiny.

I will help guide you through my own experience as well as the power and willingness of the living God to set you free forever. Whatever you think you know or don't know about God and about yourself is about to change as the Holy Spirit begins to do His work in your life by opening your eyes and mind, and preparing the soil of your heart to accept the seed that will spring forth, a tree of life within you overflowing with good fruit.

It would be most beneficial for you to get a Bible for the rest of this journey. Don't worry about what other people say or think. This is your preappointed time. God has drawn boundaries around your life. It's in here where you can listen, where you can receive. Believe it or not, you're in the right place at the right time to change your life forever as the storehouse doors of heaven open to you, where an unending supply of mercy, grace, love, and provision wait to be poured out on you—not only on you but on everyone who comes in contact with you; they too will be blessed. You will become a wellspring of life fully equipped for all of life's challenges, lacking nothing. Others will seek you out, wanting to hear your words, even to just touch you and get some of what you have, because what you'll have is undeniable, transforming, real, and permanent.

So let's talk about God—who He is, what He is up to, and how we contact Him.

When I was young, I was raised in a church (as I stated earlier). This meant a lot of kneeling, standing, repeating, or answering during what is called the "liturgy." This is when the priest reads from a format that has been handed down for hundreds of years. He says something, and then everyone responds with a prescribed response. Although I went to church regularly, I didn't know anything about God, His Son, or the Holy Spirit. I knew nothing personal, nothing life changing, nothing permanent. I'm not casting blame on anyone but myself for not learning more. Remember, I was unable to receive God's truths because I was looking through the eyes of selfishness. But I needed to go through something before I was ready to really seek Him.

All of us are born with an understanding that there's something greater out there and a desire to connect to it. We know God exists. Somehow and on occasion, usually when we are in trouble, we cry out, "God, help!" Why do we do this if there is no God? Well, because there is a God and we know that only He can help in a hopeless situation. We were designed to seek Him out, and He didn't do that to us in vain. Listen to what the Bible says. Jeremiah 29:12–14 says, "Then you will call upon Me and go and pray to Me, and I will listen to you. And you will seek Me and find Me, when you search for Me with all your heart. I will be found by you, says the Lord, and I will bring you back from your captivity. I will gather you from all the nations and from all the places where I have driven you, says the Lord, and I will bring you to the place from which I cause you to be carried away captive."

Did you hear that? He said that when we call, God will listen. But there is a condition, a requirement. He says, "When you search for Me with *all your heart*" (emphasis added). It has to be a sincere effort and desire to know Him, not just for a favor. That isn't to say that God doesn't answer your requests—He does—but He also knows you'll soon quickly forget Him and say to yourself, "Look what I have done. I got myself out of this mess."

He desires an intimate, working relationship in which both parties are engaged in meaningful dialogue and actions. He's not just the grocery store or bank where you can just drive up and get what you need and then drive away. Even so, a bank or store must have money and food put back into them for resupply. God's storehouse never runs out, but He wants you to put back effort into the relationship in the form of worship, praise, thanksgiving, faith, and belief.

What are the promises God makes in that passage? He says, "I will listen," "You will find me," and "I will bring you back from captivity." So right about now, you've got to admit that sounds pretty good—promising, in fact, and hopeful even.

Why has God allowed us to be taken captive to begin with? Because He wants us to seek Him out in earnest so He can reveal Himself to us and restore us back into a right relationship. For example, you get into a bad argument with your spouse, family member, or good friend. You say some pretty hurtful things, and insults are exchanged. Maybe even some property is broken or destroyed. You are both hurt and upset; you're really mad, but deep down inside, you both really value the relationship, the friendship, and you know it's worth salvaging.

Well, it's like that. We've done some pretty awful things in the past; we've denied and rejected God's love for us. Maybe we even cursed Him and said He didn't exist. Seeing that He created us, we can conclude that that could probably hurt some. It's as if your own child got upset with you and said, "I wish you weren't my mom or dad." Or maybe you said this yourself during a bad argument. Or maybe your loved one screamed at the top of his or her lungs, "I don't love you!" You know that hurts. You want that pain to go away. You want things restored like they were. You want your relationship back intact. It's the same with God. Despite all our rejecting and resisting God, He still desires to restore His children back to a right relationship.

So God allows us to get to a place where we can be still and think about what we've done; it's in that place of brokenness that we truly seek Him because deep down, we know that only He can fix our broken hearts. Some of you might say, "I called on God, even cried out to Him with tears, 'Please save my mommy. Please don't let Daddy die. Please don't let Mommy and Daddy get divorced. Please don't let me get molested anymore. Please God, make them stop!'" These are all valid and legitimate requests without doubt. Seemingly unanswered prayer can leave us disbelieving, doubtful of God's existence, or angry with God, even to the point of waging war against Him.

Listen to what the Scriptures have to say. Isaiah 65:24 says, "It shall come to pass that before they call, I will answer; and while they are still speaking I will hear."

Did you hear that? God has already answered, even before you spoke. Before your situation even existed, God was working out your solution. He can do this because He is all knowing (omniscient), all powerful (omnipotent), and everywhere (omnipresent).

So your next logical question is, "Okay, if God is all those things, then why did He let that stuff happen to begin with? Why didn't He just stop it before it even started?" Again, these are legitimate and valid questions. And it's here where we will go into greater depth of who God is and what He is doing through our origin, our fall from grace, our restoration, our purpose, and our future. Amen.

Consider these verses.

> Before the mountains were brought forth, or ever You had formed the earth and the world, even from everlasting to everlasting, You are God. (Ps. 90:2)

> Have you not known? Have you not heard? The everlasting God, the Lord, the Creator of the ends of the earth, neither faints nor is weary. His understanding is unsearchable. (Isa. 40:28)

> The Eternal God is your refuge. And underneath are the everlasting arms; He will thrust out the enemy from before you. (Deut. 33:27)

The general theme here is that God is eternal, with no beginning or end. He has always been and always will be. He is not created, but He is the Creator of all things, both seen and unseen. He isn't the figment of man's imagination. Man does indeed need to worship. It's part of his DNA. It's the most crucial part of his DNA, not his physiological

DNA but his spiritual DNA. Some might say that God is the creation of man's imagination to meet his need to worship and have a deity rule over him, making himself somehow connected to the greater theme of the cosmos. There are a few flaws in this theory, but we will discuss the most important one for this study.

If God is man's invention, then He was created in man's mind. This is where the road gets slippery. Man has three parts to him: spirit, soul, and body (in that order). The spirit is first. Have you ever walked or driven by one of those yoga or so-called spiritual wellness places? Their motto is either mind, body, spirit or mind, body, soul. The first puts the spirit last, and the second is even more confusing.

Let me illustrate. John 4:23–25 says, "But the hour is coming, and now is, when the true worshippers will worship the Father in spirit and truth: for the Father is seeking such to worship Him. God is spirit, and those who worship Him must worship Him in spirit and truth." So first understand that God is a spirit.

Next, Genesis 1:27 says, "So God created man in His own image, in the image of God He created him, male and female He created them." Genesis 5:1 says, "This is the book of the genealogy of Adam. In the day that God created man, He made them in the likeness of God." Zechariah 12:1 says, "The burden of the word of the Lord against Israel. This says the Lord, who stretches out the heavens, lays the foundation of the earth, and forms the spirit of man within him." So here we clearly see that God Himself is a spirit. He is *the* spirit from which all life comes.

Second, we (men or women) are all spirits beings created after and in the likeness of God's own spirit. (We will discuss what it means to be created in His image soon). So the beginning of man, the first part of man, the order of man is *always* spirit first. This is the part of man, the *only* part of man that is God conscious, the *only* part of man that can hear from and speak to God. Period.

Next, Genesis 2:7 says, "And the Lord God formed man of the dust of the ground and breathed into his nostrils the breath of life; and man became a living soul." Many people think this verse describes the moment man was created in his entirety, but I have just shown you that the spirit man was created first in heaven before the man of the dust was created. All the elements that formed or completed the physical body of man and all life on earth can be found in the earth's crust.

So we know what man is made of, but how was he made? And I'm not referring to the reproductive system. The Bible states that all life came from the earth in its basic rudimentary composition, but it didn't become sentient until the breath of life was introduced. Scripture says that after God formed the man of the dust (the physical body), God breathed the breath of life into man's nostrils, and man became a living soul, (Genesis 2:7 KJV). That breath of life was the spirit man still inside God and part of God, and when it was sent forth into the man of the dust, that physical body was now a sentient being. He was fully aware and conscious of his surroundings. He was a spirit living in a physical body with a conscience (the soul).

Many people think spirit and soul are one and the same, but they aren't. The spirit is the actual life-giving essence of God Almighty, the very best of God. Love, wisdom, knowledge, understanding, reason, compassion, faith—these attributes, coupled with the supernatural life-giving power that is God, are what the spirit man is.

I don't know about you, but I find this pretty exciting to discover that somewhere inside me is the very best of a supernatural God, the one and only true God, our Creator and Father. He loves us more than we can imagine because we are His image.

Just as man is composed of three parts—spirit, soul, and body—the soul is also three parts. The intellectual and emotional parts will make up the soul. This is very important for us to understand. Because of man's current fallen condition, it is the soul plane that governs him until the spirit is reawakened.

Remember earlier when I told you about how I stole my friend's girlfriend? And that every subsequent relationship following that one until love was revealed resulted similarly? That's because I saw something, I wanted it, and I acted on it. The soul plane led and governed me.

My mind received certain knowledge. In this case, it was about my friend's girlfriend. She was taken and unavailable. My emotions (pride and greed, which are both lust) wanted to take something that wasn't mine to take.

My will caused me to act, and I hurt my friend and entered into a doomed relationship. Does this sound familiar? It doesn't have to be a relationship; it can be anything. The mind sits on the throne of the soul, receiving information and processing it into knowledge to be used.

The emotions are stirred feelings that come and go, such as happiness or sadness, anger or the giddy response we experience toward the opposite gender that we mistake for love. The Greek language describes love in three ways: (1) *phileo*, the kind of love you have for friends and family; (2) *eros*, the kind of love shared in the bedroom (marriage), and (3) agape, the God kind of love that is unconditional, forgiving, and eternal. The first two, *phileo* and *eros*, are found in the soul plane. Agape love can come only through the spirit from the source of love, which is God. We cannot generate this kind of love on our own, and that is why the spirit must be awakened—so God's love can flow through us.

Finally is the will, the final step in our downfall. The process begins when we see something we think we want or need; that vision is processed into usable knowledge. Then our emotions are stirred to the point that our very actions are under its control, and we do the things we know will cause us harm.

So being led by the soul plane isn't a good thing, especially for those of us who are more broken than others (for example, druggies, drinkers, gamblers, sexually promiscuous, and so on). The soul has its purpose so long as it is pulled into subjection by the spirit.

Let's take a closer look at the parts of man or woman. Our spirits are created in God's image, containing the very best of His essence and made to reflect His attributes. Since they are actually part of Him, our spirits are always conscious of their origin, always seeking communion with their creator. They are God conscious.

The soul is made of three parts: mind, emotion, and will (in that order). It is able to receive and process information into usable knowledge and then apply that knowledge through the act of the will. It is sentient—able to reason and problem solve. It is self-aware, self-conscious.

The earthen physical body contains (1) potassium, (2) calcium, (3) magnesium, (4) phosphorus, (5) iron, and (6) manganese (same as the earth). The physical body uses these elements through a very complex laboratory, called the "body," to generate cell growth, reproduce those cells, and then change some of them into specialized cells and systems that use oxygen and nutrients to sustain its functions just like all other life on earth.[1] It knows only what the five senses tell it. It knows only what it can see, smell, hear, feel, and taste. That's it. Period. It is world conscious.

So when man was created in God's perfect, pristine, holy condition, he was a God-conscious spirit that was self-aware, could receive and process information, and could act out his will because he now lived in a physical body, complete with everything he needed to function and prosper in the earth's atmosphere.

Okay, we've covered a lot of ground since we introduced the supposition that God was a creation of man's imagination to feed his need to worship and be somehow connected to the greater theme of the cosmos.

I have shown you step by step the order of man:

1. The spirit is God conscious and, to our eyes, invisible. (The spirit is the essence of God in us).

2. The soul (mind, emotion, and will) is self-conscious and able to reason, receive information, and process it (sentient).

3. The earthen body, though complex and a marvel of bioengineering, is still just elements arranged in a way to make mass, muscles, bones, and connective tissue. Without the sentient soul, the body would just be a piece of meat. And without the breath of life (the spirit), it would die and decay.[2]

So, you see, the order of man must be spirit, soul, and body. So if the mind makes up God's existence, then it denies its very own spirit or, worse yet, doesn't even know it exists.

CHAPTER 4

THE LEGITIMACY OF THE BIBLE

What we are really talking about is the legitimacy of the Bible as God's inspired Word, which reveals Himself to man: who God is, who man is, and the ultimate destiny of the universe.

Let's take a look at three relevant verses, but first let's bear in mind that what I'm teaching you took me forty years to learn. I had to learn it the hard way—failure after failure, heartbreak after heartbreak, jail cell after jail cell. I'm giving you the benefit of a lifelong journey of pain and suffering to the ultimate deliverance, freedom, and success that can come only from knowing God. Amen.

First, Romans 1:19–20 says, "Because what may be known of God is manifest in them [men] for God has shown it to them. For since the creation of the world His invisible attributes are clearly seen, being understood by the things that are made, even His eternal power and God head, so that they are without excuse."

Second, 2 Timothy 3:16–17 says, "All Scripture is given by inspiration of God, and is profitable for doctrine, for reproof, for correction, for instruction in righteousness, that the men of God may be complete, thoroughly equipped for every good work."

Third, 2 Peter 1:19–21 says, "And so we have the prophetic word confirmed, which you do well to heed as a light that shines in a dark place, until the day dawns and the morning star rises in your hearts; knowing this first, that no prophecy of scripture is of any private interpretation, for prophecy never came by the will of men, but Holy men of God spoke as they were moved by The Holy Spirit."

Our Father has been reaching out to us since we were created. In the garden of Eden, all was perfect. Man was aligned as he was intended to be—God over man; that is, man subject to God. Man's spirit was aligned directly under God's Spirit to receive holy communion (communication). Man's soul was subject to His spirit, and his body was subject to His soul and perfectly aligned. In that perfect and holy state, man received vast amounts of holy, intimate knowledge from God and creation itself.

All of creation spoke its mysteries to man. The stars were saying, "I am a star, and this is how I was made." The trees and rocks had a voice and told Adam, "We are rocks and trees, and this is how we were made." (Does this sound silly?) In Adam's perfect condition, he was the greatest scientist and mathematician the world had ever seen—next to God, of course. But man has fallen from grace and his first estate. We will talk about that in a second. What I want you to understand is that since that fall, God has been reaching out to humanity and working out a plan to restore him back to his rightful place in the universal order.

God has been revealing Himself to us through creation and the Scriptures by His Holy Spirit. Observe Hebrews 1:1–4.

> God, who at various times and in various ways spoke in times past to the fathers by the prophets, has in these last days spoken to us by His Son, whom He has appointed heir of all things, through whom He also made the worlds; who being the brightness of His glory and the express image of His person, and upholding all things by the word of His power, when He had by Himself, purged our sins, sat down at the right hand of the Majesty on high, having become so much better than the angels, as He has by inheritance obtained a more excellent name than they.

I cannot convince you of the reality and existence of God. Those are the work of the Holy Spirit to make contact with your spirit and awaken it, to reveal the truth of God's Word and make it alive to you. All I can do is point the way, be His witness, and testify of His goodness and the miracles He has performed in my life.

The greatest miracle, of course, is my salvation; God granted me forgiveness for my sins and eternal life with Him. But second are the daily miracles and advancements of my life.

The fact that I don't use drugs is a miracle. The fact that I haven't had a drink in nine years is a miracle. The fact that I work and hold a job is a miracle. The fact that I've turned from a life of crime to serve the living God from behind the pulpit is a miracle and a testimony of the power of God not only to change your life for the better but to deliver you from the chains that bind you forever.

Our very lives are a miracle. The earth is a miracle. The universe is a miracle. God is a miracle maker. He is in the miracle business, and He wants to perform miracles in your life. He wants to set you free.

So creation itself testifies to us through its grand scale and beauty. The marvel of life itself in all the wonderful and diverse species that fill the earth, coupled with the perfect life-sustaining atmosphere, proves that there is an intelligent master designer at work.

The Bible is a miracle unto itself. It contains sixty-six books that have two major divisions: the Old Testament and the New Testament. The word that best translates the meaning of *testament* is "covenant." A covenant is an agreement between two parties that cannot be broken.

Because man is imperfect and at times has a hard time keeping his promises, God himself initiates and upholds this covenant agreement.

In the Old Testament (covenant), the people of Israel were to obey and keep the regulations and statutes God gave them through Moses. God promised that they would be a "special treasure" to Him and that He would make sure they were protected and provided for. If they broke their part of the covenant, however, God would withdraw His provision and protection. Unfortunately, they did.

But the ultimate goal of the Old Testament was to prepare the way for the coming Messiah (which means "Anointed One"). *Anointed* means "authorized" or "set apart."

An angel sent to Joseph (Jesus's stepfather) gave the historical figure we know as Jesus His name in a dream. Matthew 1:20–21 says, "But while he thought about these things, behold, an angel of the Lord appeared to him in a dream, saying, 'Joseph, son of David, do not be afraid to take to you Mary your wife, for that which is conceived in her is of the Holy Spirit. And she will bring forth a Son, and you shall call His name Jesus, for He will save His people from their sins.'"

The name *Jesus* is the Greek translation for the Hebrew name *Yehoshu'a* or *Joshua*, which means "God is salvation."

Christ is the Greek translation for the Hebrew "Messiah." T h e historical figure Jesus is often referred to as "Jesus Christ." *Christ* is not His last name, so His title is better written and understood as "Jesus, the Christ."

The proper Hebrew title for Jesus is *"Yeshua Mashiach,"*[3] which is translated "God is salvation, and this is the One who has been authorized and set apart for this work."

The Bible is a historical record of many things: the creation event, man, and peoples of the ancient world.

Jesus is the central figure in the entire Bible, though he is concealed in the Old Testament. He is revealed in the New Testament.

He fulfilled every single one of the Old Testament prophecies concerning the Messiah. The odds of one man fulfilling even only eight messianic prophecies are beyond astronomical. One tiny human being cannot really comprehend this number, but I will write it for you anyway.

It is 1×10 to the 28th or 1 in 10,000,000,000,000,000,000,000,000,000. That is over a quintillion! I didn't even know such a number existed. Jesus fulfilled not just eight prophecies but over three hundred.[4]

Jesus fulfilled and ratified both testaments in His life, burial, and resurrection. God upheld His covenant with man, and the Bible reveals Him to us as humans through a historical written account.

The Bible is the best-selling, most copied, and best-preserved book in the history of man, bar none. It is ancient yet timeless in its message and practical application. No other book on earth has the power to awaken your God-conscious spirit to receive the revelation of God.

No other book in history has been sought after or persecuted so much. The Roman Emperor Diocletian tried to destroy the Bible and set forth an edict that all Christian churches and literature be destroyed. Those named Christians were considered outlaws. They were seized and tortured in the crudest of manner and then burned. This persecution lasted ten years.

Dioceltian's reign of terror and efforts to extinguish the Word of God ironically came to an end. Under the banner of the Cross Diocletian's successor, Constantine, eventually became the sole Emperor of Rome. Constantine's favorable embrace of Christianity led to the edict of (313) which stated that all confiscated church property be returned at the expense of the imperial treasury. Moreover, the edict of (313) would pave the way for Christianity to flourish and become the official religion of the Roman Empire.[5]

The Bible is known as the Word of God. The Holy Spirit inspired every single letter, and God promised that His Word, His revelation to us, would stand forever. This is how it has been able to endure all attempts of its destruction and even flourish amid persecution.

> Forever, O Lord, Your Word is settled in heaven. (Ps. 119:89)

> The grass withers and the flower fades, but the Word of Our God stands forever. (Isa. 40:8)

> For whatever things were written before were written for our learning, that we through the patience and comfort of the scriptures might have hope. (Rom. 15:4)

Brothers and sisters, dear friends, I'm trying to establish in your hearts the very hearts that are hurting, scared, unsure, and searching for hope. I'm saying that your best chance, your only chance at turning your life around, is found between the two covers of the Holy Bible. It's not just an ordinary book written by ordinary men. It's the very words of God Almighty, written by holy men and inspired by the Holy Spirit. It has the power to change you, to transform you, to reposition you from the prison house to the palace. It has the ability to touch your heart because it meets you where you are. It knows your needs and can speak to you because it is alive. Hebrews 4:12 says, "For the word of God is living and powerful, and sharper than any two-edged sword, piercing even to the division of soul and spirit, and of joints and marrow, and is a discerner of the thoughts and intents of the heart."

Oh, glory to God! My words aren't adequate; my speech is unable to convey the depths of joy, hope, and deliverance the Word of God has brought me. If only I could reach into my heart and bring forth but a single speck of the hope and peace God's Word has given to me.

Wait ... wait. I can! Listen to what God is saying to you. I want you to understand that right now, this very second, God's heart is hurting for you. His heart aches to bring His children home. Jeremiah 29:11–14 says, *"For I know the thoughts that I think toward you,* says the Lord, thoughts of peace and not of evil, to give you a future and hope. Then you will call upon Me and go and pray to Me, and I will listen to you. And you will seek Me and find Me, when you search for Me with all your heart. I will be found by you, says the Lord, and I will bring you back from your captivity"* (emphasis added). It took me forty years of wandering in the wilderness before I let God into my life. Don't make the same mistakes I did.

The Bible isn't some big rule book man made up just to keep you from having fun or to control you. God has given you a free will to make your own choices. If He wanted to control you, He wouldn't have given you a will. He has lovingly and graciously given His Word (the Bible) as a revelation of Himself. It isn't meant to enslave us but to set us free. Free to love our families, free to form meaningful and lasting relationships, free to be able to see trouble coming and avoid it. Free from drugs, alcohol, gambling, violence, pornography, and everything that causes your family to worry and eventually separate you from them or them from you. Your families look up to you and have trusted you time and again—and so has God. The difference is that God isn't giving up on you. The proof is that you're still reading this book.

Look around you right now. How is that free will working out for you? You need God's Word to help you make better choices. But it's more than that. You need God's Word to awaken your spirit so you can realize the greatness that is in you and just waiting to burst forth. There is another you in there, the *real* you.

CHAPTER 5

ISRAEL IN THE PAST AND TODAY

The real you is a spirit being created in the image of the living God. Your purpose is to bear that image and reflect His attributes, to be His representative here on earth. And He has revealed Himself through the Holy Bible and the Hebrew people of the ancient world. That is why there will be no room in your heart for bigotry and racism. Who are we to question God's method by which He has chosen to reveal Himself to us?

Through those people and their mistakes and diligence, we have received the full historical (present and future) accounts of man and his eternal destiny. We owe our gratitude to those brave men and women who came before us to pave a way and instruct us in the revelation and worship of the one true God.

Let's just take a brief moment to discuss this topic.

The actual origin and meaning of the name *Hebrew* is unknown. It is used first in Genesis 14:13 to identify Abram and his family group by the other peoples. This is a mystery because Abram was a Syrian from Mesopotamia (present-day Iraq). So even though today the name *Hebrew* connotes ethnicity, in Abram's day it may not have had such value. Perhaps the designation of Hebrew by the other peoples of the area can be better understood in the view that Abram was a believer and a worshipper of the one true God in the midst of a polytheistic culture. (This is purely the author's view.)[6]

The name *Jew*, which again connotes ethnicity, was used primarily to describe the people living in Judah after the kingdom of Israel was split in two: Israel to the north and Judah to the south. After the Babylonian captivity, the returning exiled Israelites were all referred to as Jews and were so designated in the New Testament. This designation separated them from the rest of the surrounding cultures, collectively known as "the Gentiles." Out of these peoples, the Hebrew people, God called men to proclaim His truths and warnings of judgment on Israel for their disobedience and the breaking of His covenant.

A prophetic warning always preceded judgment to give the Israelites a chance to turn away from their backsliding and turn back to Him. Their mistakes and disobedience mirror ours. These men, whom God called for this purpose, were known as "the prophets." They spoke only what God had told them to, and it *always* came true. Their prophecies of God's judgment and restoration were confirmed in Jesus's life, death, burial, and resurrection. But there are prophecies of the End Times yet to be fulfilled. That is why it's so important for us to be in a right relationship with God the Father through His Son, Jesus, the Christ. Amen.

This relationship, once restored, is what allows us to leave the failures and wreckage of our past for a bright and hopeful future, a life of victory over everything that once enslaved us.

So we have very briefly covered the origin and universal order of man. We've also covered the legitimacy of the Holy Bible as God's inspired, inerrant, infallible, and preserved Word that reveals Himself to us. We also looked at His eternal plan to bring us back into a relationship and restore our rightful place in that universal order.

And we've also covered the portion of the Bible referred to as being prophetic. Many people have claimed to be prophets or seers like Nostradamus. There are objects that have been described as prophetic, such as the Mayan calendar. Nostradamus and others like him have come and gone. Their so-called prophecies, which were nothing more than vague ramblings, have fallen flat and came to nothing. The Mayans no doubt could read the stars and had methods of counting and building that were extremely accurate. Their prophetic voice, however, echoed hollowly. December 12, 2012, came and went, with no cataclysmic end of all things; it was just another day in December.

Only the Word of God can be trusted for its prophetic accuracy. The reason God has given His prophetic voice is so that, when it comes to pass just as He said it would, we as humans have no excuse not to believe in Him.

Here are some verses that show how God Himself tells us He is the source of prophecy and that what He says will happen will indeed happen:

> Declaring the end from the beginning and from ancient times the things that are not yet done, saying, "My counsel shall stand, and I will do my pleasure." (Isa. 46:10)

> Tell and bring forth your case; Yes, let them take counsel together. Who has declared this from ancient time? Who has told it from that time? Have not I, the Lord? And there is no other God besides Me, a just God and a Savior; there is none besides Me. "Look to Me, and be saved. All you ends of the earth! For I am God and there is no other." (Isa. 45:21–22)

> So shall My word be that goes forth from my mouth; it shall not return to me void, but it shall accomplish what I please, and it shall prosper in the thing for which I sent it. (Isa. 55:11)

> For false christs and false prophets will rise and show great signs and wonders to deceive, if possible, even the elect. See, I have told you beforehand. Therefore, if they say to you, "Look, He is in the desert!" do not go out; or "Look, He is in the inner rooms!" do not believe it. (Matt. 24:24–26)

This last prophecy comes from Christ Himself regarding those who would come after His ascension and try to trick people into thinking that Christ had come again and drawn people away from the truth. Jesus will no doubt come again, but no one knows when it will happen.

The entirety of Matthew 24 is prophetic, and verse 34 declares, "Assuredly, I say to you, this generation will by no means pass away till all things take place." If you read Matthew 24 and Mark 13 side by side, you will see that the event the Jews referred to for that generation was the coming persecution under Nero and subsequent destruction of the temple in AD 70 under Titus.[7] These events came to pass just as Jesus said they would, and there is more to come.

CHAPTER 6

MAKING MY OWN WAY

But for right now, the writer and the reader, it's prudent for us to continue to get to know each other. We've established a good foundation using creation, the Bible, and the prophets to prove not only God's existence but also His deep interest and activity in human affairs. After all, four thousand years of recorded human history pointing to one event (the crucifixion) has got to have some kind of credibility, right?

Like I said before, I can't make you believe in anything, but there's one thing for sure you can't deny … Your life is a mess, your future is uncertain, and if you don't make some improvements, you'll be right back in there.

I started using drugs the summer between the sixth and seventh grades. Back then the prominent strain of marijuana was called Columbian or Columbian Gold. It was very potent and didn't take much to mess you up. I smoked all that summer, and when the school year started, I would walk to school with someone else who smoked pot. He was in the ninth grade. We would stop behind the grocery store near our school and smoke a bowl. I had pre-algebra first period and suffered from a learning disability in math. So, needless to say, smoking some really powerful weed right before my hardest class was a bad idea.

As anybody who has ever smoked weed before knows, you're pretty much useless afterward except to daydream and eat. When the high wears off, you're all tired and burned out. I suppose there are folks out there who say marijuana is natural, God made it, He gave it to us to enjoy, and it gets creative juices flowing and the like. Yeah, I said all that as well to justify my wanting to get high, but the truth is, it just made me really dense and very lazy.

I struggled during my seventh, eighth, and ninth grades (repeating the eighth grade), all because I was too stoned to do the work. And by that time I was too convinced in my own mind not to even care anymore about grades or my future. I dropped out of high school at the beginning of the tenth grade. The only time I quit smoking pot was when I was in the service. When I took the ASVAB (Armed Services Vocational Aptitude Battery) test, I didn't do so well. I scored low in math and needed to get some college credits to supplement my score.

So I did. It wasn't easy, but I wanted to serve my country and become a paratrooper more than anything. And on January 7, 1987, I boarded a bus in Phoenix, bound for the induction center at Fort Benning in Georgia. Back then, they could still yell at you and say horrible and mean things, which, when they weren't directed at you, were pretty comical. I had packed on quite a bit of weight between the ages of seventeen and nineteen from all the beer and alcohol I drank, so I was pretty chubby. My drill instructors were very vocal about my weight and let me know daily their disapproval of my physical condition and appearance. They singled out the fat guys and troublemakers, and made examples out of them. Their intention was to break you and make you either quit or become a soldier.

I had quit at everything in my life, especially school or anything that took a lot of effort or wasn't something I was any good at. The one thing I disliked most was running. I was in poor physical condition with zero stamina. I felt like a bucket of chum in a shark tank. The drill sergeants would get in my face and say, "Why are you here, Private? You're never gonna make it!" When they found out I was trying to get to the airborne, they really started in on me. I mean, it got bad. I wanted to quit. I tried to talk myself into quitting. I practiced the words I would say and tried to convince myself that it was okay to quit, but I didn't.

With each passing day, the PT (physical training) got a little easier. I began to see the value in their approach, and deep down, I started to feel like I belonged to something, something greater than myself. I can't tell you how good it felt to graduate from basic and AIT (advanced infantry training), but I still had to make it through airborne training, known as "jump school." Upon my graduation, my drill instructors shook our hands and signed our graduation books. I was so excited to see what the senior drill was going to write in mine. I thought it would be something encouraging and hopeful like, "Way to go. You've had great improvements this cycle. Good luck in the airborne!"

But all it said was, "Learn to lead." It was such a blow. He didn't even mention one single thing I did right. Just when I didn't think it could get any worse, the other drill instructor walked up and said, "You're never gonna make it through jump school, let alone to the 82nd Airborne Division. I was crushed—beyond crushed, near tears—but I wasn't going to give him the satisfaction of my sorrow. I purposed right there and then in my heart that I would do whatever it took to make it.

The one thing they couldn't take from me was the confidence I now had by graduating. I had passed all the tests and had been found acceptable according to their standards. I would build on this confidence and succeed, I told myself, no matter what they said.

It was mid-May in Georgia and already hot. They marched us from the graduation parade field over to an area off to the side and informed us that there would be an advanced class being pushed through. That meant that whoever wasn't chosen would have an additional week tacked on before getting assigned to his or her duty station.

Back then, jump school consisted of three weeks or phases known as "ground week" (when demanding physical and mental training was employed to prepare the student to meet the basic qualifications of a paratrooper), "tower week" (when the student honed the skills he or she had learned and began to learn how to exit the aircraft in a mass tactical formation and land safely; this meant the use of mock aircraft and a harness and pulley system that allowed the student to actually jump from a thirty-four-foot tower and experience the simulated opening shock of a parachute), and "jump week" (when the remaining students, who had successfully passed all prior requirements and physical tests, finally got to exit an aircraft at twelve hundred feet five times, one being at night).

If you made all five jumps without getting hurt or disqualified for unsafe practices, you were now jump qualified and considered airborne. This also meant that you got to dress differently than the rest of the regular army. You wore a maroon beret, and when you were in your dress green uniform, you got to wear highly polished jump boots and tuck your pant legs into the boots. We looked so cool!

The confidence I gained there at jump school would stay with me for the rest of my life. I was no longer a quitter, but a hard-charging, high-speed, low-drag airborne soldier who could run two miles in thirteen minutes with no problem.

Once at my duty station at Fort Bragg, the real training started. I thought jump school had made me airborne, but I was wrong. Jump school only qualified me. Being airborne meant maintaining a high level of physical readiness. The PT got harder, the training was more intense, and the jumps … Almost all of them were at night.

Being airborne is a lifestyle. For those of you who don't know who or what the 82nd Airborne Division is or what their mission is, I'll briefly explain. The paratrooper was born out of necessity during World War II to be able to put highly motivated and trained soldiers on the battlefield as fast as possible by the use of parachutes or gliders.

Nearly all the parachute or glider drops at the invasion of D-Day took place "behind enemy lines" to overrun the enemy, secure vital strategic pieces of land, and isolate or cut off command and control centers or important places like airstrips or bridges.

The 82nd is the hub of America's quick reaction force and can have a complete military contingency on the ground anywhere in the world en route within eighteen hours of notification. Everything an army needs to win the battle, including tanks, artillery, trucks, cooks, and of course the soldier himself, is brought to the battlefield by way of parachute.[8]

The 82nd is completely self-contained, and to the best of my knowledge, it is the only whole airborne division in the free world. It is a sight to behold, the low-approaching thunder of aircraft after aircraft flying in mass tactical formation, and then to see the small black dots being released from the bellies of the planes. Each dot blossoms into a canopy, and the enemy knows the full might and broadsword of American power has come for him or her.

Yes, I had become quite confident in myself indeed. Although self-confidence is a good thing, it would prove ultimately detrimental to me. I drank profusely, downing as much alcohol as was set before me. As I stated before, my heavy drinking and poor relational choices created the inevitable circumstances that would destroy my career. Now, I'm not casting the blame on anyone but myself. If I had been more mature, I could have avoided those circumstances that led to everything just crumbling before my eyes. Before I knew it, I received two field grade article 15s, lost all my rank and possibility of promotion, and my pay. I ultimately chaptered out of the service just two months shy of being able to receive any veterans' benefits.

CHAPTER 7

TOUCHED BY EVIL

During this time, when all that disappointment was happening, I began to search everywhere for answers. One day one of the guys suggested we get an Ouija board. I had never even heard of one before. So we went, of all places, to a toy store, and there it was, right there on the shelf, for any child to purchase. I'm not going to get into the history of this so-called toy save to say that it's not just an innocent novelty.

We gathered in a room on the second or third floor of our barracks and followed the instructions. The oracle, (an independent piece of the board that glides across the board when touched), began to indeed move and spell out words and sentences just as advertised. But it would work well for only one particular soldier. When his hands were on it and he was the one asking the questions, it would answer.

Everybody took his turn asking questions via the soldier the board picked to communicate through. He was starting to get pretty freaked out and wanted to quit, but we pressed him to continue. I had a lot of questions because my life at the time was all messed up, so I was seeking answers. At first the board claimed to be the spirit of a famous silent movie actor long since dead. Then, strangely enough, the alleged spirit changed to that of a boy slave who issued a warning, saying he was in some sort of limbo. If he spoke a warning to us, he would be granted passage out and entrance into heaven.

It told us to quit seeking answers from the board and said the board was bad and that there were many bad spirits there. Then, as if that wasn't enough, it asked whether we had a Bible and directed us to the gospel of John 3:19–21. "And this is the condemnation, that the light has come into the world, and men loved darkness rather than light, because their deeds were evil. For everyone practicing evil hates the light and does not come to the light, lest his deeds should be exposed. But he who does the truth comes to the light, that his deeds may be clearly seen, that they have been done in God."

As soon as the warning was given, the boy disappeared. The board fell silent, and we all stared at each other in wonderment. We looked at each other when the oracle began moving again. "Wait!" it said. "Don't you want to play anymore?"

We said no.

It became agitated and said, "Why?"

We said, "Because we were warned not to," and it really got annoyed, demanding that we tell it the name of who issued the warning. We asked it its name, and its response was so horrifying that I won't repeat it. It kept asking who had issued the warning, but we were too afraid to say.

Finally, it asked, "Who?" one last time, and one of the soldiers sitting in on it said something really smart alecky, and it became hyper agitated. The oracle began doing figure eights on the board, faster and faster. The soldier who had his hands on it and was asking the questions was terrified. His eyes were as wide as saucers and fixed on the board, a look of petrified disbelief plastered on his face. Suddenly, with a final blazing fast figure eight, the oracle flew off the board all by itself and exploded into pieces in midair.

That was one scared bunch of soldiers, let me tell you. After the shock wore off, I searched for someone to help me destroy the board. We took it outside and burned it while reciting Scripture over its burning carcass.

But that isn't all that happened. A short time later—I'm not sure how many days later—I went home, as I lived off post. I hadn't wanted to go home to an empty house, battling loneliness, but they told me I had to go home; that I couldn't stay in the barracks. I sat there, sad and confused, hurt and mad. Aside from those normal feelings of betrayal, something else was nagging at the back of my mind. Something was telling me not to go home, but I had no choice.

I remember pulling up to the little house and feeling like something was watching me from inside the house and outside the house at the same time. It was everywhere. The house was really small. I felt compelled to make a search of the house. Something was wrong. I had a large bowie knife I kept under the seat of my truck. I took it out and entered the house through the kitchen door.

Immediately past the kitchen were the living room and a tiny bathroom just to the right. My bedroom was a mere few feet across the living room. The kitchen was clear, and so was the bathroom. There was a spare bedroom between the bathroom and my bedroom, but I always kept the door closed because I got weird vibes from it.

I quickly opened the door and snatched the light on. To my utter shock, the window was open. I want to say the window was either stuck or nailed shut. It was almost thirty years ago, twenty-six to be exact, at the time of this writing. Either way, the window was open. Nothing appeared to be missing, just that window open and a cold draft coming in. I closed the window and continued my sweep of the house; I had just one more room and one more closet to check.

It was all clear, but I was really rattled. I turned on the TV and tried to stay awake until the sun came up. I grew very tired, and it was late, like one or two o'clock in the morning. I had been through basic and AIT, I'd jumped into the night's skies, and I'd even been deployed to Honduras, but nothing shook me up like that night. I was a paratrooper, for goodness' sake. What was I scared of? So I talked myself into going to bed.

My aunt had given me a glow-in-the-dark rosary a bishop had blessed. I used to keep it in a small plastic pouch in my breast pocket along with a small pocket New Testament. Every time I made a jump out of an airplane, I would put my hand over it and say, "God, please protect me, but if my parachute fails, Your will be done." Then I would jump out. I took the rosary and set it on the nightstand next to my bed. It glowed so brightly that it would illuminate the room on the darkest night. I settled beneath the covers and almost instantly became super peaceful. It's as if I was sound asleep and completely awake at the same time My room was transformed into a lush, green Eden (for lack of better words).

A figure appeared, wearing a long, black trench coat with a tall top hat and a half moon for a face. I wasn't scared at all but extremely relaxed, peaceful, and *awake*. The figure began to communicate to me telepathically. It said, "Turn around." In the vision, I did. There, in front of me where I now faced, a large bookcase floated in the air. The figure summoned a large red book from the shelf. It flopped open and floated. The figure told me (again, in my mind) to read the book. I knew immediately what was happening. I had been searching for answers in that unholy Ouija board, and now I came face-to-face with evil. The figure said, "Read the book."

And I said, "No! I know who you are, and this is the book of knowledge, and I have no business in it. I command you in the name of Jesus Christ to leave my house at once!"

Now remember, during the whole vision, I was completely at peace and totally awake. But the moment I said, "In the name of Jesus," I was no longer in that lush, green, peaceful Eden but transported back into my bed. I was crushed into my bed with such force that I couldn't move a muscle, and the overwhelming feeling of fear and helplessness engulfed me.

I was wide awake while half of my head was smashed into my pillow so only one eye could see. The weight and pressure are beyond description. I was truly paralyzed with fear. It gripped me at my very core. I knew I was in serious trouble. I had been looking for answers in the wrong place, and evil had come calling. It was right there in my room with me, pressing me into my bed and letting me know how utterly helpless I really was.

I felt like I was going to disappear into oblivion. One more second, and I would dissolve into the darkness, not that I would physically disappear but be overtaken. I believe it was seeking my surrender, wanting me to just give up and let it consume me. My extreme desire to know my future had brought something to the surface from the deep. And now I was in the water with it, paralyzed, ready to drown. With every ounce, my last ounce of resistance and will, I made my trembling vocal chords work to say the only words I knew would, could help. I said, "In the name of Jesus Christ, I command you to get out of my house!"

I was instantly released. I sat straight up. The residue of fear was dripping from me like a bucket of cold grease had been poured over me. The room was pitch black, and terror started to grip me again. I looked over at the nightstand in search of my rosary to grab it and start praying, but I couldn't see it.

The distance between my bed and the doorway where the light switch was located was probably no more than ten feet, but it seemed like miles. I was so scared, and each passing second in the darkness brought more fear. I had to get to that switch and expose the darkness to the light. I had to find my rosary and pocket New Testament. I had to hold them and pray.

With every ounce of courage I had, even more than it took to jump out of an airplane—in fact, way more—I jumped out of bed and sprinted the two measly steps it took to reach the switch and snatch it on, I can't tell you how much comfort the light brought. It was only electricity harnessed in an incandescent lightbulb, not even sunlight, but it felt wonderful.

I was badly shaken and needed to find my rosary and New Testament. I looked over at the nightstand, and there they were, right where I'd put them. I didn't understand why I hadn't seen them when I was on the bed only inches away from them. Why was it so dark? Had I just been dreaming? Was it just a bad nightmare?

I walked over to the nightstand and grabbed the rosary, still in its little clear plastic bag. I walked back over to the light switch and, cupping my hand over the rosary, held it up close to my eye and turned off the light. The rosary had quit glowing and never glowed again.

It wasn't a bad dream; it had actually happened. I had been visited by evil, and the darkness had touched my life in a very real and tangible way. My mind went back to that Bible verse a few days before. "For everyone practicing evil hates the light and does not come to the light, lest his deeds should be exposed. But he who does the truth comes to the light, that his deeds may be clearly seen, that they have been done in God." (John 3:20-21).

Jesus's name is truth, and it was more than enough to make the darkness flee but not before it left a stain on my soul. I have no idea where the knowledge came from to invoke Jesus's name during that situation. Well, I didn't know then, but now I do. It was the Holy Spirit giving me the right words and the only name that could have saved me.

CHAPTER 8

HEAVENLY VERSUS DEMONIC WISDOM

I shared this story to show you the dynamics between the spirit realm and the soul plane and how our physical bodies get caught in the crossfire. My spirit was still dead asleep, and I was being led about by the soul. I had been hurt and betrayed, and my emotions wanted answers, which caused my body to go to the store and buy that board and participate in something very dangerous.

But because I had said those words about accepting Jesus as my Lord and Savior years before, I belonged to Him. So when darkness came for me, Jesus sent His Holy Spirit to nudge mine awake long enough to tell my soul what to say. My soul had been gripped by fear, my body paralyzed; rendering my soul and body useless. It was my spirit that had forced my mouth to invoke Jesus's name and send the evil fleeing.

The Bible strictly condemns the use of mediums, sorcery, witchcraft, astrology, necromancy, and the like as a means of fortune-telling or inquiring of one's future—and for good reason. These methods open up the individual to demonic influence, sometimes called "possession." The ultimate goal of evil is to draw you away from God. It promises everything and delivers nothing but death.

God wants you to ask Him about your future. He wants you to include Him in your plans and ask for His blessing in all things. This ensures our success and keeps us from stumbling and getting caught up in trouble. The stronger and deeper your relationship with God becomes, the better and clearer you will hear His voice and see His hand at work in your life. He is at work right now through this book, drawing you to Him as He reveals Himself through my own experience and, most importantly, through His Holy Spirit-inspired Word, the Bible.

It's no mistake that you're right here, right now, reading this book. It is your divine appointment. Isn't it awesome to know that even when you were doing everything you could to mess up your life, God was working out the solution? This book isn't the solution; it only points the way. The Bible has your answers, and once you receive it by faith as God's inspired Word, it begins to expose those areas of your life that need attention and then gives you the power to do it.

Let me show you an example. As the story I just told you illustrated, I was hurt and looking for answers somewhere other than God. This is what the Bible has to say about that situation. Proverbs 16:24–26 says, "Pleasant words are like honeycomb, sweetness to the soul and health to the bones. There is a way that seems right to a man, but its end is the way of death. The person who labors, labors for himself, for his hungry mouth drives him on."

God's Word has a way of reaching you right where you are at. Observe. I was seeking pleasant words about my future to comfort my soul (mind, emotions, and will), to make myself feel better. But the consequences of using that board were very dangerous and could have ended tragically. I was laboring to find answers and feed my soul some peace. God wants us to ask Him and Him only. His ways are always best and lead us on the right path, the path to eternal life in the kingdom of God complete with every provision … no wants, no needs, no worries.

That is not to say that life won't happen to us. We will always have bills, our kids will get colds, and somebody will open his or her car door into ours. Life will continue to happen, but once we've entered into the kingdom of God, we can be at peace and rest, assured that God will *always* provide exactly what we need when we need it 100 percent of the time without fail, guaranteed. Matthew 6:25–34 says,

> Therefore I say to you, do not worry about your life,
> what you will eat or what you will drink; nor about your

body, what you will put on. Is not life more than food and the body more than clothing? Look at the birds of the air, for they neither sow or reap nor gather into barns; yet your Heavenly Father feeds them. Are you not of more value than they? Which of you by worrying can add one cubit to his statue?

So why do you worry about clothing? Consider the lilies of the field, how they grow: they neither toil nor spin; yet I say to you that even Solomon in all his glory was not arrayed like one of these. Now if God so clothes the grass of the field, which today is, and tomorrow is thrown into the oven, will He not much more clothe you, O you of little faith?

Therefore, do not worry saying, "What shall we eat?" or "What shall we drink?" or "What shall we wear?" For after all these things the Gentiles seek. For your heavenly Father knows that you need all these things. But seek first the kingdom of God and His righteousness, and all these things will be added to you. Therefore do not worry about tomorrow, for tomorrow will worry about its own things. Sufficient for the day is its own trouble.

Jesus Himself spoke this passage right after He received the anointing of the Holy Spirit for His intense three-year ministry on earth. I encourage you to get to know the historical Jesus, for in so doing, you will come face-to-face with the Messiah, the Savior, and judge of the world, the King of Kings and Lord of Lords. There is none like Him in all the earth. Bless His holy name!

CHAPTER 9

WAKE ME UP

Worry is an emotion, and excessive worrying can cause us to act impulsively. Let's face it; our impulsiveness is what drives us to places we later on regret. That is why it's so important for our spirits to be awake, so they can take charge of our souls before we make an unhealthy choice. God's Word plus an awakened spirit equals good, healthy, correct choices. You can make the right decisions, but you can't do so alone. You need the Bible's direction and the Holy Spirit's revelatory discernment.

Some of you may have already read parts of the Bible before or are reading it now and have found it hard to understand. There is a reason for this. First Corinthians 2:9–14 says,

> But as it is written: "Eye has not seen, nor ear heard, nor have entered into the heart of man the things which God has prepared for those who love Him." But God has revealed them to us through His Spirit. For the Spirit searches all things, yes, the deep things of God. For what man knows the things of a man except the spirit of the man which is in him? Even so no one knows the things of God except the Spirit of God. Now we have received, not the spirit of the world, but the Spirit who is from God, that we might know the things that have been freely given to us by God. These

things we also speak, not in words which man's wisdom teaches but which the Holy Spirit teaches, comparing spiritual things with spiritual. But the natural man does not receive the things of the Spirit of God, for they are foolishness to him; nor can he know them, because they are spiritually discerned.

The natural man is the combination of the physical earthen body being led about the soul plane (mind, emotion, and will) whose spirit is yet asleep.

Two things are needed to understand the Bible: (1) a desperate and broken condition of the heart with an intense desire to seek out God (the understanding that you need God and that there is no place else to look but up) and (2) the Holy Spirit's unction or anointing to open your understanding. The Holy Spirit has been wooing and drawing you to Jesus. He has been leading you all this time to a place where you would and could seek out a relationship with God the Father, our Creator.

Remember all those close calls you've had? That was Him protecting you because you are chosen specifically, individually, for His purpose. Once you receive Jesus as Lord and Savior and accept that He is God and that He died for *you*, you will enter into the kingdom of God and become a son or daughter of the Most High. Amen.

Remember all those weird people around town handing out Bible tracts and talking to you about Jesus? Well, that was the Holy Spirit at work through those believers. Some of those weirdos were just like you—lacking hope, locked up, and unsure. But now they have a life, a good job, the right spouse, a home, bills paid, and every need met, living a life in service to God Almighty. There is no shame in serving the one who died for you. Jesus suffered the most brutal and tortuous death you could ever imagine. He deserves your love, honor, respect, and devotion.

Do you know anyone else who would allow himself or herself to be nailed to a cross for you? And that was the end of the torture. He was beaten so badly that He wasn't even recognizable anymore. The suffering He endured for you and me is unimaginable, yet He did it gladly. Hebrews 12:1–3 says,

Therefore we also, since we are surrounded by so great a cloud of witnesses, let us lay aside every weight, and the sin which so easily ensnares us, and let us run with endurance the race that is set before us, looking unto Jesus, the author and finisher of our faith, who for the joy that was set before Him endured the cross, despising the shame, and has sat down at the right hand of the throne of God. For consider Him who endured such hostility from sinners against Himself, lest you become weary and discouraged in your souls.

There is *no other way* to God. There are many religions out there, but none of them can make or meet the claims of Christianity. All other religions attempt to reach up to a god they can never know, but Christianity is God's reaching down to man through His Son, Jesus the Christ, so we may have a living relationship with God. In Jesus, the prophetic Word was and is confirmed, and the revelation of God is realized.

"Let not your heart be troubled; you believe in God, believe also in Me. In My Father's house are many mansions; if it were not so, I would have told you. I go to prepare a place for you. And if I go and prepare a place for you, I will come again and receive you to Myself; that where I am, there you may be also. And where I go you know, and the way you know." Thomas said to Him, "Lord, we do not know where You are going, and how can we know the way?" Jesus said to him, "I am the way, the truth, and the life. No one comes to the Father except through Me. If you had known Me, you would have known My Father also; and from now on you know Him and have seen Him." Philip said to Him, "Lord, show us the Father, and it is sufficient for us." Jesus said to him, "Have I been with you so long, and yet you have not known Me, Philip? He who has seen Me has seen the Father; so how can you say, 'Show us the Father'? Do you not believe that I am in the Father, and the Father in Me? The words that I speak to you I do not speak on My own authority; but the Father who dwells in Me does the works. Believe

Me that I am in the Father and the Father in Me, or else believe Me for the sake of the works themselves. (John 14:1–11)

> He is the image of the invisible God, the firstborn over all creation. (Col. 1:15)

> Also I will make him My firstborn, The highest of the kings of the earth. (Ps. 89:27)

> In the beginning was the Word, and the Word was with God, and the Word was God. (John 1:1)

> He [John the Baptist] was not that Light, but was sent to bear witness of that Light. (John 1:8)

> For whom He foreknew, He also predestined to be conformed to the image of His Son, that He might be the firstborn among many brethren. (Rom. 8:29)

> Whose minds the god of this age has blinded, who do not believe, lest the light of the gospel of the glory of Christ, who is the image of God, should shine on them. (2 Cor. 4:4)

> Now to the King eternal, immortal, invisible, to God who alone is wise, be honor and glory forever and ever. Amen. (1 Tim. 1:17)

> By faith he forsook Egypt, not fearing the wrath of the king; for he endured as seeing Him who is invisible. (Heb. 11:27)

These words were written for our profit so we could see the love of God poured out on the people of the earth. It also will stand as a testimony in the day of judgment against all those who rejected the truth of God's Word and His Christ. God the Father has made every effort to reveal Himself and His plan of redemption to His creation. Those who choose to resist and reject Him will have no excuse, but those of us who receive His Word with gladness and accept His free gift of salvation will receive everlasting life. Amen.

But meanwhile, here on earth there is much to do and much to learn. God wants us to be engaged in holy activities and to form deep, meaningful relationships with those in need so He can live and love through us.

So what do you say? Is it time to wake up that spirit of yours? If you're still reading this book, it's because you're serious about making some much-needed changes in your life. You know your way isn't working so well, and you're open to suggestions. It also means you're not resisting the Holy Spirit's tugging at your heart and that you're ready to do what it takes to get your life back on track and start moving forward. Congratulations! I'm proud of you.

CHAPTER 10

IN THE GARDEN

How did our spirits become asleep? Earlier we discussed who man or woman is and where we came from. We, being the very best of the essence of God, enjoyed a life in the presence of God in a place called the garden of Eden. This isn't some fairy-tale place but a real place here on earth, and the Bible gives its exact location in Genesis 2:8–15. I want you to read from chapter one through chapter two, verse twenty-five. Come back here when you're done.

Okay, great, glad to see you back! Some of you may not have access to a whole Bible but only to the New Testament. Don't worry; I'll be as thorough as I know how. Also, my wife and I will be praying that whole copies of the Bible will be made available to you through your chaplain, in Jesus's name, amen.

The creation events are told in narrative form, read from Genesis 1:1–2:3, and cover the universe including the earth. They are told to us in narrative form for two reasons: (1) simplicity and (2) a standpoint of faith. If we believe in God, then it's enough for us to know that it's God who is telling us it was Him who created it. We don't need scientists proving or disproving theories to make us believe. Even still, science is on our side; quantum physics proves God's existence any way, but for now we move in faith. Amen.

From now on, faith will be the means by which you allow the Holy Spirit to bear witness with your spirit that God's Word is true. God has given us a free will either to believe or not to believe, either to have faith or not to have faith. But understand this: God is moved by your faith, not your circumstances. He uses your circumstances to bring you to faith.

Hebrews 11:6–7 says, "But without faith it is impossible to please Him, for he who comes to God must believe that He is, and that He is a rewarder of those who diligently seek Him. By faith Noah, being divinely warned of things not yet seen, moved with godly fear, prepared an ark for the saving of his household, by which he condemned the world and became heir of the righteousness which is according to faith."

Faith is essential for spiritual growth, enlightenment, action, and what you are most interested in right now ... answered prayer. "Please God, get me outta this mess." As we move forward, ask God to increase your faith and just come to Him as a little child with no reservations or preconceptions. I want you to do a little test that will help you better understand the faith that is already inside you. Walk over to your or your cellie's bunk or to the stool at your desk/table or even to the toilet. Stand with your back to it, close your eyes, and sit down. Sit there for a second with your eyes closed and then come back here.

If you followed instructions, you sat down with your eyes closed and put your trust in an object you couldn't see to support you and not let you fall to the ground. Of course you know that the object was there, so it was easy for you to trust in it. But the object itself is made up of millions of atomic particles you cannot see. They are totally invisible to the naked eye. But God has made a way for those atoms to be able to bond together to form mass, and that mass becomes a chair, stool, or whatever. But ultimately you've chosen to put your trust in something you cannot see: the atom. So it is with your faith in God; He is invisible, but He has taken atoms and formed them into a man named Jesus so you could see Him, the One who is there to support you when you need it most. Amen.

As for the creation event, they are numbered in days, but science clearly proves that the universe and earth are very, very old indeed. So how can this be? Observe what the Scriptures have to say:

> For a thousand years in Your sight Are like yesterday
> when it is past, And like a watch in the night. (Ps. 90:4)

> But, beloved, do not forget this one thing, that with
> the Lord one day is as a thousand years, and a thousand
> years as one day. (2 Peter 3:8)

These references to time aren't literal increments of time. Those
would date the earth only ten thousand years or so. The reference is
the author's way of showing us that God not only sees things but also
operates from and in an eternal perspective. He is eternal. We are
mortal. We have a beginning and an ending, but God is and always
will be in a state of eternity. To Him and for those of us who are saved,
we are eternity present. The creation event took place in eternity past.
We must use timelines as a reference point because the universe is in a
state of constant movement and decay. We are born, we grow old, and
we die. All life has this same cycle until Jesus comes back and restores
all things back to Himself in the original universal order.

> For I consider that the sufferings of this present time
> are not worthy to be compared with the glory which
> shall be revealed in us. For the earnest expectation
> of the creation eagerly waits for the revealing of the
> sons of God. For the creation was subjected to futility,
> not willingly, but because of Him who subjected it in
> hope; because the creation itself also will be delivered
> from the bondage of corruption into the glorious liberty
> of the children of God. For we know that the whole
> creation groans and labors with birth pangs together
> until now. (Rom. 8:18–22)

> Now I saw a new heaven and a new earth, for the first
> heaven and the first earth had passed away. Also there
> was no more sea. Then I, John saw the holy city, New
> Jerusalem, coming down out of heaven from God,

prepared as a bride adorned for her husband. And I heard a loud voice from heaven saying, "Behold, the tabernacle of God is with men, and He will dwell with them, and they shall be His people. God Himself will be with them and be their God. And God will wipe away every tear from their eyes; there shall be no more death, nor sorrow, nor crying. There shall be no more pain, for the former things have passed away." Then He who sat on the throne said, "Behold, I make all things new." And He said to me "Write, for these words are true and faithful." (Rev. 21:1–5)

And finally, concerning the creation event and our faith, this Scripture should be enough so we can move on. Deuteronomy 29:29 says, "The secret things belong to the Lord our God, but those things which are revealed belong to us and to our children forever, that we may do all the words of this law."

God will indeed reveal to us more and more mysteries of the universe, but for now, what He has revealed we are responsible for, and we have no excuse not to believe in Him. Whatever He has chosen to keep secret for now is for our own good, just like we keep secrets from our own children.

In Genesis 2, we see the institution of the Sabbath day, a holy day, a day of rest. We will talk more about this later. Then in verse 7, the man of the dust was formed, and God breathed the breath of life (the spirit man ushered forth by the Holy Spirit), and he was living in the garden of Eden we spoke of earlier.

Eden means "delight" or "pleasure." It was the geographic location, the region of the earth, Adam and Eve lived in. Its name meaning is best understood as "the garden of God in which He delights." This wasn't a small backyard garden, but a vast, lush, well-watered garden that supported a great multitude of wildlife and vegetation. Adam was first and walked the earth alone for a time. As God brought forth all living creatures from the earth, He brought them to Adam for him to name.

This story is important for us to discuss and gives us a glimpse into the awesome brilliance and greatness Adam possessed before his fall from grace. By virtue of naming all the animals, we can clearly see that Adam received intimate, sacred knowledge from creation itself. The creation spoke its mysteries to him, and he understood. Adam was the greatest scientist the world would ever see next to God Himself. He had to be; to be able to identify and name something indicates intimate, working knowledge. Adam knew, just by looking at creation, what it was and how it was made, and he didn't even have a microscope or petri dish.

That is how awesome he was, and that is the same kind of greatness that is still inside us, just waiting to be set free at the appointed time … But I'm getting ahead of myself. Just understand this and receive it deep down in your spirit. You are the greatest of all creation. Nothing in all the cosmos was ever created in the image of almighty God except man or woman. We carry the very best of God inside us. The love, wisdom, knowledge, understanding, reason, compassion, and faith of the living God are inside us, waiting to be released. We are the image of God. That image fell, and God Himself has come to restore that image to its rightful place of honor in the whole universe.

So if Adam was so great, why and how did he fall? The answer is going to surprise you, and it's more complex than assuming Adam was some half-baked creation or that God just didn't get it right the first time. God never makes mistakes, and everything He does or allows to happen has an ultimate purpose for the greater good. Romans 8:28 says, "And we know that all things work together for good to those who love God, to those who are called according to His purpose." So what good could come out of the fall? First, we'll see how, and then we'll know why.

Go back and reread Genesis 2:15–25. Verse 15 shows us God giving man his first job, but it was more than just getting up early and slaving away all day. God instructed Adam in good stewardship principles. Adam took care of the Lord's garden. He was nurturing the living things therein. God was teaching Adam responsibility. Besides, before the fall, Adam didn't sweat; he didn't get fatigued. It wasn't too hot or too cold. Everything was perfect. Adam gained a great love and respect for all life in the garden, and he took very good care of it.

Verses 16–18 go together and introduce some very exciting theology. They have to be read and understood together as two separate events that would bring forth man's fall from grace, but it is much more than that. From a human perspective, it might seem cruel or unjust that a loving God would set before His choice creation an object that could ultimately cause his demise and introduce such misery into the world. But as I just stated, that is a human, worldly perspective.

The Tree of Knowledge of Good and Evil is first mentioned in Genesis 2:9 and scripturally it is placed right next to the Tree of Life. The Tree of Life represents an existence in the presence of God with every need supplied out of God's never-ending economy. This also includes immortality. The Tree of Knowledge of Good and Evil represents a life separate from God, apart from Holy Communion, apart from God's glory.[9] Adam was advised that both trees existed in his new garden home; he was not only warned but also commanded: Genesis 2:17 says, "But of the tree of the knowledge of good and evil you shall not eat, for in the day that you eat of it you shall surely die." This death was all inclusive as a result of man's autonomy, affecting spiritual, soul, and physical dimensions. It ultimately brought forth all manner of decay and corruption for all living things as sin entered in and replaced God's glory.

But before we start bashing Adam and accusing God of being unjust, let's continue our study. Right after God commanded and warned Adam, He said, "It is not good for man to be alone; I will make him a helper comparable to him" (Gen. 2:18). The King James Version of the Bible calls her a "helpmeet." Both *helper* and *helpmeet* are interchangeable. The Greek word for "helper" is so rich with meaning that our English word *helper* doesn't fully express its depth. A helper is one who stands by, assists, comforts, encourages, strengthens, uplifts, and so on. The word denotes more than a good intention but rather a purpose.[10]

This doesn't indicate, as some say, that Adam was somehow incomplete or insufficient. If Adam had been created in the image of

God, in His likeness, how then could he have been insufficient? He couldn't be; he was perfect. The bringing forth of Eve as a helper reveals a greater purpose, a plan. God didn't design us to be alone but rather to work together in unity as the Father, the Son, and the Holy Spirit do. We'll learn more about the Trinity or Godhead later. It is vital that your faith be strengthened in the knowledge of God's purpose—that is, to know that God has a purpose for you and that He is working it out on your behalf.

Let's continue. Verses 18–20 show us three truths:

1. God had a purpose.

2. Adam was brilliant and exhibited some of God's essence, knowledge, understanding, and wisdom.

3. God's purpose wasn't yet realized.

Verses 21–24 focus on the unity and eternal relationship between man and woman. It reveals the deeply entrusted responsibility that man has toward woman. She, being taken from a rib, shows she is equal in value to him in every way. God lives and loves through both the man and woman in ways that maximize and benefit His creation and purpose the best. Both have intrinsic and inherent values that complement the other, bringing perfect unity and purpose in the will of God. In verse 23, Adam instantly recognized that she was as much a part of him as he was. There is no indication that she was somehow inferior in Adam's response. On the contrary, the value Adam placed on Eve is so intense that it is second only to the value he placed on God Himself. The bottom line is that man's greatest responsibility next to the Godhead is woman. I want you to take a second here and reflect on how you view yourself and the opposite sex. It's imperative for both of you to understand how valuable you are to God and to each other.

Men, how have you been treating your wives, girlfriends, mothers, or sisters? Do you see them as the best part of you or something to be exploited, an object to be toyed with and then discarded? Who are you?

What is a man? When someone is asked these questions, a common response may be, "A man is someone who pays the bills, takes care of his family, and handles his business." But these responsibilities (when taken care of properly) are only a by-product of a man's character. If a male steals, sells drugs, or does any other illicit activity to gain money, then he's really not handling his business, is he? Yes, crime can be a means to an end, but that end usually results in an unwanted consequence. If the result of your actions lands you in jail or prison, then you aren't there for your family and have left them for predators, all alone.

In light of what we've just learned as men, how we've treated women thus far should be at the forefront of our reflections. Belittling attitudes and language toward women must stop. Abuse on any level must stop. Pouring drugs into women and using them for selfish desires must stop. And most gravely I think all forms of exploitation and any dialogue using words to glorify dehumanization must stop. One of the most shameful acts of the Devil that can be devised toward any human being is the human sex slave trade industry. We as men should be at the leading edge of protecting the innocent and vulnerable.

A man who has stepped into his greatness makes an honest effort to remain humble at all times. He will not even consider exploiting another human being, especially a woman, because he knows where she came from. Many of us haven't had the benefit of a good male role model, but that season has ended and can no longer be used as an excuse. As we've learned from our study thus far, human fathers can fail, but our heavenly Father *never* fails. At times it can seem that God isn't listening or doesn't care, but He is only working out our futures, and that takes time, His time. And His timing is *always* perfect.

Moreover, man in God's design has been given the responsibility of stewardship over the earth and all that is in it. Observe the following:

> And God said, Let us make man in our image, after
> our likeness: and let them have dominion over the fish
> of the sea, and over the fowl of the air, and over the
> cattle, and over all the earth, and over every creeping
> thing that creepeth upon the earth. So God created

man in his own image, in the image of God created he him; male and female created he them. And God blessed them, and God said unto them, Be fruitful, and multiply, and replenish the earth, and subdue it: and have dominion over the fish of the sea, and over the fowl of the air, and over every living thing that moveth upon the earth. (Gen. 1:26–28 KJV)

This "stewardship" extends to all creation and is a reflection of God's character, as indicated by the words "Let us make man in our image, after our likeness." Since God is ascribed a male gender in Scripture and is further described as a father, then it's safe to conclude that men should follow the example their Creator set. All the things a good father does and says are summed up in love. The protection, provision, wisdom, and instruction of a father issue forth from a heart of love. Observe the following:

Be watchful, stand firm in the faith, act like men, be strong. Let all that you do be done in love. (1 Cor. 16:13–14 ESV)

But as for you, O man of God, flee these things. Pursue righteousness, godliness, faith, love, steadfastness, gentleness. (1 Tim. 6:11 ESV)

First Corinthians 13 contains the most profound dissertation on the subject of love and contrasts the brevity of even spiritual gifts to the enduring presence of love.

If I speak in the tongues of men or of angels, but do not have love, I am only a resounding gong or a clanging cymbal. If I have the gift of prophecy and can fathom all mysteries and all knowledge, and if I have a faith that can move mountains, but do not have love, I am nothing. If I give all I possess to the poor and give over my body to hardship that I may boast, but do not have love, I gain nothing. Love is patient, love is kind. It does not envy, it does not boast, it is not proud. It does not dishonor others, it is not self-seeking, it is not easily angered, it keeps no record of wrongs. Love does not delight in evil but rejoices with the truth. It always protects, always trusts, always hopes, always perseveres. Love never fails. But where there are prophecies, they will cease; where there are tongues, they will be stilled; where there is knowledge, it will pass away. For we know in part and we prophesy in part, but when completeness comes, what is in part disappears. When I was a child, I talked like a child, I thought like a child, I reasoned like a child. When I became a man, I put the ways of childhood behind me. For now we see only a reflection as in a mirror; then we shall see face to face. Now I know in part; then I shall know fully, even as I am fully known. And now these three remain: faith, hope and love. But the greatest of these is love. (vv. 1–13 NIV)

Here we see the definition of real love and learn that a real man isn't afraid to let this attribute shine forth. When love is at the forefront of every action, you cannot help but succeed. When love is in control, there is no need for a tough front, and the facade of machismo melts away. Violence and intimidation only breed fear and contempt in others. Respect isn't demanded but earned. A true leader invokes the desire to follow in those being led. When we genuinely lead out of a heart of love, others recognize this, and trust is formed.

Our wives and girlfriends look to us to lead and know we should be leading. When our loved ones get on us for falling short, it's because they know we can do better. We must let the Word of God be the final rule of faith and conduct for us concerning all things. Our approach to marriage should be thus:

> Husbands, love your wives, just as Christ loved the
> church and gave himself up for her to make her
> holy, cleansing her by the washing with water through
> the word, and to present her to himself as a radiant
> church, without stain or wrinkle or any other blemish,
> but holy and blameless. In this same way, husbands
> ought to love their wives as their own bodies. He who
> loves his wife loves himself. After all, no one ever hated
> their own body, but they feed and care for their body,
> just as Christ does the church—for we are members of
> his body. "For this reason a man will leave his father
> and mother and be united to his wife, and the two will
> become one flesh."(Eph. 5:25–31 NIV)

These verses leave no room for error. Love is summed up by
sacrifice. That means time, money, and—most importantly to your
wife—emotional and spiritual support. Next we see the following:

> Drink water from your own cistern,
> And running water from your own well.
> Should your springs overflow in the streets,
> your streams of water in the public squares?
> Let them be yours alone,
> never to be shared with strangers.
> May your fountain be blessed,
> and may you rejoice in the wife of your youth.
> A loving doe, a graceful deer—
> may her breasts satisfy you always,
> may you ever be intoxicated with her love.
> Why, my son, be intoxicated with another man's wife?
> Why embrace the bosom of a wayward woman? (Prov.
> 5:15–20 NIV)

Why embrace the bosom of a wayward woman? These verses too
make it perfectly clear that one's wife should, *must*, be sufficient for

her husband in every way. Whether she is short, tall, or slim makes no difference, just as it should be for her toward you as well. Once we have chosen a mate, that is it. We should stick to our guns and be a man. All too often men get with a woman, and she gets pregnant, and her body changes; then to our great shame, we become disinterested. She now carries with her the scars of childbearing and the emotional scars of betrayal and abandonment. Don't be like that. Love her for her sacrifice and *never* leave her side or just stay away from her altogether. Don't start something you can't finish. Be a man.

Women, how do you see the men in your lives? Are they just dumb, easily manipulated pieces of meat you use to get your way? Do you cater to their ego and need of praise to get what you want? Do you jump from man to man because the next one fits your fancy better? Do you use your body to get back at those who mistreat you? Women! The sum of your self-worth is *not* your sexuality. How you dress, walk, or talk isn't what defines you. I know this is how the world has made things, but it isn't who you really are.

Almost every industry exploits women to sell their products. This has been going on for so long now that many women actually believe there's nothing wrong with it and fall right into its destructive power, ever searching to be more beautiful and desirable. The Devil has completely corrupted the true beauty of woman and deceived her on every level; and to top it off and compound the problem, he whispers his final poison into her ear so she feels she's never pretty enough, slim enough, or desirable enough. So she holds all other women in contempt with an envious eye, judging herself against them. No matter how much makeup she puts on, no matter how many men she sleeps with, no matter how slim she is or how well her clothes cling to her, she will never be good enough. She will never feel truly loved, appreciated, and valued.

Wake up, sisters, and take hold and control of your future. If you had any idea of the greatness that is in you, you wouldn't be sitting there now. But soon you will know and never be used or abused again. You will get your children back, and your lives will be restored. This is what the Bible has to say about you: "So God created man in His own image;

in the image of God He created them, male and female He created them" (Gen. 1:27). Did you hear that? Both men and women were created to bear the image of God, His likeness, and His holy attributes. We are equals. But there is much more to this. Let's continue.

Proverbs 12:4 says, "An excellent wife is the crown of her husband." It doesn't say a crown but "the crown." The word *crown* is a military term, meaning to encircle for attack or protection. It is related to wisdom. Proverbs 4:7–9 says, "Wisdom is the principal thing; therefore get wisdom. And in all your getting, get understanding. Exalt her, and she will promote you; She will bring you honor, when you embrace her. She will place on your head an ornament of grace; A crown of glory she will deliver to you."

Put these two verses together, and we see that women in God's design are fierce protectors who encircle the minds of their husbands and feed them the wisdom of God they receive from God. What else does the Bible have to say about women in God's design?[11] Proverbs 31:10–31 says,

> "Who can find a virtuous wife? For her worth is far above rubies." The heart of her husband safely trusts her; So he will have no lack of gain. She does him good and not evil all the days of her life. She seeks wool and flax, and willingly works with her hands. She is like the merchant ships, she brings her food from afar. She also rises while it is yet night, and provides food for her household, and a portion for her maidservants. She considers a field and buys it; from her profits she plants a vineyard. She girds herself with strength, and strengthens her arms. She perceives that her merchandise is good, and her lamp does not go out by night She stretches out her hands to the distaff, and her hand holds the spindle. She extends her hand to the poor, yes, she reaches out her hands to the needy. She is not afraid of snow for her household, for all her household is clothed with scarlet. She makes tapestry for herself; her clothing is fine linen

and purple. Her husband is known in the gates, when he sits among the elders of the land. She makes linen garments and sells them, And supplies sashes for the merchants. Strength and honor are her clothing; she shall rejoice in time to come. She opens her mouth with wisdom, and on her tongue is the law of kindness. She watches over the ways of her household, and does not eat the bread of idleness. Her children rise up and call her blessed; her husband also, and he praises her: "Many daughters have done well, but you excel them all." Charm is deceitful and beauty is passing, but a woman who fears the Lord, she shall be praised. Give her of the fruit of her hands, and let her own works praise her in the gates.

The word *virtuous* has many meanings. It can mean "moral purity," "upright," "orderly," "correct," but here it means something completely different. *Virtuous* is derived from the Hebrew word *chayil*. Again, it's a purely military term meaning "strength, soldiers, company, great forces, goods, host, might, power, riches." It comes from the root word *chul*, which means "endure" and "prosper." Put these two together, and it forms the complete meaning: an elite army with the strength to endure and prosper! How about those apples? You have living inside you and at your disposal an elite army ready to do battle on your behalf with the strength and support it needs to not only endure the fight but also win the battle and then prosper.[12]

There are twenty-two verses dedicated to women here alone. These verses include the duties, responsibilities, actions, and attributes of a wife or mother, which complement her husband, manage her home, secure her own good reputation, and leave no one feeling left out. That is why she is called a "virtuous wife," a *chayil* wife, because she attacks the daily issues of life with an urgency and military mind. She has a mind of strategy focused on conquering the day and draws on the strength of her God, who has a limitless supply.

This should encourage you beyond measure. I know you may not feel like a conqueror right now, but you will the more you draw into a closer relationship with the living God. Amen. God is beginning to unlock the mysteries of who you really are and reveals to you the power within and the wisdom to succeed and find the right man who will treat you as God has intended for you to be treated.

"Lord, right now in the name of Jesus, I pray for all these women reading this book and being touched and led by your Holy Spirit. I pray that every yoke would be broken, every bondage lifted, every lie exposed; and that You, Father, would take these, Your daughters, and set them free so they will no longer fall prey to godless men and the lies of the Devil. Help them to clearly see and understand that their sexuality isn't the sum of their self-worth but that their identity is found in the risen Christ, who is the husband of all. Amen and amen."

Let's go back to the garden and see what else we can learn about our first parents. "Therefore a man shall leave his father and his mother, and shall cleave unto his wife; and the two shall be one flesh" (Gen. 2:24). This verse explains God's design for marriage. There is a leaving and a cleaving in the process. Both men and women form close bonds with their parents, and though Scripture commands us to "honor our father and our mother," we should do so while maintaining a healthy distance that allows the married couple to flourish in their own set of marital applications and maturities. There must be a drawing away from the parental boundaries and instructions to form their own style of parenting while applying what they've learned from their parents. Men or women who continually allow the influence of their parents into their marital relationship are unhealthy. That isn't to say that we cannot or shouldn't seek advice from those who have the wisdom to help but rather that we are careful not to allow parents to dictate every decision regarding their marriage.

Some parents have a difficult time letting go of their children and try to maintain control of their child's every move. Some young adults are too afraid to make a move without the parents' consent or are unable to firmly but respectfully ask the parents to allow them to make their own choices and mistakes. For a couple, a husband and wife, to be effective and fulfill God's purpose, they must leave one set of instructions to cleave or cling to each other and form their own.

Last, this verse expresses a mystery of the spirit and flesh becoming one. In the flesh, the joy of sex may be realized and God ordained as a relational expression that joins the two together in a way that represents a deep spiritual unity. They are to enjoy this union in the sight of God, and it is sanctified in holiness. It's never to be given to another, or it becomes the opposite of its intended purpose, and because the two have become one, when one of the spouses commits adultery, he or she has unwittingly joined another flesh and spirit to his or her own. This union becomes an abomination.

The spirit of adultery is just that, a spirit or demon; so when one lies with someone other than his or her spouse, the two join with the demon as well. I suggest that you take this issue very seriously, because when you join yourself (have sex) with another, you transfer all his or her spiritual garbage into your own spirit. It is a spiritual STD, and it's no joke. That's why there's so much confusion, jealousy, hatred, and violence in the midst of relationships formed out of sex and not marriage. The most critical element is missing: God. God sanctifies sex in marriage and makes it holy. Apart from marriage, sex is filled with every vile demon of lust and always ultimately ends with death.

> All things are lawful for me, but all things are not helpful. All things are lawful for me, but I will not be brought under the power of any. Foods for the stomach and the stomach for foods, but God will destroy both it and them. Now the body is not for sexual immorality but for the Lord, and the Lord for the body. And God both raised up the Lord and will also raise us up by His power. Do you not know that your bodies are members of Christ? Shall I then take the members of Christ and make them members of a harlot? Certainly not! Or do you not know that he who is joined to a harlot is one body with her? For "the two," He says, "shall become one flesh." But he who is joined to the Lord is one

spirit with Him. Flee sexual immorality. Every sin that a man does is outside the body, but he who commits sexual immorality sins against his own body. Or do you not know that your body is the temple of the Holy Spirit who is in you, whom you have from God, and you are not your own? For you were bought at a price; therefore glorify God in your body and in your spirit, which are God's. (1 Cor. 6:12–20)

The good news is that God has made a way to forgive the big mistakes we've made. By the way, a harlot is anyone, man or woman, who is having sex outside of marriage. Period. As we continue our journey, we will discover that God has made a way to pass over our sins and transgressions so we aren't consumed by guilt. In a nutshell, for now, all you need to know is that Jesus is that way. He is the Only Way, and by accepting Him as Lord and Savior, our sins are forgiven. Ask Jesus right now to show you more and to begin to reveal Himself to you more fully through the ministry of the Holy Spirit. If you feel the Holy Spirit drawing you to repentance and the lordship of Jesus right now, and you know you're ready to do what it takes, go to the back of this book and recite the sinner's prayer the Lord has provided for you. If not, please continue reading.

Genesis 2:25 says, "And they were both naked, the man and his wife, and they were not ashamed." The reason they weren't ashamed or embarrassed isn't because they were nudists at heart but because of two reasons: (1) They were innocent and untainted by the stain of sin; and (2) though they were naked, they were still clothed with something … the glory of God. In their pristine condition, they both reflected the light and glory of God. They were like lightbulbs glowing in the radiance of holiness and godliness. This is very important to understand for our study. When Adam looked at Eve and she looked at him, they saw the most beautiful light radiating from one another. The beauty they saw in one another is beyond our understanding, but suffice it to say, they were a sight to behold—in fact, breathtaking.

One can only imagine the bliss they enjoyed and the deep, meaningful relationship and bond that grew between them. They loved a love the likes of which this world has never seen since, a love so pure and strong that it was second only to God's love for them.

CHAPTER 11

MEAT AND POTATOES

Now we're going to get to some serious meat-and-potatoes study. Remember the three pointes we discussed back in Genesis 2:18–20? That God has a purpose, that Adam was exhibiting some of God's attributes, and that God's purpose hadn't yet been realized? Well, here we go.

Genesis 3:1–24 deals with the temptation and fall of man so naturally for some of you that the question will arise: "So if God knew this would happen, why did He let it?" Or "Why did God set this temptation before Adam if He knew Adam would fall?" These are the questions that need to be asked:

1. What was God's purpose?

2. What was God's plan?

THE PURPOSE

> For thus says the Lord, who created the heavens, who is God, who formed the earth and made it, who has established it, who did not create it in vain, who formed it to be inhabited: "I am the Lord, and there is no other." (Isa. 45:18)

Then God said, "Let Us make man in Our image, according to Our likeness; let them have dominion over the fish of the sea, over the birds of the air, and over the cattle, over all the earth and over every creeping thing that creeps on the earth." So God created man in His own image; in the image of God He created him; male and female He created them. Then God blessed them, and God said to them, "Be fruitful and multiply; fill the earth and subdue it; have dominion over the fish of the sea, over the birds of the air, and over every living thing that moves on the earth." (Gen. 1:26–28)

Declaring the end from the beginning, and from ancient times things that are not yet done, saying, "My counsel shall stand, and I will do all My pleasure." (Isa. 46:10)

So shall My word be that goes forth from My mouth; it shall not return to Me void, but it shall accomplish what I please, and it shall prosper in the thing for which I sent it. "For you shall go out with joy, and be led out with peace; the mountains and the hills shall break forth into singing before you, and all the trees of the field shall clap their hands." (Isa. 55:11–12)

For I know the thoughts that I think toward you, says the Lord, thoughts of peace and not of evil, to give you a future and a hope. Then you will call upon Me and go and pray to Me, and I will listen to you. (Jer. 29:11–12)

"And God will wipe away every tear from their eyes; there shall be no more death, nor sorrow, nor crying. There shall be no more pain, for the former things have passed away." Then He who sat on the throne said, "Behold, I make all things new." And He said to me "Write, for these words are true and faithful." (Rev. 21:4–5)

God's purpose was to create all the universe and then place the earth in just the right place with just the right atmosphere to sustain life. Then His purpose was to create man in His image and give man dominion over the earth. Another part of God's purpose was to create the heavens, the earth, and man because they pleased Him. It made Him happy to give so graciously to His creation and have communion with man. And though this isn't an exhaustive list of God's purposes, finally we see for this study that God's purpose is to establish His sovereignty in the heart of man. So that man would choose to love and worship God of His own free will. And ultimately God would grant obedient men an eternal future in the presence of God, where sin doesn't exist, nor corruption, decay, or death. Amen.

THE PLAN, PART 1

This is where most folks get lost or decide there's no God or that if there is a God, He is cruel and unjust or just plain uninterested in and far removed from man and his circumstances. Nothing could be further from the truth. First, let us consider this: What does it mean to be created in the image of God? Is it that God created two people, Adam and Eve, and placed them on the earth and that they are now deities unto themselves, mini gods? No, not exactly.

While the historical Jesus walked the earth during the three years of His earthly ministry, He no doubt performed miracles like raising the dead, giving sight to the blind, restoring limbs, casting out devils (demons), and exhibiting power and authority over nature itself. After Jesus's death, burial, resurrection, and ascension back to the Father, His disciples continued to walk in the power of God by performing the exact same type of miracles, including raising the dead. People are still being raised from the dead today in places like Africa, where holy men and women of God preach the true gospel of Jesus the Christ under the anointing of the Holy Spirit.

The great need of humanity to be connected to their Creator is always present regardless of the time or place. In this fertile soil of the heart, God plants the seed of His Word, then waters it with His Holy Spirit and the power of God, complete with signs, wonders, and miracles; it bursts forth through the lives of the believers. When we allow the attributes of God to rise to the surface, when our spirit is awakened, the image of God is reflected through us, and the character of God is revealed in the earth's realm. Bless His holy name.

The love, wisdom, knowledge, understanding, reason, compassion, and faith of Jesus are the same attributes that flow through us. We bear the same image. We share the same anointing. Jesus performed miracles because He was and is God. The apostles and disciples performed miracles because Jesus, who is God, was working in them through the power of the Holy Spirit.

So where was Adam's power? What was God's plan for him? How did Adam exhibit the attributes or image of God? First, in Adam's pristine condition, every second was filled with God's glory, power, and wisdom. Adam and his wife were a sight to behold. They were beautiful beyond words, covered in the glory of God and radiant. With all this going for them, what could have pulled them away from God and made them disobey God's command? The choice to disobey is more complex than one might first think. First, let's deal with the thought that temptation was some cruel joke.

James 1:13–15 says, "Let no one say when he is tempted, 'I am tempted by God'; for God cannot be tempted by evil, nor does He Himself tempt anyone. But each one is tempted when he is drawn away by his own desires and enticed. Then, when desire has conceived, it gives birth to sin; and sin, when it is full-grown, brings forth death." This verse clearly states that God isn't doing the tempting; evil Satan is. Moreover, the temptation in itself is harmless until the soul plane processes it, and then it is acted on. For our first mother, Eve, the temptation alone wasn't enough to draw her away. Observe Genesis 3:1–6.

> Now the serpent was more cunning than any beast of the field which the Lord God had made. And he said to the woman, "Has God indeed said, 'You shall

not eat of every tree of the garden'?" And the woman
said to the serpent, "We may eat the fruit of the trees
of the garden; but of the fruit of the tree which is in
the midst of the garden, God has said, 'You shall not
eat it, nor shall you touch it, lest you die.'" Then the
serpent said to the woman, "You will not surely die.
For God knows that in the day you eat of it your eyes
will be opened, and you will be like God, knowing
good and evil." So when the woman saw that the
tree was good for food, that it was pleasant to the
eyes, and a tree desirable to make one wise, she took
of its fruit and ate. She also gave to her husband with
her, and he ate.

The elements necessary for temptation to take hold are the following:
(1) doubt, (2) an intentional distortion of the truth, (3) a lie, (4) a desire,
and (5) an act of the will. Eve knew the Tree of the Knowledge of Good
and Evil was there in the midst of the garden. But it wasn't until the
serpent, possessed by the Devil, cast doubt into Eve's mind (the soul
plane) that she reacted. A careful study will reveal not only that our first
parents fell from grace but more importantly that the Enemy employs
his strategies against us today.

Genesis 3:1 (KJV) says, "Now the serpent was more subtle than any
beast of the field." The word *subtle* means "cunning, crafty, shrewd." It
isn't by accident that Satan chose the serpent to possess and approach
Eve. All serpents (snakes) are by nature ambush predators. They lie in
wait for their prey to come by, unsuspecting and alone; then they strike,
and it's too late.

First Peter 5:8 says, "Be sober, be vigilant; because your adversary
the devil walks about like a roaring lion seeking whom he may devour."
Here Satan is called "your adversary" and depicted as a lion, a terrifying
and powerful predator. Again, lions are ambush predators who hunt in
prides. They seek out the weak, sick, and old. When the chase starts,
they separate their quarry from the rest of the herd and isolate it. There,
when the defenseless animal is alone and without help, lions completely

devour it. There is no hope or escape, and that is exactly how Satan attacks. He wants you isolated, apart from any help. The things that isolate us are our desires. The Devil uses them against us, but they're more subtle than that. He is the one who plants the seeds of desire in the first place, and then we act on them and become weak, sick, and isolated. Once we're isolated, he really goes to work by telling us we're no good and useless, that we deserve to be mistreated and abused, so we dive further into despair and depravity until only a shell of us remains. He wants us too weak to say no to drugs, too sick to have meaningful relationships, and too isolated by our own actions. Watch how Satan employed his tactics against Eve.

Satan had Eve alone and isolated. How do we know that? First Corinthians 11:9–11 says, "Nor was man created for the woman but woman for the man. For this reason the woman ought to have a symbol of authority on her head *because of the angels*. Nevertheless, neither is man independent of woman, nor woman independent of man, in the Lord" (emphasis added).

Contextually this verse is talking about head coverings in the church, but the allusion is to Eve being uncovered when Satan approached her. To be "covered" means to be protected, as if Adam were her covering. Then we see that this verse clearly states that Eve was uncovered, unprotected, and alone.

So the tempter approached Eve, who was alone in the garden, minding her own business. "And he said to the woman, *'Has god indeed said* you shall not eat of *every* tree of the garden?'" (emphasis added). The first thing he did was plant a seed of doubt. "Has God indeed said?" (Did God really say that? Is that what He really meant?) Then he implied that there was something more, that God was holding something back from her. "Every tree?" This is exactly how Satan comes at us today. Watch what happened next.

Genesis 3:2 says, "And the woman said to the serpent, we may eat the fruit of the trees of the garden, but the fruit of the tree in the midst of the garden, God has said, 'You shall not eat it, nor shall you touch it, less you die.'"

Eve's response wasn't completely accurate. She added to what God had originally told Adam in Genesis 2:16–17. She added, "Nor shall you touch it." This shows us, first, that Eve was alone. If Adam had been there at that moment, he would have corrected any variance from the truth. Also, remember that Adam had already named all the animals. He had intimate working knowledge of his surroundings. He knew how they were made, so the second he saw the serpent, whom he had just named, he would have known at once that there was something very different about him. He would have said, "Hey! I named the serpent yesterday and you're not him. You look like him, but you sure don't act like him. Get outta here, imposter, and leave my wife alone!" So Eve was alone.

Second, Eve intentionally distorted the truth. The seed of doubt was already taking root. Her autonomous response clearly shows that she was seeking either sympathy or confirmation from the serpent. And he was more than glad to oblige. Genesis 3:4 says, "Then the serpent said to the woman, "you will *not* surely die" (emphasis added). Satan, through the serpent, blatantly lied to Eve's willing ears and directly challenged God's command. Then he drove home the poison and said, "For God knows that in the day you eat of it, your eyes will be opened, and you will be like God knowing good and evil" (Gen. 3:5).

Eve allowed the seed of doubt to take root, and then, seeking justification for her own desires, she sought someone to agree with her. And when she had completely accepted and received in her heart a lie in exchange for the truth, she acted on it. Genesis 3:6 says, "So when the woman saw that the tree was good for food, that it was pleasant to the eyes, and a tree desirable to make one wise, she took of the fruit and ate" This is how Satan approaches us still today, and it's always the same. It never changes. So once you learn to recognize his tactics, you can avoid them; moreover, you can call them by name and expose them. Satan fears being exposed, and he will flee every single time he is. This is how he came at Eve, and this is how he comes at us every single time. Understand this!

First John 2:16 says, "For all that is in the world—the lust of the flesh, the lust of the eyes, and the pride of life—is not of the Father but is of the world."

"The woman saw that the tree was good for food" (the lust of the flesh).

"That it was pleasant to the eyes" (the lust of the eyes).

"And a tree *desirable* [emphasis added] to make one wise" (the pride of life).

These are three tactics Satan uses against us every single time. I keep saying this because I want you to get it. It's only three measly methods, but they are very powerful. They operate in the soul plane. That is why your spirit *must be awake* to pull your thoughts into subjection.

Now we're talking about God's plan. Remember, we said that Genesis 2:16–18 needs to be studied together. Well, here it is ... Verses 16 and 17 are God's command to Adam. It is specific, detailed, and concise: (1) provision, (2) a warning in the form of commandment (an order), and (3) the consequences for breaking the commandment.

But then, curiously falling on the heels of verse 17, the thought seemingly shifts to a different idea. Verse 18 says, "It is not good that man should be alone." On the surface, this statement seems to be an afterthought, such as, "Oh, I didn't think about man being lonely. I'll just whip him up a companion to keep him company." Verse 18 is an extension of God's plan. If man was going to be the only one of God's creation to bear His image, he would have to be tested and found worthy. Remember, God chose us (man or woman) to be in His likeness. Not even the most powerful angels in heaven were created in the exact image of God, only us. And that is why Satan hates us so much.

Here comes that pesky question again: "If God knew man was going to fall, why didn't He just make man better so he wouldn't or couldn't fall?" The answer is simply free will. God wanted His choice creation to love, serve, and worship Him of his or her own free will. All of God's creation has free will, including the Devil. Satan chose to go his own way, and so can man. So can you.

CHAPTER 12

THE LOVE TEST

But it's more complex than that. Let's follow the trail of bread crumbs and see where they lead. Man had to be tested on two levels. The first test is the love test, and the second test is the obedience test. Why did man have to be tested? What would it prove? It comes down to being the bearer of God's image. When we think of God, we naturally think of majesty. He is big, vast, unreachable, and unknowable; and though His ways are past finding out, we certainly can reach Him and know Him because our spirits are part of Him, and Jesus reveals Him to us. But the word we will focus on for this study is *holy*. Holy is defined as "moral perfection, wholeness, soundness." [13] It is the sum of God's character because all the other attributes of God are found and perfected in it. And God's people are called to pursue holiness, to pursue perfection. Holiness is the complete, absolute, and immediate rejection of evil. God created man to be just like Him, and he would have to be tested and proved.

Our first clue is found in Genesis 3:5: "For God knows that in the day you eat of it your eyes will be opened, and you will be like God, knowing good and evil." The key words are "be like God, knowing good and evil." There are two perspectives here that must be understood: God's perspective versus Eve's perspective. Eve had everything provided for her, but the seed of doubt and the accusation of the Devil that God was withholding something good from her (self-rule) proved to be too much. In Eve's perspective, to know good and evil meant to have more knowledge, a knowledge that would somehow give her more than God was offering.

God's perspective is totally different. To know means "to detect, discover, discern." Satan used a word play on the term "to know": to Eve, there was one meaning; and to God, there was another. So if God is completely holy and rejects the presence of evil, how can God know evil? And how does this tie into the image of God and man being tested?

Consider an inventor who creates a useful invention. He draws it out on paper and does all the math. He gathers all the best material and puts his invention together, then finally moves into the test phase. No inventor in his or her right mind would try to sell an unproved invention. He has to make sure it works properly and safely, and functions for its purpose. Our purpose as God's creation is to love and worship God of our own free will and to be able to detect and reject evil as soon as we see it just like God does and to be able to withstand evil and temptations, even when confronted with it face-to-face, just like God did.

There was a moment in eternity past when God Himself was confronted with evil and even tested in His very own house. Before we continue this study, let us pray together for understanding. Say this prayer with me: "Holy Spirit of the living God, we come in the name and by the precious blood of Jesus. Open the eyes of our understanding according to Your Word, which cannot lie, so that whatsoever we should ask in Your name according to Your will shall be done. Reveal to us now, according to the holy Scriptures, the fall of Lucifer and the testing of men so we might be perfected as You are perfect, Most Holy Father. Amen.

> How you are fallen from heaven, O Lucifer, son of the morning! How you are cut down to the ground, you who weakened the nations! For you have said in your heart: "I will ascend into heaven, I will exalt my throne above the stars of God; I will also sit on the mount of the congregation on the farthest sides of the north; I will ascend above the heights of the clouds, I will be like the Most High." (Isa. 14:12–14)

83

Son of man, take up a lamentation for the king of Tyre, and say to him, "Thus says the Lord God: 'You were the seal of perfection, full of wisdom and perfect in beauty. You were in Eden, the garden of God; every precious stone was your covering: the sardius, topaz, and diamond, beryl, onyx, and jasper, sapphire, turquoise, and emerald with gold. The workmanship of your timbrels and pipes was prepared for you on the day you were created. You were the anointed cherub who covers; I established you; You were on the holy mountain of God; You walked back and forth in the midst of fiery stones. You were perfect in your ways from the day you were created, till iniquity was found in you.'" (Ezek. 28:12–15)

From these two Scripture passages, we learn that prior to Satan's being cast to earth, his name was Lucifer, which means "light bearer" or "light bringer." Ezekiel 28:14 calls him "the anointed cherub who covers." These two names indicate his high office and estate in heaven as the angel who reflected the light and glory of God, and was responsible for protecting God's holy mountain, even God's throne. A cherub is an order of angel, not a cute, little, winged naked baby, as depicted on some artwork, but a powerful being, terrifying in sight. Ezekiel 28:13 suggests that another role of Lucifer was to lead the choirs of heaven in worship of the Most High.

Lucifer was perfect in his ways, the Scripture says in Ezekiel 28:15 *until* "iniquity was found in [him]." *Iniquity* means rebellion against God and His holy standards. As we see in Isaiah 14:13–14, Lucifer's heart changed toward God. All that God had given and entrusted him with wasn't good enough, and he rebelled. Five times he exclaimed that he would either exalt himself above or be equal with God. At that very moment, God, sitting on His throne, came face-to-face with this rebellion, and He knew, detected, discovered, and discerned evil. Of course, Lucifer was immediately expelled from heaven. The point is that evil tested God in His own house. God is too holy to tolerate evil on any level, so He rejects it and removes it instantly. Now man who was created in the image of God had to be tested. Since we are not God, there had to be a testing process to a perfect man, God's choice creation.

This leads us to what may have motivated Lucifer into rebellion. First, consider that he was one of the most powerful, wisest, talented, responsible angels in heaven. All that fame could get to anyone's head. But one particular event took place that just set him off, and I think it was just too much to find out that, as awesome as he was, there was another created being moving in who would be chosen to bear the image of God. Amen.

Psalm 8:4–6 says, "What is man that You are mindful of him, And the son of man that You visit him? For You have made him a little lower than the angels And You have crowned him with glory and honor. You have made him to have dominion over the works of Your hands; You have put all things under his feet."

Here we see that God considers man just like we think about our loved ones; so does God long for us. Then it says that He visits us, and that means He forms relationships with us. James 2:23 says that if we believe in God, our faith is counted as righteousness to us and that we are called friends of God. If the living God, the Creator of all who is seen and unseen, calls you a friend, that is a relationship. Then it says that we were created a little lower than the angels, yet God crowned us with glory and honor, and that we have dominion over the works of His hands and that all things have been put under our feet. That, my friends, was the last straw for Lucifer: to know that man, being created, wasn't as powerful as he was, yet was chosen to be the image bearer and to have dominion. I can imagine what Lucifer may have said...

"Who does man think he is anyway? All puny and stuck in that earthen vessel. He can't even fly! I'll show You that man isn't worthy. I'll show You that man is a mistake, and I'll take my rightful place in the order of things. I'll show you!"

THE PLAN, PART 2

So God's plan was set in motion.

1. Lucifer was expelled. Luke 10:18 says, "And He said to them, 'I saw Satan fall like lightning from heaven.'"

2. Lucifer (now Satan) was placed in the garden. Ezekiel 28:13 says, "You were in Eden, the garden of God; every precious stone was your covering: the sardius, topaz, and diamond, beryl, onyx, and jasper, sapphire, turquoise, and emerald with gold. The workmanship of your timbrels and pipes was prepared for you on the day you were created."

3. Man was placed in the garden. Genesis 2:7–8 says, "And the Lord God formed man of the dust of the ground, and breathed into his nostrils the breath of life; and man became a living being. The Lord God planted a garden eastward in Eden, and there He put the man whom He had formed."

4. Man was given responsibility and a choice. Genesis 2:15–18 says, "Then the Lord God took the man and put him in the garden of Eden to tend and keep it. And the Lord God commanded the man, saying, 'Of every tree of the garden you may freely eat; but of the tree of the knowledge of good and evil you shall not eat, for in the day that you eat of it you shall surely die.' And the Lord God said, 'It is not good that man should be alone; I will make him a helper comparable to him.'"

5. Man was tested to receive a reward. Jeremiah 17:10 says, "I, the Lord, search the heart, I test the mind, Even to give every man according to his ways, According to the fruit of his doings."

6. Our test is that we may be proved, because we are God's glory, and He won't give His glory to another. Isaiah 48:10 says,

"Behold, I have refined you, but not as silver; I have tested you in the furnace of affliction." First Corinthians 11:7:7 says, "For a man indeed ought not to cover his head, since he is the image and glory of God; but woman is the glory of man."

So now we have explored God's purpose and His plan to test man. Remember, there are two basic tests: the love test and the obedience test. Obviously Adam failed miserably at the obedience test, or did he? In the purest sense of obedience, yes, absolutely he disobeyed God's command not to eat of the Tree of the Knowledge of Good and Evil. But it was necessary that he did disobey so that the rest of God's plan could unfold. I know this can be hard to wrap our head around, but I'll try to be very clear.

The decision for Adam to disobey wasn't of choice but of necessity. Adam was perfectly content with his existence and home. He wasn't looking for more or to be free of God's rule. Observe what 1 Timothy 2:13–14 says. "For Adam was formed first, then Eve. And Adam was not deceived, but the woman being deceived, fell into transgression."

This Scripture, along with Genesis 2:19–20 and 1 Corinthians 11:9–11, proves that Adam wasn't present when Eve was deceived. Adam would have immediately recognized that there was something wrong with the serpent. Eve was uncovered (unprotected), and a fallen angel named Satan took advantage of her. First Corinthians 11:11 says that neither woman nor man is independent of the other. They are eternally joined. You must understand this key point to fully grasp the fall of man. When Adam returned to Eve, his heart was broken in two. She was no longer clothed with the glory of God. There he stood, radiating and glowing, and there she stood, dull and dirty, hair greasy, wrinkles forming, with bad breath. Every stain of sin was upon her. I can only imagine the tears he must have cried and the sorrow that overwhelmed him at the sight of his beloved consumed with the onset of death and decay. But Adam's love for her wouldn't die. He knew he was eternally joined to her and that God would make a way to bring them back. He couldn't let his best friend and beloved die in her sins. So he did the only thing he could to save his wife. He went and got her. He cried, and, trusting God to fulfill His plan and redeem them both, he took of the fruit and ate.

Immediately, the glory of God departed from him, and sin and time entered the earthly realm. He felt the sun beating down on him, the earth beneath burned his feet, and the back of his throat became parched. And in his heart formed an unquenchable thirst to know God again, to be back into a relationship with Him. And since we all came from one man, we share this thirst. This is why drugs and alcohol always leave us feeling empty and worse off than before we started using them. We try to fill the void with substances and chemicals, but that spot is reserved for the Spirit of God. Apart from physiological effects of drugs and alcohol, like hangovers, there is a residue of deep despair on our spirits that leaves us feeling ashamed and guilty.

So Adam failed the obedience test, but it wasn't his to take anyway. That test belonged to Jesus. But Adam passed the love test with flying colors and exhibited the attribute of God … love. Our first father sacrificed everything for his wife. Adam is a type of Christ.

> Nevertheless death reigned from Adam to Moses, even over those who had not sinned according to the likeness of the transgression of Adam, who is a type of Him who was to come. (Rom. 5:14)

> Husbands, love your wives, just as Christ also loved the church and gave Himself for her. (Eph. 5:25)

Both Adam and Jesus removed their crowns and glory to come, and they rescued those whom they loved. Throughout Scripture, the church, which is composed of every believer on earth, is also known as the body of Christ and the bride of Christ. These metaphors are used to illustrate the deep relational value God places in His people. Jesus is called the bridegroom and husband. These metaphors are used to illustrate not only relational value but also provisional values and responsibility. Jesus is responsible for the whole of humanity, and He willingly left His home in heaven to put on human clothes and be one of us so He might win us back to Himself through His death, just like Adam did for Eve. The blood that flows from the sacrifice at Calvary's cross washes away the stain of sin, qualifies us to become sons and daughters of the Most High, and entitles us to everlasting life with Him. Amen.

CHAPTER 13

THE FRUIT OF FREEDOM

We will cover many more topics in the pages to come. We've come a long way, you and I. I sincerely hope that you're enjoying and benefiting from this book.

Remember, brothers and sisters, that I love and care for you deeply. It wasn't so many years ago that I sat exactly where you sit or lie now. I ate the same foods and worried the same worries. I struggled in life through one failure after another. I couldn't stop using drugs. I didn't want to. And ultimately I ruined everything around me. The river of lies, broken promises, and the wreckage of my past was wide and deep. It meandered for miles and miles under one burned bridge after another. I had given up on life. I couldn't trust anybody, and you sure couldn't trust me. What I didn't fully understand is that there was somebody chasing after me, someone I couldn't see, someone who genuinely cared for and loved me, and He wasn't going to stop or give up until I was rescued. That somebody was Jesus. He had a purpose for bringing me into this world and a plan to carry it out, but first He had to get my attention.

He has a purpose and plan for you too, every single one of you. If you're still reading this book, that fact is evidence that God's plan is unfolding in your lives at this very moment. There are doors being opened and closed in the spirit realm on your behalf to secure your future. Some of these doors will transfer into the earthly realm as God manifests His power and willingness to set you free. God grants us increments of His manifestation to build our faith and draw us into a relationship. It is our responsibility and honor to thank and praise God vocally, in the presence of all, when these manifestations appear. Don't worry about what others may say or think. Our public declaration of thanksgiving to God is our testimony to both the earth and spirit realms that we acknowledge and give all praise, honor, and glory to God, the only One worthy of it and the One who is working on our behalf.

This book is my personal testimony of God's grace and deliverance. It is my own effort and responsibility to declare the goodness of God to all who would listen. But it is more than that. God is speaking through me to you so that He might gain your trust and devotion through my experience. It's one thing to hear a preacher on TV or radio, but when one can see and hear the message of God's love from one who has come from his or her own ranks, there is certain credibility there. Make no mistake, and let me be clear, I didn't do anything. It was all God. I am only a messenger—but a messenger who was in the exact same place where you are right now. By the love and grace of God, I have been set free. Each and every one of us has a story to tell, an experience to share. Our life's experiences help to shape who we are. The most prolific and beautiful experience we can have and share is knowing God. The very moment God reveals Himself to us, He begins the work of getting back out to reach others and awaken their spirits as well. Second Corinthians 5:17–21 says,

> Therefore, if anyone is in Christ, he is a new creation; old things have passed away; behold all things have become new. Now all things are of God, who has reconciled us to Himself through Jesus Christ, and has given us the ministry of reconciliation, that is, that God was in Christ reconciling the world to Himself, not imputing their trespasses to them, and has committed to us the word of reconciliation. Now then, we are ambassadors for Christ, as though God were pleading through us: we implore you on Christ's behalf, be reconciled to God. For He made Him who knew no sin to be sin

for us, that we might become the righteousness of God in Him.

These verses reveal three main truths:

1. By faith in Christ, we have become a "new creation." According to John 3:1–21, we are born again; that is, the Holy Spirit has awakened our spirits. The work of the Holy Spirit is to make the Word of God alive to us by revealing the love of God that was poured out on us by His Son, Jesus, the Christ. Once we realize the awesome sacrifice Jesus offered up by giving His own life for us, a change starts to take place, and we understand that we're indebted to Him for our lives. The devotion that stems and grows from this understanding compels us to begin living holy lives, and the Holy Spirit again enters into His ministry with us by revealing more and more of God's Word to us. He enables and empowers us to apply these truths to over lives, thereby leading us to victory. Bless His holy name!

2. These verses also reveal that we've been given the "ministry of reconciliation." The King James Version says, "He hath committed to us the Word of reconciliation." The Greek term for "hath committed" (*tithemi*) is defined: put, set, establish, appoint, destined (KJV).

   A. The term "to us the Word" is translated by the Greek word *logos*, which means "divine utterance."

   B. The term *reconciliation* is translated by the Greek word *katallage*, which means "restoration of favor."

   So it can be read and understood like this ... "I have set before you a destiny; I have appointed you and will establish in you My divine utterance, which will restore favor and precisely exchange your sin for My righteousness and bring you back into a relationship with Me."

First and foremost, this ministry of reconciliation is us telling others about Jesus and how He changed our lives forever. It is us sharing the transforming power of God that has made us new creations. It is us sharing with others by our own experience the new birth that ushered us forth into the kingdom of God and all its provisions. Second, this ministry, our ministry of reconciliation, is our standard for daily living. By keeping a willing attitude to forgive in our heart, others see God living through us and are drawn to Him through our genuine acts of love.

3. The last truth these verses reveal, which I wanted to go over, is that we are called "ambassadors for Christ." The Greek word that translates "ambassador" is *presbeuo*, and it is defined as "I am aged"; act as an ambassador. "I am aged" means to be mature.[14] In short, an ambassador is one who is trusted and respected, being mature enough to carry the authorization to speak for the king. He or she represents not only the kingdom but the king himself. Revelation 19:16 calls Jesus the "King of Kings and Lord of Lords." How awesome a picture and to think that He has chosen us—yes, *you*—to carry His message and be His trusted ambassador.

God sees value in you that you cannot see right now, but He can. The fact is that you're sitting in a jail or prison cell right now, but the truth is that Jesus holds the keys to the prison. The fact is, you've got yourself caught up, and the law is against you, but the truth is, Jesus has come to set you free and whom the Son sets free is free indeed. Facts can change, but the truth remains the same. Jesus is called the way, the truth, and the life. Hebrews 13:8 says, "Jesus Christ is the same yesterday, today and forever." The fact is that people have given up on you, and you feel lost and without hope, but the truth is that the resurrected Christ, the Prince of Peace, the Lord of life, and the King of Kings is alive and well; and He's come to get you and bring you home. Amen.

Yes, God has a plan for you just like He does for me. It is my firm belief that no one has something to say for God like the one He has rescued. I made God chase me for forty years before I finally stopped running away. God allows us to act like fools and go our own way because He loves us, but like a good father, He also corrects us. Sometimes when the child just refuses to accept correction and continues in his or her destructive self-will, the parent has to love enough to let go and let the child come to the end of himself or herself. That is what happened to me and what is happening to some of you right now. Some of you are at the end of the rope and have no place else to look but up. Good, then you're ready to do what it takes. Don't worry. God is there, extending His mighty arm to you. He won't let you fall.

CHAPTER 14

A CHANGE OF HEART

Back in 1988, I was chaptered out of the service with a general discharge under honorable conditions. But drinking, immaturity, and poor relational choices had brought the demise of my military career.

Mad at the world that my career had ended before it started, I carried a big chip on my shoulder. I returned home as a broken and defeated shell of a man with nothing to show for nearly two years of service to my country except more poor choices and severe alcoholism. I drank heavily—and I mean heavily. I drank and smoked all the weed I could get to try to mask my shame of getting kicked out of the army. I held a good job a couple of times, but when I got laid off, I became depressed, just gave up, and dove deeper and deeper into alcoholism.

I tried going to college, but the drinking was more important, and I ended up dropping out. Feeling like the ultimate failure, I even tried to sell my soul to the Devil in exchange for financial security. I mean, I even got books on the subject and everything. I was so mad at God that I cussed at Him and even went so far as to urinate on a statue at a local church.

But God loved me anyway because He knew I was lost. Some of you might think your crimes and sins are too great to be forgiven, but that is a lie of the Devil straight from the pit of hell. The Devil does *not* want you to receive salvation because he knows that the moment you accept Jesus, you no longer belong to him but to God. He also knows that once you receive Christ, you start walking in the power of the Holy

Spirit, and his authority over you is taken away and given back to us. Watch this.

> That if you confess with your mouth the Lord Jesus and believe in your heart that God has raised Him from the dead, you will be saved. For with the heart one believes unto righteousness, and with the mouth confession is made unto salvation. For the Scripture says, "Whoever believes on Him will not be put to shame." For there is no distinction between Jew and Greek, for the same Lord over all is rich to all who call upon Him. For "whoever calls on the name of the Lord shall be saved." (Rom. 10:9–13)

> If we confess our sins, He is faithful and just to forgive us our sins and to cleanse us from all unrighteousness. (1 John 1:9)

> As far as the east is from the west, So far has He removed our transgressions from us. (Ps. 103:12)

> Then the seventy returned with joy, saying, "Lord, even the demons are subject to us in Your name." And He said to them, "I saw Satan fall like lightning from heaven. Behold, I give you the authority to trample on serpents and scorpions, and over all the power of the enemy, and nothing shall by any means hurt you. Nevertheless do not rejoice in this, that the spirits are subject to you, but rather rejoice because your names are written in heaven." (Luke 10:17–20)

> Then I heard a loud voice saying in heaven, "Now salvation, and strength, and the kingdom of our God, and the power of His Christ have come, for the accuser of our brethren, who accused them before our God day

and night, has been cast down. And they overcame him by the blood of the Lamb and by the word of their testimony, and they did not love their lives to the death. (Rev. 12:10–11)

You see, the Devil can read you know. He has no doubt read the Bible from cover to cover. If he can keep you from reading it, you'll always be his slave, powerless over the chains that bind you and helpless to change course. The cycle can be broken, and your life can be restored to you in full and then multiplied. It's actually quite easy; you just need to be ready to do what it takes.

In the aforementioned verses, we learned that the only things we need to start our lives over are a confession and a believing heart. Then God does the rest. He says that if we come to Him with those two things, He will be just, faithful, and forgiving; and He'll even give us power over our enemy so that we are overcomers.

For some of you, the old ways are hard to shake. Right now, this sounds good and makes sense. You want to do good; you know you should start doing the right things, but there is this nagging little part of you that thinks you can still mingle with the old crowd. I know; I did too. The problem is that, until Jesus is established in your heart and the vested interest God has in you becomes profound, you aren't strong enough to withstand those temptations that surely come with that company.

Now is the time God has granted you to seek His face and begin to cultivate a relationship with Him. We give all our time and energy into forming relationships that will ultimately benefit us. That special girl or guy who catches our eye begins to get all our attention. We stand in front of the mirror, trying on different clothes and preening our hair just in hopes that he or she will look our way, and then we will hold his or her gaze. We say to ourselves, "Hey! Over here, look at me. I'm the one for you!" It's the same thing with other relationships; we try to get people to see a quality in us that draws them to us, to make them say, "I want to be this person's friend. I need them and their special quality in my life." Likewise, we seek out these qualities in others to enhance our lives.

God wants us to put that kind of effort into a relationship with Him. To some of you, this may sound strange or even impossible. How can you have a relationship with something or someone you cannot even see? Have you ever heard of the term "doubting Thomas"? Well, that term was derived from an event in the Bible. After Jesus's crucifixion and burial, three days later He rose again, just like He said He would. He presented Himself to His disciples as proof of His resurrection. (By the way, it wasn't just one time—He appeared over and over again in the course of forty days, and over five hundred people saw Him. This is recorded history). Anyway, a certain disciple named Thomas wasn't there, and when the others told him about Jesus appearing to them, he said, "Unless I see in His hands the print of the nails, and put my hand into His side, I will not believe" (John 20:25).

Consequently, eight days later, Jesus showed up again, and this time Thomas was present, and He said to them, "Peace to you!" Then He said to Thomas, "Reach your finger here, and look at My hands; and reach your hand here and put it into My side. Do not be unbelieving, but believing." And Thomas answered and said to Him, "My Lord and My God!" Jesus said to him, "Thomas, because you have seen Me, you have believed. Blessed are those who have not seen and yet believed" (John 20:26–29).

We are unfortunately by nature creatures that must either see, hear, smell, taste, or feel something before we believe it. This is called "tangibility." We look for tangible proof, something we can hold or see. Thomas was the same way. Jesus used Thomas as an example to us to teach us to have faith. Our tangible proof that God is real, that Jesus is who He says He is, is found in history, in the writings of the Bible, and in other historical records, such as the writings of Josephus and many, many others who wrote down records at the time Jesus walked the earth. Another tangible proof is the fact that Jesus and His story didn't fade into obscurity but became a movement that changed the world. He is the central figure and object of worship that God has ordained to bring the whole of creation back into alignment with the will of God.

And last but not least, the tangible proof that Jesus is who He says He is comes from the transformed lives of millions of people who were just like you and me, unable to stop the destruction of their lives until they met Jesus.

CHAPTER 15

ESCAPE AND EVADE

Right around 1993, my constant drinking proved to be too much for any relationship. Consequently I ended up in jail and lost everything, including my home. In the course of that time, I entered into another doomed relationship, and it always ended the same way: there was a big fight, and the cops were called.

One argument took place in a bar. We had intended to go to the movies, but we missed the start time by about half an hour, so I suggested we go shoot a game of pool. Obviously, that was a poor choice since the only place to shoot pool was a bar. As we walked in, Jolene my girlfriend strolled up to the bar, visibly pregnant, and ordered a White Russian. It's made with vodka.

I went off. "Why don't you just get a glass of milk?" I yelled.

She started her usual mischief and tried to get every guy in the bar involved by yelling, "Help! This guy is bothering me!" So, of course, every drunken fool in the joint wanted to be a hero, not taking into consideration the condition of the trouble-making pregnant woman with the drink in her hand. Hello ... What's wrong with this picture?

Well, I was in no mood, and things got out of hand, including snatching the bartender up, who just so happened to be the owner, who just so happened to be a retired cop from Phoenix. So, needless to say, the cops came, but I had already left the scene and was making my escape when the po-po spotted me.

The chase was on. I ran as fast as I could to a wooded area of town. There was a creek that bordered the business district and the lower income district, separating the two. Its inhabitants endearingly refer to the area as "Creekside" or just plain "The Creek." Its population was mainly Mexican or a mixture of Mexicans, Indians, and whites. This is where my grandmother's humble little shack was located, nestled right in the center and surrounded on all sides by Mexican families, who were willing to turn their heads when a local kid came tearing through their yard at full speed with a cop hot on his heels.

Don't get me wrong. It's not that Mexican people condoned crime; it's just that social and class differences cause them to band together under a protective umbrella of silence. But be assured: when the dust settles, their own brand of justice would be administered to whatever fool was causing the police to run through their yard.

So when the cop saw I was heading that way and couldn't drive any farther, he jumped out and followed me on foot, leaving the door to his cruiser wide open, keys in the ignition, engine running, and everything. He kept yelling, "Stop! Stop!" I found this rather insulting, considering all that had just happened in the last fifteen minutes. I knew what my outcome would be, and it wasn't favorable; and here he was, chasing me on foot through the woods, and I was just supposed to *stop*? Well, that's what I was thinking then anyway. But he was motivated and tenacious—I'll give him that. I could hear his equipment and another set of keys hanging from his utility belt jingling wildly as he gave it all he had. I could hear his breath huffing and puffing as he got closer. We passed under an old train trestle that spanned the creek; the earth beneath my feet was uneven, rocks and roots jutted out from its surface like ancient fingers of the dead reaching up from the grave to pull down an unsuspecting passerby.

My lungs burned in my chest with each heaving breath, and my legs were like rubber that could barely hold me up. He was gaining on me, and then the unthinkable happened. One of the fingers of the dead reached up, perfectly caught the tip of my shoe, and sent me sprawling hard to the ground. Fear, panic, and anger boiled through my entire being as the ground came closer and closer. One thought overtook my mind in the whirlwind of emotions and physical stress. *Absorb the impact, recover quickly, get to your feet, and make your stand. Don't go out covered in dirt and mud, handcuffed with nothing to show for it.*

He saw me trip, and I could feel the smile broaden across his face. I could hear the victory in his voice as the ground came up fast before my face. He said, "You're going to jail!" That was it. That was all I needed to hear to solidify my resolve. After everything that had just happened, after everything I had just gone through, there was no way I was going out like that. Everything just went into slow motion. I could hear my own heartbeat; I could hear his footfalls, heavy to slow him down, his keys shifting on his belt, the creek running. I could hear everything, especially the jubilant inflection in the tone of his voice through the heavy labored breaths. "You're going to jail!"

It all just became one moment in time coming to a screeching halt, stopping, and then speeding up again, all one fluid motion born out of chaos. I hit the ground hard, my toe throbbing from whatever had tripped me, but I let myself fall into a combat roll. And just as quickly as I had fallen, I regained my footing. It was just one fluid motion, one moment in time ... trip ...

"You're going to jail!" ... *Ka pow!*

I rolled to my feet, turned, and said, "Not today, I'm not." A look of total disbelief replaced the smirk of satisfaction on his face. His momentum continued to carry him closer. This was before every cop carried a Taser (luckily for me), but he did have pepper spray. It was the biggest can of pepper spray I had ever seen. It was about the size of a can of bug spray or the old hair spray cans.

I guess he decided he should employ some of that good police training and spray me first before we grappled. This measure also buys time for backup. Well, he got me all right; he emptied the whole can on me. I'll never forget it. He got so close while spraying that I could feel my eyelids shuddering from the blast of the propellant, like if you stick your head out of a very fast-moving car or screaming roller coaster. But that wasn't enough for him, no sir. Then, after he got my face, he actually pulled the waistband of my sweat pants open and emptied the rest of the can on my private parts. His training sergeant would have been real proud of him.

Time stood still again. We stood there, facing each other, both affected by the spray. He had gotten too close, and residual overspray, swung by the wind, had gotten him too. Of course, I had gotten the worst of it. If you've never had the pleasure of being the target of pepper spray, you really can't appreciate the physical pain I was in. It truly does burn like fire on your skin. And your eyes ... Well, forget it. One little micron is all it takes to blur your sight, but for all intents and purposes, I was completely blind. It was like someone had taken superheated sand and ground it in between my eyes and eyelids. It hurt so bad, and every blink generated more heat and pain.

The experience really is quite nasty. But he'd underestimated two things: my resolve and my own military training. I had been exposed to CS Riot Control Agent in large doses in a closed building without any mask. Then I was made to do physical exercises while reciting details such as my weapon serial number and its maximum cyclic rate of fire and max effective range. The army does this to get you used to the chemicals and still able to function without panicking.

He was waiting for me to fall over, curl into a little ball, and cry for my mommy. But instead, since I was blind, I used my hearing to orient myself. I could hear him breathing and shuffling a few feet away, fighting off the effects of the overspray. I could hear the creek about ten to twelve feet below me, and to my right was the edge of the high wall that banked the creek. The creek was thick with trees and undergrowth that had all gone dormant for the winter. I could hear the sirens getting closer. It was now or never. I wasn't positive, but I was pretty sure he wasn't going to follow me into the blackness of night, not knowing what treacherous ground lurked below. I made my scariest face and let out my best war cry, waving my arms in the air like a madman. My ploy had worked.

I heard him scurry backward a few steps, and that was all the distance I needed. I blindly bounded toward the edge and leaped off. Dry, brittle branches snapped and cracked beneath me as I crashed my way through, down to the waiting earth. Anything could have happened. I could have broken a leg, caught a broken branch in my eye or neck, but somehow I survived the jump. I made my way through the thick undergrowth toward the edge of the wood line that broke into a clearing. The creek bed was a minefield of debris from previous floods, thick brush, and clumps of tall grass that hid huge, dangerous holes, and tons of loose, slippery stones. I had made it. All I could hear were my own sounds, which I tried to minimize so they couldn't track me by hearing. But once I was on the other side of the creek, it was quiet and peaceful. The dense vegetation was an excellent sound barrier. I couldn't hear the cars or their yelling. I couldn't even see their flashlights, which I knew by experience were frantically searching the wood line for movement. But I wasn't out of danger yet.

Though my little ghetto neighborhood was surrounded by the creek and woods, there was a street leading into it from the other side; actually there were two, and one of them I would eventually travel for a short distance to get to safety. But for that moment I needed some safe place to hide and try to recover.

By the time I reached the far end of the creek, where the clearing began to rise into a rocky hill dotted with houses, I was literally crawling on my hands and knees, my eyesight was severely impaired, and the effects of the spray were just getting worse and worse. Every once in a while, I tried to open my eyes to catch a glimpse of something familiar, but each time was like taking a piece of decomposed granite and raking it across my eye. It hurt so bad.

I felt my way up a walkway and some steps. I hoped the inhabitants would be sympathetic to my cause and grant me some reprieve; to my delight, they did. They allowed me to wash my face and gave me a few minutes to recuperate. They asked whether I was hungry. That is how Mexican folks are—kind of like Italian people, I suppose. They are very family oriented and always trying to feed you, even with snot dripping down your freshly pepper-sprayed face. I didn't want to impose any further, so once I felt it had been long enough, I peered out the door into the blackness of night. So far so good, but I wouldn't know for sure until I was farther away from the house. Sometimes when the police have you cornered but aren't quite sure where you are, they sit and wait until you think it's all good. Then wham! ... You're busted. But that night, the coast was clear.

I cautiously made my way up the rocky path toward my grandmother's property. We had long since torn down the house. It had been abandoned for years, and winos and vagrants had made it a shelter along their byways to and fro. I can't tell you how sad it had been to tear down the walls of my childhood home. Those were the best memories. Years filled with carefree play and the wild imaginations of a young boy disappeared with each removed plank and floorboard.

I sat atop the hill where the foundation remained and surveyed the night from burning, raw eyes. I could see well enough to identify a slow-moving cruiser, but the night was quiet, and the roads betrayed no such dangers. I could see my destination on the next hill over, where my aunt and uncle lived. I would be safe there. They would be asleep, and I could just go in and hide in the darkness until the morning came. But first I would need to cross about five to six hundred yards of relatively open space. I could skirt the property line, which was strewn with trees, until I came to the dirt road that came from the main street. I could cross there and disappear into a small clump of scrub oak, tall grass, and rock outcroppings for concealment. But I had two problems: (1) once I came down from my perch, I would lose all visibility and be stuck in the lowland; and (2) once I was in the second clump of trees, I would have to expose myself to the streetlight and about another three hundred yards of open ground. If a cruiser came from any direction, he or she would see me for sure, and I didn't know whether I could outrun the cruiser in my present condition.

I waited in that second area forever, it seemed, trying to talk myself into just going for it. The longer I waited, the more I worried that a cop was going to come around the corner any second. I was a sitting duck where I was. I couldn't wait any longer. I shot out of the tree line at full sprint, my feet falling lightly to reduce any noise. One hundred yards—almost there. Huff, puff, sprint. Two hundred yards. "I can make it!" Huff, puff, sprint.

Oh no—there were lights approaching. *I gotta make this turn up the dirt road. If I can just make it to the dirt road, I can cut in and be out of sight before he crests the hill.* Huff, puff, sprint. I made it, but I still wasn't out of the woods. I had to get inside. With all my strength, I ran up the hill and quietly entered the house. I was breathing so hard, and my heart was pounding in my chest so bad that I thought they would hear it and wake up. I didn't need to involve them, and I sure didn't want to do any explaining. I stared out the window from behind a curtain, waiting to see a cruiser any second, but it never came. The lights must have belonged to a resident up the street somewhere, who had turned to go home.

I spent the rest of the night peering out of windows and expecting the door to be knocked on any second, but the knock never came. With the first rays of sunlight came a sense of relief. Isn't it funny how the coming morning washes away the fears of the night? This event has spiritual connotations, but we'll continue with the story. I just couldn't help mentioning it.

Upon rising, my aunt and uncle knew was something wrong. It wasn't unusual for me to show up anytime of the day or night, but they could tell I was agitated, and the pepper spray still clung to me heavily, leaving an irritant in the air that is unmistakable. To my absolute horror, my antics appeared in the paper. Whatever comfort the morning sun had promised soon faded into oblivion. I knew there was no chance of this just going away. I would end up in jail for sure, but I was resolute to make it as far from there as possible. I even called the police station and tried to plead my case, hoping to find a sympathetic ear. But they just said, "It's all good. Why don't you just come on down, and we'll figure it out." Yeah, right. I had to get out of town and fast, but where could I go?

I was devastated, hurt, angry, betrayed, and in serious trouble. I finally caught up with Jolene. We fought and yelled, but nothing changed. All I wanted was for things to be normal, but it was way too late for that.

Jolene and I managed to slip out of state to seek refuge elsewhere, but it was all short lived, as alcoholism and its destructive behavior patterns would override any common sense. Stability eluded me, so inevitably we went back to Arizona, where trouble and disappointment awaited.

I knew every inch of my hometown and was confident that I could stay concealed there if I lay low. My plan was to put as much time between the events of the pepper spray incident and now as I could and hope things blew over. But by that time, the police and the county DA had had enough of me. They issued a warrant and knew sooner or later they'd get me.

CHAPTER 16

THE METH MONSTER

This is when things went really bad. My brother-in-law, now deceased, was into meth. I had always talked down about anybody who used any powders or heroin. I knew some heroin users, and I talked really bad about their use of needles. After all, I only drank booze and smoked weed. There was nothing wrong with that, right? Even though my whole life had been ruined, consumed by alcoholism, I totally denied that alcohol was the problem, so how could I be as bad as any junkie?

Well, I was at my wit's end back in town and hiding from the cops, broke as a joke. I didn't know what to do or where to turn, so when my brother-in-law told me I could make some quick cash by peddling meth, I said okay. He started me out with a small line. The line turned into a glass pipe, and the glass pipe turned into a needle and spoon. And before you could say, "Oops," I was a hard-core junkie, needle freak, just like what I used to talk-trash about. Funny, huh? No, not really. It didn't help that my aunt was a diabetic, a situation that afforded me an unlimited supply of new syringes.

The police finally caught up with me in a motel room. I'm not positive but pretty sure that my brother-in-law had tipped off the cops on my whereabouts. Usually when the cops are informed of where you are, especially a motel room, they just kick the door in, rough you up, and off you go. But this time, they had front desk call with a question about billing and lured me out of the room, where I was met by a bunch of drawn weapons and "Get on the ground." They caught me with some weed, some empty bindles, some baggies, and a scale. My brother-in-law had just left, and my girlfriend didn't get charged at all.

They gave me one and a half years in county and then probation. Of course, I absconded the moment I left the probation office and directly looked for Jolene. I eventually realized that that relationship wasn't going to work, and now I was getting a good dose of my own medicine.

They eventually caught up with me again in a motel room with a quarter gram of speed on me. They gave me six and a half years in the Department of Corrections. It seemed that my run had come to an end—for a while anyway. While there, I went to school and worked out like crazy. I started going to Bible study again, but I still didn't know who Jesus was. I did three and a half of my sentenced years and got paroled. I was doing pretty well on the outs. I joined a gym and went to school to be a certified fitness trainer. But soon thereafter I entered into another doomed relationship. I hadn't known it at the time, but I soon found out my new girlfriend Maggie was using meth. I begged her to stop because that was my drug of choice, and I was all about it. I begged and warned her, but she wouldn't listen, and then it was too late. We lost everything.

After every bridge was burned and another run-in with the cops became inevitable, I left Phoenix and booked back north. I was lying in my old bed, asleep at my parents' house, when a car came screeching up, the driver yelling. "I have everything I own in the car and fifty bucks for gas. I am leaving, and you are going with me," Maggie said.

I said, "No way am I going with you. You can forget it."

She said, "If I don't make it and something happens to me, it will be your fault." And so I was guilted into going with her. I packed anything of value that could be pawned along the way for gas.

We literally rolled into a town in the Midwest on fumes and a few copper pennies in change. My mom sent me about $300 by Western Union a few days later. She started working at a restaurant, and I landed a job with a plumbing company. Things seemed to be looking up—that is, until I started drinking a couple of beers after work and maybe a bowl of weed. I wasn't using meth, at least not at first. Soon my life was consumed again. I got laid off, and I turned to drugs full-time again.

We broke up, and I again got into another doomed relationship. This time it was with someone who'd had to survive on her own all her life. Because of this upbringing, she was very resourceful. I convinced myself that it was all right to steal to survive. I ended up catching a theft beef there and was sentenced to one and a half years in the Department of Corrections.

While in jail, awaiting the due process, my girlfriend left me hanging. Obviously she didn't want to feel guilty for having to do what she had to do to survive. I don't blame her, and as much as I thought she would never do me dirty, I guess I still don't blame her. That was all she knew. I met this guy in there, and he had a girlfriend who would do anything he asked. But he was young and immature, and he would yell at her over the phone. *How ungrateful*, I thought. Here this guy has someone taking care of him on the outside—he gets mail and calls on the daily—and here he is chewing her out every time he talks to her. They moved him to a different dorm, but he wanted to stay in touch, so he started to write to me through her. Now I had her address and phone number.

So before you knew it, those were my phone calls and mail. I got out of prison, and they had me on probation to boot, house arrest even, ankle bracelet and all. I hadn't known it while we were writing, but she liked speed, so off to the races I went again, and five years almost to the day, we returned to the scene of the crime, my hometown. It seemed that each subsequent girlfriend was more broken than the one before. The pattern never changed, only the people. No matter how hard I tried, I couldn't fix their brokenness, mainly because they didn't want to be fixed, only to exist and dish out as much as they could of what they themselves had been dealt all their lives. It was a vicious cycle, to say the least. Somebody, stop the ride and let me off this thing!

The stress got to be too much, so I put her back on the bus bound home. She'd be fine. She had family there and plenty of likeminded people who were zealous for that lifestyle. My life was one big mess after another.

I had graduated to fraud to support my habit and got thrown in jail again. It was there that I did something that would change my life forever. Sitting in my cell, I started reading the Bible again, but this time there was something different. The words had more meaning to them. I didn't understand it at the time, but my own spiritual state of brokenness was crying out for the solution it knew was true. My spirit, that is, knew what it needed, just like the body, when depleted of a certain nutrient, will cause you to crave certain foods, because it knows it can get what it so desperately needs from it; so it is with the human spirit.

CHAPTER 17

THE VOW

As I was reading the Bible, I felt a sense of urgency to tell others, and before I knew it, I said, "God, if You get me outta this mess, I promise that I will tell every living creature about You, leaving no stone unturned." I had done it. I went and did it, the one thing that would seal my fate. I made a vow to God—not just any ol' vow but the one thing that is within His will the most: to tell others about Him. Well, sure enough, He softened the heart of all involved, and the judge released me on time served and supervised probation. First of all, as many of you already know, probation is for first timers, maybe second timers, but definitely not for somebody who's already been to DOC twice in two different states. But there I was, walking out of jail. I was stuck in Phoenix with no way back north. I called my mom, who wasn't too happy with me and wasn't about to come all the way down there to get me just so I could start my shenanigans all over again. I stayed there for a couple of days, but the perpetual nagging of unfinished business soon drew me back north, back to my stomping grounds.

Needless to say, everyone was let down, disappointed, and hurt that I couldn't get it together. I guess, in retrospect, I felt useless and ashamed. I was a big mess. I had no job, I was on probation, I was severely dysfunctional, and I was completely addicted to meth. It wasn't just the drug, but everything that went with it—the lifestyle, lies, and grandiose notions that I was somehow something other than a broken-down junkie— consumed me. I had been believing my own lies for so long that I was truly trapped, a prisoner who couldn't break free. I didn't want to break free because I was afraid of freedom. Freedom from drugs meant responsibility, and I didn't know how to do that. I had been a failure all my life, so I ran away from everybody who needed me most.

Of course, this only bred a greater shame. That much spiritual destitution leads only to greater depravity. I had turned away from the vow I made to God and went back to that horrible lifestyle. I had no home, no money, no friends, no hope. I tramped from one drug house to another, looking for shelter and drugs, but I spent most of the time living in the woods and traveling at night, always skirting the wood lines to conceal me as long as possible until I had to make a break through open ground. Of course, I had a warrant for breaking probation, so I was constantly paranoid of getting busted. I never sat still for very long. I was always peering out the windows.

People will put up with your blowing in unexpectedly, all spun out and insisting that they turn all the lights out while you sketch out the windows, only so long before they tell you to leave and not let you back in again. Yep, you sure learn who your friends are, all right. I lost all hope and sank so far down that I stole the credit card of the only person who would open her door to me no matter the time of day or night: my mother. I knew I was going back to jail, so I figured in my very sick mind that I would run her card up and just tell her after the fact. I would admit to stealing it, and they would reimburse her. What I didn't know was that it wasn't a credit card but her debit card. I took all the money she had and blew it on goods I would trade for dope. She went to make her house payment and discovered all the money was missing. I can only imagine how she must have felt; it was the ultimate betrayal and slap in the face. But that's how sick I was; I even justified it all in my own mind. It was time to get out of town again. It was the same cycle year after year: running, hiding, finding nowhere to turn, and coming back and getting busted. It was the same story, just a different day.

But there was one significant difference this time ... the vow. You see, the Lord takes vows, oaths, promises, and covenants very seriously. He always keeps His promises—*always*. So when we involve Him, we have set ourselves on a collision course with the living God.

When you make a vow to the Lord your God, you shall not delay to pay it; for the Lord your God will surely require it of you, and it would be sin to you. But if you abstain from vowing, it shall not be sin to you. That which has gone from your lips you shall keep and perform, for you voluntarily vowed to the Lord your God what you have promised with your mouth. Apart from that, the vow I made was within His will which compounded the seriousness of the vow. (Deut. 23:21–23)

Now this is the confidence that we have in Him, that if we ask anything according to His will, He hears us. And if we know that He hears us, whatever we ask, we know that we have the petitions that we have asked of Him. (1 John 5:14–15)

These two Scriptures, read together, show us the following:

1. The spoken Word has power;

2. When we invoke God in a vow, it cannot be broken; and

3. The sovereign will of God is to answer prayers.

It was certainly within God's will that I tell everyone about Him, but first I had to be made fit and then equipped for this huge honor and task. At that time, in the condition I was in, I was totally unfit. How can somebody be trying to talk about God and still be living a life full of sin? You can't. I didn't really know enough about God to be an effective representative. First, I would have to be broken and then shaped and molded.

Take, for example, a potter. He takes the vessels he makes that crack and haven't been baked yet and returns them into a container with water to soften them back up and reform them. If a piece doesn't come out to his satisfaction while on the wheel, he pounds it back into a lump of clay and begins again with the same lump. He does it as many times as necessary until his clay becomes a masterpiece. So it is with God's people. He takes the raw, unruly clay of humanity and works it until it takes shape. Clay has amazing properties. In its raw form, it can be pounded, molded, and even stretched. And if it tears, it can be pounded back together again. It has the ability to absorb paints and finishes. It can take tremendous heat and come out of the fire as a beautiful work of art. Does that sound familiar? That is how people are! But the most desirable quality of raw clay is its ability to be shaped and reshaped. That is how we must be. We must remain willing to be shaped and thrown on the potter's wheel as many times as necessary until God, the great potter, has finished His masterpiece in us and removes us from the fire as a vessel worthy of the master's use.

A vessel laden with cracks cannot hold its contents; they spill out onto the ground as soon as they are poured in. The contents never make it to the table but are wasted on the floor. That is how I was, a vessel full of cracks; and as soon as the Word of God was poured into me, it ran right back out the cracks. God wanted to use me, but I had to be thrown back on the potter's wheel. It took forty years. What a loving and patient potter our God is. He won't force us to do anything; we have to be willing to be broken and reshaped. Sometimes this process can be very painful, but the impurities that cause cracks to develop must be removed.

Some of the impurities that cause cracks are addictions (of any kind), anger, resentment, unforgiveness, illicit sex (any sex outside of marriage), gossip, lying, hatred, racism, fear, doubt, accusation, mistrust, and unbelief (to name a few).

I know right now it may seem like you're full of cracks, and that's okay, so long as you're willing to be shaped and molded. We must remain in a constant state of willingness to yield to God's hands. We must be malleable and shapeable. It took me forty years to figure out that God was trying to shape me. It would have been much easier if I had just let Him do it earlier. But the experiences I've had in life aren't a total waste. God uses the worst of us to bring out the best in Him.

That is to say that He lives through us. His character begins to surface in us as the impurities are removed and replaced with the pure material of God's attributes. Love, wisdom, knowledge, understanding, reason, compassion, and faith replace all the junk in our lives; and we become fit for the kingdom of God, equipped for service to the King! Bless His holy name.

So with warrants from two different counties looming over me, I ran. It was just a matter of time. Absconding from probation was bad enough, but now I had a boatload of new charges in a different county. I was one big mess. It was January and bitter cold. I was scared, Elisa my new girlfriend had heard of a treatment program in the northern part of the state. My mother, despite what I had done, scrounged up enough money to get Elisa and I up there and into a motel room until the program had room for us.

Elisa went in for an interview first, and when she came out, she said she wasn't allowed to have a boyfriend while in the program; they wouldn't accept her until she dumped me. I felt so alone. I knew that the only chance she had was to get rid of me. I was as sick and broken as you could get. The world was crashing in on me. We had only two more nights paid for; we would have to face the brutal winter in a town we didn't know and had absolutely no resources. I knew her only hope was to go into treatment, and I would have to fend for myself on the streets. I was used to that, but there in that city, I didn't know anyone. It would be very difficult and cold.

We made our way back to the motel, not saying much. We knew the end had come. She had a warrant as well, but her stuff was nothing at all, some unpaid fines or something like that. In a couple of days when she got into treatment and the court saw that she had voluntarily admitted herself, they would go easy on her. I was another matter altogether. I remember from the moment we had gotten there how hopeful she was, and I had this never-ending feeling of impending doom. I kept telling her that God was coming for me. She couldn't understand what I meant. I think she thought I was finally losing it, but I knew God was surely coming. I had made a vow to God, and He wasn't letting me off the hook—no way, no how.

In a last-ditch effort, I called my mom and told her what was happening. I was frantic, lost, and hopeless. I had felt like a sitting duck for the last year. My paranoia had gotten so bad that I trusted no one. I would use my cell phone for a quick call and then immediately take the battery and SIM card out and disperse the components in different locations, hiding them in the woods or under rocks. Then, when I needed to make a call, I would have to go, retrieve them, and do the process all over again.

I cried out to my mom, looking for some kind of consolation, but what could she do? She had no money because I had spent it all. I was convinced that the police were going to try to kill me and make my death look legit. I had certainly made plenty of enemies, especially in the law enforcement community. She said, "Turn yourself in, Son."

I said, "No way! Are you crazy? They are going to kill me!" I finally said, "I am going to try to make my way back home on foot."

We hung up, and I just sat there, contemplating the logistics of the long march back home. I didn't doubt that I could make it. The army had trained me well and put enough confidence in me to last a lifetime. What worried me was being spotted by the po-po. The unnerving feeling kept nagging at me that something was about to go down.

I put on all my gear, as was my custom, and went to the bathroom window to plan my escape, if necessary. I was on the second floor and would have to jump—not the most favorable of conditions. When I opened the small window, to my delight there was scaffolding near the window. If I weaseled my way out feetfirst and hung by my fingers, I could use my feet to push against the building, turn in midair, and catch the scaffolding. It would be risky, but what choice did I have? *She would be all right*, I thought. *Just a slap on the wrist.* "Blame everything on me," I'd told her. "They'll believe you."

She said, "You're trippin'. Just chill. No one is coming. No one knows we are here."

I said, "You don't understand. They want to kill me. They're coming, and so is God." I didn't know who I was more scared of—the cops or God—but I was sure that either way, I was going to die. I wasn't ready to die. I was so scared.

"You're freaking out," she said. "Just relax."

I just shook my head in disgust. How could she not get it?

I had all hotel lights off, of course, and went to the window to peer out, and there in the parking lot was one cop car after another. I switched sides of the window to see whether they were making their way around the back of the building, where my escape route was, but there was no way of knowing for sure until I landed on the ground.

Elisa said, "What's wrong?"

"Cops," I said. I turned to go into the bathroom and looked over at her. Elisa was as white as a sheet, and in a trembling voice, she said, "I'm scared."

I thought, *Oh, now she gets it.*

I slowly and quietly opened the small bathroom window. It was high above the shower. I would have to go out headfirst, hold on for dear life, and somehow turn to face the building. Then I could use my feet to push off and turn again in midair to catch the scaffolding. I peeked out. There were no cops, just the dark, cold night and about a twenty-foot drop. I ran back to the front window. The parking lot was empty except for all the cars, lights swirling red and blue. Then, down at the corner of the building, where the staircase was, I saw a big, burly cop step out from under the second-floor walkway and look up at the second floor and over at my room. Another cop stepped out, this time a woman. I could tell this was a command element and that there were troops already coming, one behind the other, guns drawn.

I didn't want to get caught half in and half out of the window, and I considered just making a break for it and jumping off the second-floor balcony, but I wasn't sure whether a cop was hiding there below. If I hurt my ankle even for a second, by the time I recovered, I would be swarmed. My heart was pounding, my mouth dry. I was shaking all over from adrenaline. I opted for the window. When I got into the doorway of the bathroom, the front door slammed open. They saw me go into the bathroom, and a ton of flashlights and red dots danced across the bathroom wall. There was no way I was going to make it out the window now. I was done for. They were all yelling at once like they do. "Get down! Police! Come out with your hands up!"

This is it, I thought. Soon my blood would be pooling in red, sticky puddles on the bathroom floor of this foreign-owned dive of a motel on the Flagstaff strip. "Come out with your hands up!" This time more urgent and audibly shaken came the command. Red dots continued their frenzy across the bathroom wall, betraying the tense, nervous condition of the army in blue just fifteen feet away.

"Okay, okay," I said. "I'm coming out. I am unarmed. Just relax." I slowly stepped out into the front room. There were so many cops in there. It looked like the Dunkin' Donuts at shift change. The sheer number of police multiplied my fears. It was obvious they'd been told I was dangerous and probably armed. This had happened once before to me, and the SWAT team had come to serve a warrant. I would say that was a little overkill for just one skinny, dehydrated dope fiend. But here we were again. For those of you who have ever been in that situation know, the very air is thick with adrenaline and electricity. The tension and fear on both sides are so high that you can physically feel them. All those guns pointed at me, all those little red dots collecting on my chest and head. All I needed was just one nervous rookie, and it could end very badly.

But the commands kept coming. "Get on your knees! Lock your fingers behind your head."

So far so good, I thought. I started running it all through my head: handcuffs, questions, the ride to the jail, the long booking procedure. I knew it all so well, exactly how it would go. What I didn't know was which agency would be coming for me. Which county? Maricopa, where I had violated probation? Or Yavapai, where I had new charges waiting? I didn't even know what the charges would be in totality, but I did know they were very displeased with me.

Any agency has the potential for corruption, and in my sick mind, everyone was out to get me. I was so scared, and for me, in my state of mind, death lurked around every corner. It was just a matter of time before some guard played his role in the death of another convict no one cared about. When someone is killed on the street, it's all over the news. There is outrage and a demand for justice. Even when gang members are killed in a drive-by or a bank robber is killed in a desperate shootout, society cries for justice and mourns his or her death. But once the person is inside the razor wire and walls of a prison or jail, no one cares. For all intents and purposes, that person ceases to exist. No one cries, and no one mourns. No one even cares about some convict or inmate who dies behind the walls. It happens all the time.

And county jails are notoriously violent places run by the hierarchy of fear. The institutions play the inmates against themselves in a type of controlled chaos. Using racial segregation as a means of fear and control, the system knows that by using this segregation the inmates will micromanage themselves. All the staff have to do is kick back and watch, and if things get too out of hand, they come in like storm troopers, bust some heads, and set things back in order again until the next time. But who cares about a single incident? As long as it isn't a riot or escape, who cares? I had already experienced what the guards would do if they didn't like you or you were a troublemaker. I knew firsthand the levels of corruption. I would have to be smart if I wanted to survive.

I want to take just a few seconds here to reflect on two things: the vow and my spiritual, physical, and mental state. Now, if you were to have asked me then, I would have told you that I was healthy and in complete control of my faculties. But the truth is that my spirit was struggling to wake up. It was like when you are in a deep, deep sleep; and you open your eyes, but they barely blink from heaviness. It's a struggle and takes all your effort just to barely open them, only to slam them shut again. That is how my spirit was. My mind was filled with terror and fear. It wouldn't stop racing. I was in constant turmoil. One bad thought after another in my mind churned up murky waters like a paddle wheel on a steamship. My every thought was consumed by fear, doubt, and mistrust.

My physical body was breaking down. It was barely functioning. I had put so much dope in it for so long that I was as skinny as a rail. I'm naturally around 215 to 220 pounds, and I was down to 180 or so. So no food plus no sleep plus dope plus trouble with the law equal one skinny, paranoid, burned-out, messed-up dude.

I wouldn't have admitted there was anything wrong. It was the cops' fault. It was everybody else's fault but mine. I was innocent. I just wanted to be left alone and get high. After all, it's my life, right? It's my body, right? I can do whatever I want with my life. I'm not hurting anybody … Ummm, hello … When you steal anything that isn't nailed down to support your drug habit that is slowly killing you, no one else's feelings matter to you whatsoever. That isn't innocent. You're a dope fiend stuck in a rut; just face it.

With that being said, let's consider the vow. I had made a promise to God, a promise that was within His will that He was surely going to hold me to. I wouldn't learn this juicy nugget of wisdom until way later, but there are a couple of Scripture verses that totally explain what was happening to me.

During the period of time when God led Israel out of Egypt (a historical fact, by the way, called the Exodus), God gave Moses what is called the Law, or (*Torah*), the first five books of the Bible. This law or rather a set of laws concerned the governing of the newly forming nation of Israel. If they kept and obeyed these laws, they would find favor in the sight of God, and He would bless them in whatever they put their hands to. These blessings and promises can be found in Deuteronomy 28:1–14.

On the other hand, if they didn't obey and keep the laws of God's covenant, then curses would replace the blessings. The curses can be found in Deuteronomy 28:15–68. You will notice that there are a lot more verses concerning the curses, and that's because there's a prophetic voice added to the descriptions of the curses. All the curses did fall upon Israel eventually time and time again because they kept falling into idolatry. Yes, they broke God's covenant. A covenant is an oath, an agreement between two parties. It is a vow.

So I made a vow, an agreement, a covenant with God that if He delivered me out of trouble, I would in turn tell people about Him, but I had broken that agreement just like the children of Israel did. So guess what? Yep, that's right, I got a whammy. And when God gives you a whammy, you know you got a whammy. Listen to this:

The Lord will cause you to be defeated before your
enemies; you shall go out one way against them and
flee seven ways before them; and you shall become
troublesome to all the kingdoms of the earth ...
The Lord will strike you with madness and blindness
and confusion of heart. And you shall grope at
noonday, as a blind man gropes in darkness; you
shall not prosper in your ways; you shall be only
oppressed and plundered continually, and no one shall
save you ... Your life shall hang in doubt before you;
you shall fear day and night, and have no assurance
of life. In the morning you shall say, "Oh, that it were
evening!" And at evening you shall say, "Oh, that it
were morning!" because of the fear which terrifies your
heart, and because of the sight which your eyes see.
(Deut. 28:25, 28–29, 66–67)

This is exactly what was happening inside me. I was totally defeated,
terrified, petrified, totally convinced in my mind that I was being
pursued by an enemy that was waiting everywhere to ambush and kill
me. You've heard the saying, "There's no rest for the wicked." Well, that
was certainly true in my case. Not everyone makes a vow, but I would
probably bet safely that most of you have at some point in your life,
especially now. So if you're one of those folks who just entered into a
vow or someone whom God just brought back and placed on your knees
before the cross, take heed.

Some of you who have just made this vow are about to find favor
seemingly out of nowhere. Your case will either be dismissed or released
time served. You will remember the words in this book, how it happened
just like this: a vow, an answered prayer, release, and freedom. As you
gather your property and get dressed in your own clothes, you will
rejoice and thank God. You will feel so good and know deep in your
heart that God released you. Then soon you will forget and believe in
your own heart that somehow you did this thing. And the words of this
book will come back to remind you, but you will reject it and push it

out of your mind. You will be back because you have broken your vow to the living God; then you will remember these words and mourn. So it was with me. It happened just like that. I'm trying to warn you ahead of time so you can keep your vow and avoid having to come back again and again.

CHAPTER 18

BOOK 'EM, DANNO

Once I was handcuffed and things had calmed down, they asked me my name. Of course, I lied. I had memorized other names, birth dates, social security numbers, addresses—everything—but they knew they had the right person. They said, "It doesn't matter because we are going to fingerprint you. Then we'll know exactly who you are." That I knew was for certain, and not wanting to catch any new charges in yet another county, I finally just admitted who I was. A half an hour later, I was booked into the Coconino County jail on hold for some other agency—which one I wasn't sure. I asked, and they wouldn't say, which really freaked my paranoid self out.

Morning finally came, and so did the jail food. The breakfast of losers: a couple of cold, rubbery pancakes; and a hard-boiled egg you couldn't peel without taking all the white out in big chunks that stuck to the shell. By the time you were done, there was nothing left but a watery, greenish-yellow yoke. Yep, I was in jail all right. Yuck.

The outer door buzzed and clanged open, and the sounds of chains rattled down the barren hall, echoing off the walls and into my brain. I knew they were here for me. Transport was here to take me wherever. They gathered up the rest of the prisoners getting transported and shackled our hands and feet; then they took a length of chain and wrapped it around our waists, and ran our handcuffs through the chain, in effect binding our hands to our waists. Then they took another length of chain and ran it through our feet shackles. It ran from one prisoner to another, connecting us all together about eighteen inches apart. They did the same at the waist. Once good and secure, they shuffled us out through the sally port and into the back of the transport vans. Nothing more than a Ford Econoline or standard Chevy cargo van. The only difference was that they have rear windows and hard metal benches for seats with no seat belts. It is one uncomfortable ride, let me tell you.

The van stopped at the Yavapai County jail after about an hour. They pulled out some prisoners from each van but left me inside. I awaited my turn, but it never came. The van started up and drove back out of the yard. *I guess it is Maricopa after all*, I thought. Well, that was good since Yavapai had me and let me go; they must not be pressing charges after all. *Things are looking up*, I thought. But in my mind, the cops were still trying to see me dead.

I was so paranoid that I felt everyone was looking at me. I believed in my mind that the cops would stop at nothing until I was dead. They would pay off another convict or even another race to snuff me out. I got myself thrown into the hole by refusing to lock down. At least in the hole, it's just you and your cellie, maybe two cellies, but that was it. One person could fend off one or two people but not a whole group. So I spent the next two weeks in the hole, sleeping or rather trying to sleep, with my back to the wall and a towel wrapped around my neck. It wasn't armor, but a rolled-up towel is pretty thick and enough protection from a pencil to the neck.

My day in court finally came, and I was pretty scared. You know you are in trouble when you don't get to see your public defender until you're already in the courtroom. I had been through this experience countless times. I knew how everything was going to go. But no matter how many times you go through it, there is always the fear of the unknown, what the judge might do. But aside from that, fear consumed me. I had never experienced a feeling of complete helplessness like that before. I was totally destitute.

It was my turn. I stood shackled and chained before the judge. He took forever, it seemed, to review my case. Then, to my complete surprise, he was cool. I hadn't known it then, but he was a former family court judge. These types of judges seem to be more compassionate and understanding while sentencing someone. They know the home is where it all starts, so they tend to have more pity on folks. He sentenced me to two years in DOC. I was still scared, but two years minus time served minus good time meant more like eighteen months. I could make it out alive if I was careful. I would have to spend all my time in the hole, but who cared? I would be alive.

I tried every trick in the book: I acted crazy, got on meds, told them I was of Jewish descent—anything and everything to try to position myself somewhere safe. My goal was the state hospital, but they weren't going for it. I told them I heard voices and was suicidal. All that got me was a visit to the "chair." The "chair" is a special seat with straps and buckles. It's made of hard plastic, and the seat is set at such an angle that your feet dangle, thereby cutting off the circulation to your legs and feet. The whole time you are strapped tightly to it. You can't move. Then, as if that wasn't enough, they roll you over a drain in the center of the floor directly under the air conditioner. The cold air makes you have to pee. The lessened circulation of blood numbs your extremities. The drain is for when you pee. I managed to last ten hours in that thing without peeing on myself, but they have no intention of giving you what you want. I wasn't the first guy to try acting crazy. They just keep you there until you break.

All my efforts to get to a safe place were failing miserably. I had been classified a 3–3, which meant I was a medium-risk prisoner. It goes 1, 2, 3, 4, and 5 levels. So when you get classified, they give you a PI score: P for public risk and I for institutional risk. Hence 3–3. According to state law they have to house prisoners with the same scores together. They aren't supposed to, for example, house a 2–2 with a 4–4 or vice versa. So when they sent me to a 4–4 yard, I saw an opportunity to get thrown into the hole by refusing to lock down, claiming they were breaking their own rules. I was being punished for no reason. Four-level yards are for controlled movement; prisoners aren't allowed to roam around, whereas a 3 has more freedom.

What I didn't realize was that God was forcing me into a corner—more like out on a limb with nowhere to go. He did this so I could learn to trust that He was my only refuge. I could try all I wanted, which I did, but He kept pushing me further out on the limb until there was no place else to look but up. While there in the hole, cellies come, and cellies go. Each one is met with suspicion. *Is this the one they are sending to kill me?* At that time, there was a lot of political unrest within the races. The holes in each prison all over the state were full of people running from something and people chasing after them. You never knew who you were going to get. It was an unsure time full of fear, doubt, and mistrust.

It was the hardest time of my life, without question. I had been locked up many times before, but this time was different. This time I was completely alone, or so I thought. The whole world cut me off. No money on my books, no nothing. I was at the mercy of the state to provide me with toiletries, to do my laundry, get food, everything. God allowed me to get this far down so I could realize He was my only hope.

I contemplated day and night about how I had ruined my life, how I had absolutely nothing to show for all the years I had been on earth. I had no money saved, barely anything in social security, no home to return to, no cars, no nothing. I had to do something different. I had to make a drastic change. The trouble was that everything I tried always failed, and eventually I began to believe my own lies. Then before you knew it, I was drinking and drugging again, and jail or prison always followed soon after.

Yes, I certainly had to do something drastically different. Deep down I knew God was that change I needed. He was the drastic change I had to have. I had played with God long enough. It was always, "Please God, if You'll do this, then I'll do that." God had had enough of being the only One holding up His end of the bargain, so He got my attention real good.

There, in my complete state of brokenness, totally void of comfort and having exhausted all earthly remedies, I cried out to God in earnest, this time with my whole heart. I had always been real careful about how I worded my prayers, my pleas for help. It was always "Do this, and I'll do that." But this time something broke inside me. These were the hardest words I had ever said, because I knew God would answer, and I was terrified of His response. I always wanted to hold onto my own ways and have ultimate control over my actions. I could be good for a while, but I wanted to reserve the right to pick up and use again whenever I wanted to. But this time it was different.

CHAPTER 19

FINALLY READY

This time, on my knees, face down on my mattress, I said the hardest words I've ever said. I cried out, "God, I am sorry for who and what I am. I have lied to you and not kept my sacred vow. I have cheated and stolen and done abominable things in Your sight. I am deserving of death but have mercy on me and save me from my enemies. I have made a complete ruin of my life and the lives of those I've touched. Please forgive me. I can't take this anymore. I can't go on living like this any longer. Please God … *Do whatever it takes* to change me. I am Yours; I belong to You. Take me; make me wholly Thine. Search me, try me, prove me, and remove any way of iniquity from me. Separate me from myself and restore me unto You!"

I was finally ready. I had run from God for forty years. I had made His Holy Spirit chase me all over creation and bear witness to the horrible, rotten things I had done. To think of what I made the Holy Spirit watch me do broke and still breaks my heart to this day. But I was finally ready to do whatever it took to get right with God. I was scared because I knew God would answer me. And when you say, "Do whatever it takes," that means you're letting go of all control and putting your trust in something beyond your understanding. It's total faith. You also know that having the filth from your life that you've so dearly held onto is doubtlessly going to be painful.

The Devil immediately comes rushing in like a flood to cast doubt and fear in your mind to keep you bound. We're supposed to make confessions to God with our mouths, so I went to naming all the sins I could think of. I didn't want some decaying corpse of sin to come rolling out of the closet just when things started to look up, and I was trusting God to get me out alive and put me back on track. So I went to confessing this and confessing that. And you know what? It felt great. But then here came the Devil whispering, "Oh no. Don't admit that out loud. God will hear you, and He'll never forgive you for that one. Besides, you still have dirt you could get charged for. Don't admit that!"

But immediately the Holy Spirit told me, "Remember the words the Lord has spoken to you in His Holy Book." First John 1:9 says, "If we confess our sins, He is faithful and just to forgive us our sins and to cleanse us from all unrighteousness." By this time, God was firmly replacing doubt with trust. I knew I desperately needed a Bible, so I asked God to somehow bring me one. So the chaplain came by my door. My heart started pounding when I saw him. He represented hope. He embodied what I needed most: God. He was a man of God and was an encouraging sight.

He said, "Can I do anything for you?"

I jumped up and ran to the door. With my heart pounding and a lump in my throat, I said, "Yes. I would like a *Kenneth Copeland Holy Bible, Prisoner's Edition!*"

But his response was like a punch in the stomach. He said, "We don't have whole Bibles. I might be able to find a fragment of one or maybe a New Testament, but no way a whole Bible. Care for a *Daily Bread?*"

I felt like I had just been run over by a truck, but I was happy to have any Scripture at all, so I thanked him for the *Daily Bread* devotional booklet and took one. Then something inside me said, "Finish asking him. You didn't finish your request." I thought for a moment as he gathered his briefcase, getting ready to leave. Then it came to me. I said, "Oh, ya chaplain?"

"Yes?" he said.

"New King James, please," I said.

He said, "What?"

I said, "The *Kenneth Copeland Holy Bible, Prisoner's Edition*. Make sure it's the New King James version please." He just kind of looked at me funny, put his stuff down, withdrew a piece of paper, and wrote my request down. Perhaps it was just to appease me. The look on his face was like, *Didn't you just hear what I said? We don't have any whole Bibles here of any version.* But he said, "I am not promising you anything." And with that, he scurried off before I could ask another impossible question.

After he left, I thought, *That was strange, that afterthought about what version I wanted.* That voice told me I hadn't finished my request. I was adding another requirement to an already impossible task. *Oh well,* I thought. *At least I had a* Daily Bread. I hopped back up onto my bunk and savored the day's devotional. I read it over and over, enjoying the testimony accompanying the Scripture verse. I read all the days prior, but didn't dare advance one page, as I didn't know when I might see the chaplain again, and I wanted a fresh new encouragement for each day.

I can't convey to you the amount of encouragement and peace I received each day from that little booklet. Each morning I couldn't wait to look into it and search for hope, and each day I wasn't let down. That is how much power the Word of God has. That is why it is the *only* book in the history of man that can actually change your life and circumstances: because it is alive.

As the day passed, the face of the chaplain faded from my memory, but that nagging question remained. Why had I been so specific about what version I wanted, especially after he'd told me there were no Bibles at all? The day dragged on into night, and time stood still as it often does in the hole. I struggled to go to sleep, as I had tried to sleep through the day as well, waking up only to eat and then to try to sleep my time away. Sleep finally came, and so did my rubbery pancakes, gluey oatmeal, and worthless hard-boiled egg. I ate and went back to sleep. Around ten or eleven a.m., I was jolted awake, and something told me to turn around. I didn't have a cellie at the time, so that wasn't it. I looked to the door, and there, on the trapdoor of the food port, was a black book. It was thick too, with lots of pages and reading to kill the time. *What is it?* I thought. *It can't be!* I jumped down, ran to the door, and slowly reached out and grabbed it.

I stood there, staring in disbelief and amazement. There, in my hands, was a brand-spanking-new *Kenneth Copeland Holy Bible, Prisoner's Edition* in the New King James Version! My vision blurred as my eyes began to water. I blinked the tears away, but they kept coming because I knew without a doubt that God had visited me. He hadn't cast me off for breaking my vow to Him. He still loved me and cared for me and had performed a miracle for me to give me hope. Most of you know that when a guard or staff member responds to your request and tells you "no" or "highly unlikely," it's as good as dead. But here my great need of God's Word was well within His will, and His Holy Spirit reminded me to finish my request so there would be no doubt when the answer showed up that it was from God.

God was teaching me trust, not just trust but to trust in Him alone. He knew my needs and would supernaturally meet them. What I needed most was Him, just Him. And He is found in the pages of the Holy Scriptures. It is there where He reveals Himself in the heart of man and woman. He has brought me to the place of trust. He told me, "If you can trust Me for your salvation, you can trust Me for *everything*." The place of trust is where you learn total dependency in God. I had tried it my way for forty years, and all I had to show for it was loss, ruin, and imprisonment. It was time to try it God's way. He lovingly stripped everything away from me. He removed all outside sources of support from me so I would know and see that all things come from His hand.

I began to devour the Word of God, and something amazing happened. I was beginning to see patterns emerge and like-minded themes appear in different books of the Bible. From the Old Testament to the New, passages were being connected deep in my spirit, and understanding was born.

I'll never forget the day He opened my spiritual eyes. Up until then, I had read parts of the Bible, and it was always good and encouraging. It even made me make that vow, but I still didn't know Him. He was still distant, beyond my reach. There was an invisible barrier between us, or like a fast-moving car goes by, you turn to see it and catch a glimpse of it just before it disappears behind a building. You think you recognize the car, you think you see a friend, but you can't be sure because it disappears from sight too fast. It was like that.

But that time things were different. That time something broke into the spirit realm. That time I was ready, and when I sought God with all my heart, He revealed Himself to me. It was like finally getting how to do a math problem or ride a bike. It was that moment when you finally caught something that had been eluding you forever. It was like learning how to whistle.

I remember the epiphany hitting me like a ton of bricks and then all that weight being lifted off at the same time. The Holy Spirit opened my heart, and while reading the Scriptures, I said, "This is all about Him! This is all about Jesus! This whole book is about Him." From that moment on, things were never the same. I had something special happening inside me. I now had an inside connection. I wondered whether all people who read the Bible understood it like I understood it now. I mean, I was really getting it. It all made sense: the Old Testament sacrifices, the tabernacle in the wilderness, the Passover, the exodus, everything.

God was taking me to school. School can be scary. There are tests and pop quizzes, and sometimes there are bullies in the school yard. But God had sent the best teacher and guardian ever ... the Holy Spirit!

Though I was receiving revelation upon revelation, fear still paralyzed me. I have never experienced a fear like that before, and it consumed me. God had to deal with my fear. I had a cellie come in, whose life truly was in peril. He had trouble of his own, not just for a few weeks or months but for years. And one day he told me something that cut me to the heart. He said, "God wants to use you, but you're too afraid." My heart melted when he said that because I knew it was true. Here he was, with real legitimate concerns, and his faith was unwavering. I felt useless and small. I felt ashamed, and I just wanted to disappear into thin air, where no one could see me and my shameful lack of faith.

What I didn't understand was that God was building my faith, but to do that, He had to expose my weaknesses. Years of drug abuse and my bad actions had left me paranoid and paralyzed by fear. The scared little boy crouching in the corner had finally been exposed when his wall came crumbling down.

I was even more scared now. When I realized any stranger could see me for who and what I really was, there was no place left to hide. God was pushing me further and further out on a limb. During this time, a still, small voice spoke a recurring theme into my spirit: "Trust in Me. Rest in Me." Over and over again while I was reading the Scriptures and searching for comfort, that voice would whisper, "Trust in Me. Rest in Me." It was a turbulent time while a violent struggle went on within me. My soul wanted to cling to fear. It wanted to doubt and couldn't trust, but my spirit wanted to be set free and live in confidence. It was the most difficult time of my life. There was a war going on inside me that I felt was going to kill me if someone else didn't get me first.

I wanted to trust. I needed to rest. I was in anguish. Then it happened. I got a new cellie. This time it was a guy who had just finished doing twenty years. He was about to get out, and he was having some trouble dealing with that fact, I think, after having been locked up so long. So he sought some solitude in the hole. He didn't say a whole lot and probably couldn't have cared less about me, but there we were together.

I had been diligently trying to find my courage and start keeping my vow by telling people about God. Well, as you can imagine, in jail not many want to hear it. Besides, they always say, "Why did you wait until you got in here before you got religion?" That is a fair question, and the answer is obvious. It's in there where you realize what a mess you've made, and your greatest needs begin to surface, so you naturally seek out help from the only place you can get it: God. But they really aren't seeking an answer; they're just trying to shut you up by embarrassing you. They don't want to hear about God, so they pose the question to challenge the genuineness of your faith. For some, it may ring true and just be jailhouse religion, but for some that jailhouse religion gives birth to a relationship with the living God.

CHAPTER 20

OUR FAITH AT WORK: ANSWERED PRAYER

So there we were, my cellie and me, when one day the guard came by and said, "The water is going to be shut off for some time while repairs are being made, so be advised." It was a Saturday, the Sabbath day, according to the Hebrew calendar. I had been studying the Old Testament and found that God had given man the Sabbath day, a day of rest, so that He would indwell that. That is to say that He would come down and meet His people right where they were to meet their needs: spiritual, emotional, and physical, thereby giving them rest and a refreshing. So I decided to try it. From the time the sun went down on Friday night until it went down on Saturday night, I would give extra study, prayer, and worship to God. I eventually added fasting to this formula, and it worked.

That Saturday, once the water was off, the day lingered. Minutes became hours. I looked out the small window and strained to see the ground below. A river of water ran down the security road. *No water anytime soon*, I thought. Then the unthinkable happened. My cellie said, "I can't hold it anymore. I have to go!" Well, when nature calls, what are you going to do? Out of reverence for the Scriptures, I closed my Bible and faced the wall to give my cellie some privacy and respect.

I'm telling this embarrassing part of the story to illustrate God's willingness to engage in the affairs of man and how He proved to me that there was a power living inside me, a power to tap into the kingdom of God.

At the time, my prayers were in their infancy, and I was fumbling through the concept of prayer at best. All I really knew about prayers was that God is the One who answers them. Up until then, most of my prayers were to save my own skin, but I was starting to learn about other kinds of prayer, such as intercessory prayer. That is when you intercede on somebody else's behalf. You pray for someone else's need. This kind of prayer has a reciprocal value, which we'll talk more about later. But for now, I had an urgent need.

Most of my prayers were in petition or request form. "God, it's me. I have a need. Will You help?" But recently I had run across a pattern in the Bible about prayer and discovered something I'd been missing in my prayer formula. We'll talk about formulas in a bit as well. There are four elements that are absolutely necessary for answered prayer:

1. The will of God. First John 5:14–15 says, "Now this is the confidence that we have in Him, that if we ask anything according to His will, He hears us. And if we know that He hears us, whatever we ask, we know that we have the petitions that we have asked of Him."

2. Faith. James 1:5–8 says, "If any of you lacks wisdom, let him ask of God, who gives to all liberally and without reproach, and it will be given to him. But let him ask in faith, with no doubting, for he who doubts is like a wave of the sea driven and tossed by the wind. For let not that man suppose that he will receive anything from the Lord; he is a double-minded man, unstable in all his ways." Hebrews 11:6 says, "But without faith it is impossible to please Him, for he who comes to God must believe that He is, and that He is a rewarder of those who diligently seek Him." Matthew 21:22 says, "And whatever things you ask in prayer, believing, you will receive." Mark 11:24 says, "Therefore I say to you, whatever things you ask

when you pray, believe that you receive them, and you will have them."

3. An abiding relationship with Jesus. John 15:1–8 says, "I am the true vine, and My Father is the vinedresser. Every branch in Me that does not bear fruit He takes away; and every branch that bears fruit He prunes, that it may bear more fruit. You are already clean because of the word which I have spoken to you. Abide in Me, and I in you. As the branch cannot bear fruit of itself, unless it abides in the vine, neither can you, unless you abide in Me. "I am the vine, you are the branches. He who abides in Me, and I in him, bears much fruit; for without Me you can do nothing. If anyone does not abide in Me, he is cast out as a branch and is withered; and they gather them and throw them into the fire, and they are burned. If you abide in Me, and My words abide in you, you will ask what you desire, and it shall be done for you. By this My Father is glorified, that you bear much fruit; so you will be My disciples."

4. The name of Jesus. John 14:12–14 says, "Most assuredly, I say to you, he who believes in Me, the works that I do he will do also; and greater works than these he will do, because I go to My Father. And whatever you ask in My name, that I will do, that the Father may be glorified in the Son. If you ask anything in My name, I will do it." John 15:16 says, "You did not choose Me, but I chose you and appointed you that you should go and bear fruit, and that your fruit should remain, that whatever you ask the Father in My name He may give you." John 16:23–24 says, "And in that day you will ask Me nothing. Most assuredly, I say to you, whatever you ask the Father in My name He will give you. Until now you have asked nothing in My name. Ask, and you will receive, that your joy may be full."

I would like to take a brief moment and cover these four elements before moving on with the story. When we pray, or rather when we are first introduced to prayer, it is usually out of some great personal need. There's some kind of threat to our self-preservation, or something that's really important to us is in some kind of jeopardy. When it comes down to it, our self-interest is at stake. So our first prayers are basically selfish. "God, I am in trouble. Help!" As we've stated before, God isn't moved by our circumstances but by our faith, and our faith should compel us to seek the will of God for answered prayer.

THE WILL OF GOD

So what is the will of God for us? An exhaustive study of this subject would result in a book itself, so for our study, we'll confine it to the purpose of prayer.

Since your God, the one true God, has revealed Himself in three distinct persons, His will for us is threefold as well. The concept of a triune God (one God in three persons) is easily understood by this illustration. Take an egg or an atom: they come in three parts—yoke, white, and shell. The three parts are distinct from one another, yet it is still one egg. The chicken doesn't lay a yoke, then a white, followed by a shell. That would be messy, to say the least. But rather, it comes out as one perfect unit all encased in a shell to be used and distributed accordingly when the time is right. Similarly, the atom, made up of neutrons and protons, and surrounded by electrons, are invisible to the naked eye but form and bond together to make mass that can be seen and used like a chair or table. God is One yet three distinct persons, each having a will that is in perfect agreement with the other.

The will of God is always aligned and in agreement with His Word, and it always, always magnifies Jesus. It is the Father's will that we believe in Jesus. It is Jesus's will that we believe the Father sent Him, and it is the Holy Spirit's will to reveal this truth to us. Let's look at this illustration. John 11:38–44 says,

> Then Jesus, again groaning in Himself, came to the
> tomb. It was a cave, and a stone lay against it. Jesus

said, "Take away the stone." Martha, the sister of him who was dead, said to Him, "Lord, by this time there is a stench, for he has been dead four days." Jesus said to her, "Did I not say to you that if you would believe you would see the glory of God?" Then they took away the stone from the place where the dead man was lying. And Jesus lifted up His eyes and said, "Father, I thank You that You have heard Me. And I know that You always hear Me, but because of the people who are standing by I said this, that they may believe that You sent Me." Now when He had said these things, He cried with a loud voice, "Lazarus, come forth!" And he who had died came out bound hand and foot with graveclothes, and his face was wrapped with a cloth. Jesus said to them, "Loose him, and let him go."

Jesus's prayer to the Father wasn't the act of raising Lazarus from the dead. It was for the people to believe that the Father had sent Jesus. The answer came as the Holy Spirit revived Lazarus's dead body and breathed life back into it. The result was that the people believed. John 11:45 says, "Then many of the Jews who had come to Mary, and had seen the things Jesus did, believed in Him."

If we want answered prayer, we must seek the will of God. His will for us is not hidden but revealed in the Scriptures. For example, 1 Thessalonians 4:1–8 says,

Finally then, brethren, we urge and exhort in the Lord Jesus that you should abound more and more, just as you received from us how you ought to walk and to please God; for you know what commandments we gave you through the Lord Jesus. For this is the will of God, your sanctification: that you should abstain from sexual immorality; that each of you should know how to possess his own vessel in sanctification and honor, not in passion of lust, like the Gentiles who do not know

> God; that no one should take advantage of and defraud
> his brother in this matter, because the Lord is the
> avenger of all such, as we also forewarned you and
> testified. For God did not call us to uncleanness, but
> in holiness. Therefore he who rejects this does not reject
> man, but God, who has also given us His Holy Spirit.

Sanctification means to be set apart for God's work. We are to be set apart or visibly distinguishable from the rest of the world by our conduct. So when we trust God enough to ask Him to start removing the garbage out of our lives, other miracles start to happen so we might believe that God is real.

Matthew 6:31–34 says, "Therefore do not worry, saying, 'What shall we eat?' or 'What shall we drink?' or 'What shall we wear?' For after all these things the Gentiles seek. For your heavenly Father knows that you need all these things. But seek first the kingdom of God and His righteousness, and all these things shall be added to you. Therefore do not worry about tomorrow, for tomorrow will worry about its own things. Sufficient for the day is its own trouble."

Here we see that it's God's will and command that we shouldn't worry, but rather we should put our trust in Him to meet our needs and expend our energy, seeking after the kingdom of God and His righteousness. The kingdom of God is the economy from which we draw our strength and provision. It makes sense then that we should worship the King who rules this eternal kingdom, and His name is Jesus. Jesus is called "the righteousness of God" because His death satisfied the righteous requirement of God's law that says, "The penalty of sin is death." Jesus died for us. He sacrificed Himself on our behalf so we didn't have to die in our sins, but we have eternal life through Him. Proof that His sacrifice was accepted by the Father was His resurrection. His resurrection justifies us in the sight of God and allows us into God's kingdom complete with all the benefits and legal rights of a citizen of that kingdom.

In summary, the will of God for us pertaining to prayer is that our requests and petitions would align with His Word and ultimately magnify Jesus. God simply wants us to come to Him. He desires a working relationship with us. He wants to provide for us and loves to give us things and watch our eyes grow wide in wonderment like a child at Christmas. He truly is our Father, and He acts like one, not a forgetful, neglectful father but a loving, thoughtful, gracious, giving Father who loves His children all equally and loves to lavish His love on us. Amen.

An example of a prayer with the wrong heart attitude is "God, I can't stand my cellie. He or she is always doing things to make me mad. Make something bad happened to him or her so my cellie will learn his or her lesson. Amen." The heart attitude here is all wrong. It is focused on self. Maybe you need to learn compassion and patience. God uses circumstances and other people to reveal to us the shortcomings in our lives because He wants to remove them and make us better.

Perhaps the prayer could say, "Lord, I don't know why my cellie bothers me so much. Help me to see my own faults and teach me how to better understand and connect with my cellie. Draw us both into a relationship with You and perfect Your character in both of us so we might please and glorify You. Amen." Do you see the difference? This prayer focuses on God's will, and the result will be an answered prayer that glorifies Jesus and draws you both into a life-changing relationship with Him.

FAITH

The next element concerning answered prayer is faith. This is the hardest concept for the human mind to grasp. It relies on complete and total trust in something we cannot see. The soul resists faith, and the flesh plain rejects it. The thoughts of the soul have to be pulled into subjection by the spirit for faith to overcome circumstances.

In Luke 17:5, the apostles said to Jesus, "Lord, increase our faith." Jesus responded by saying, "If you have faith as a mustard seed, you can say to this mulberry tree, be pulled by the roots and be planted in the sea. And it would obey you."

A mustard seed is very small indeed, about the size of the head on a straight pin. Some are as small as flecks of pepper. When the seed is contrasted next to the tree it grows into, we see the potential of our faith. Our faith starts out as a teeny, tiny seed. Then, when it is planted in fertile soil and watered, it grows into a towering tree with widespread branches and a healthy root system. The soil is our heart, and the water is our use of faith. The more we exercise and use our faith, the more it's watered and thereby grows bigger.

The mulberry tree is the object of faith in this illustration, and we are the subject. There is an action that happens to the object as the subject acts on it. The term "you can say to this mulberry tree" is translated by the Greek word *lego*, which means "to command." The subject commands the object. What is it commanded to do? The term "be pulled up by the roots" or "be uprooted" is translated by the Greek words *ek* and *rhizoo* to form the word *ekrizoo*. *Ek* has a two-layered meaning, "out from and to," which is translated "the outcome." It also means "out from within." *Rhizoo* means "to establish." So then we command our faith to come out from within so that the outcome may be established.[15]

Faith is simple, but we make it complex because we can't see, smell, taste, hear, or touch it. God asks only two things of us concerning our faith in prayer: (1) that we command our faith to go forth and (2) that we expect an answer with thanksgiving.

> Watch, stand fast in the faith, be brave, be strong. (1 Cor. 16:13)

> Praying always with all prayer and supplication in the Spirit, being watchful to this end with all perseverance and supplication for all the saints. (Eph. 6:18)

> Continue in prayer, and watch in the same with thanksgiving; (Col. 4:2 (KJV). Finally, concerning our faith in prayer, let us consider the whole parable in context.

And the apostles said to the Lord, "Increase our faith."

So the Lord said, "If you have faith as a mustard seed, you can say to this mulberry tree, 'Be pulled up by the roots and be planted in the sea,' and it would obey you. And which of you, having a servant plowing or tending sheep, will say to him when he has come in from the field, 'Come at once and sit down to eat'? But will he not rather say to him, 'Prepare something for my supper, and gird yourself and serve me till I have eaten and drunk, and afterward you will eat and drink'? Does he thank that servant because he did the things that were commanded him? I think not. So likewise you, when you have done all those things which you are commanded, say, 'We are unprofitable servants. We have done what was our duty to do.'" (Luke 17:5–10)

By finishing the parable, we see that we are commanded to use the faith we have been given. The size of our faith grows by our willingness to use it. But God can take a tiny amount of faith and establish His purpose. How much more could be done to expand the kingdom and purpose of God by having and using *big* faith?

AN ABIDING RELATIONSHIP WITH JESUS

The third element necessary for answered prayer is an abiding relationship with Jesus. To "abide" means to take up residence. This is not a static (unmoving) relationship but a dynamic one. When you move into a house or apartment that has a leaking roof or plumbing issues, you don't just sit there and let the dripping water continue to damage the rest of the house: you get up and fix it. It's the same with our relationship with Jesus. Jesus moves into His new house, which is our hearts, and begins to clean house. He repairs the roof, replaces the faucet, puts in a new carpet, and fixes the broken windows. He doesn't just sit there, doing nothing.

Jesus is revealed as "The Image of the Invisible God" and as "the Express Image of His [God the Father] person." Jesus's character is ultimately expressed by His obedience to the Father. Jesus obeyed all of God's commandments, even the one that led Him to the cross. Jesus requires that we obey Him. If we obey Him, then we act like Him, talk like Him, and walk like Him.

> As you therefore have received Christ Jesus the Lord, so walk in Him, rooted and built up in Him and established in the faith, as you have been taught, abounding in it with thanksgiving. (Col. 2:6–7)

> And do this, knowing the time, that now it is high time to awake out of sleep; for now our salvation is nearer than when we first believed. The night is far spent, the day is at hand. Therefore let us cast off the works of darkness, and let us put on the armor of light. Let us walk properly, as in the day, not in revelry and drunkenness, not in lewdness and lust, not in strife and envy. But put on the Lord Jesus Christ, and make no provision for the flesh, to fulfill its lusts. (Rom. 13:11–14)

> "A little while longer and the world will see Me no more, but you will see Me. Because I live, you will live also. At that day you will know that I am in My Father, and you in Me, and I in you. He who has My commandments and keeps them, it is he who loves Me. And he who loves Me will be loved by My Father, and I will love him and manifest Myself to him." Judas [not Iscariot] said to Him, "Lord, how is it that You will manifest Yourself to us, and not to the world?" Jesus answered and said to him, "If anyone loves Me, he will keep My word;

and My Father will love him, and We will come to him
and make Our home with him. He who does not love
Me does not keep My words; and the word which you
hear is not Mine but the Father's who sent Me. (John
14:19–24)

As I've stated, Jesus wants an abiding relationship with us, a dynamic
residence where broken things are getting repaired for proper service.
Jesus is known as "the Word of God." So when the Word of God takes
up residence in us, our broken lives are mended. The dripping faucet
of addiction is stopped. The leaky roof of doubt is re-shingled so the
elements don't get in and the heat doesn't get out. The broken floor
boards of pornography are replaced with new ones so we don't fall into
its trap and break a leg or the hearts of our loved ones.

When we allow Jesus to take up residence in us, our lives get
straightened out and start making sense. The Word of God now governs
us, and we are thereby in and aligned with the will of God, and prayers
are answered in Jesus's name. Amen.

Therefore, as the elect of God, holy and beloved, put
on tender mercies, kindness, humility, meekness,
longsuffering; bearing with one another, and forgiving
one another, if anyone has a complaint against another;
even as Christ forgave you, so you also must do. But
above all these things put on love, which is the bond
of perfection. And let the peace of God rule in your
hearts, to which also you were called in one body; and
be thankful. Let the word of Christ dwell in you richly
in all wisdom, teaching and admonishing one another
in psalms and hymns and spiritual songs, singing with
grace in your hearts to the Lord. And whatever you
do in word or deed, do all in the name of the Lord
Jesus, giving thanks to God the Father through Him.
(Col. 3:12–17)

THE NAME OF JESUS

The fourth element necessary for answered prayer is the name of Jesus.

All Authority

Matthew 28:18–20 says, "And Jesus came and spoke to them, saying, 'All authority has been given to Me in heaven and on earth. Go therefore and make disciples of all the nations, baptizing them in the name of the Father and of the Son and of the Holy Spirit, teaching them to observe all things that I have commanded you; and lo, I am with you always, even to the end of the age.'" Amen

The Exalted Name

Philippians 2:9–11 says, "Therefore God also has highly exalted Him and given Him the name which is above every name, that at the name of Jesus every knee should bow, of those in heaven, and of those on earth, and of those under the earth, and that every tongue should confess that Jesus Christ is Lord, to the glory of God the Father."

The Legal Name

Acts 4:12 says, "Nor is there salvation in any other, for there is no other name under heaven given among men by which we must be saved."

Sovereign and Strikes Fear in the Enemy

> Now when they saw the boldness of Peter and John, and perceived that they were uneducated and untrained men, they marveled. And they realized that they had been with Jesus. And seeing the man who had been healed standing with them, they could say nothing against it. But when they had commanded them to

go aside out of the council, they conferred among themselves, saying, "What shall we do to these men? For, indeed, that a notable miracle has been done through them is evident to all who dwell in Jerusalem, and we cannot deny it. But so that it spreads no further among the people, let us severely threaten them, that from now on they speak to no man in this name." So they called them and commanded them not to speak at all nor teach in the name of Jesus. But Peter and John answered and said to them, "Whether it is right in the sight of God to listen to you more than to God, you judge. For we cannot but speak the things which we have seen and heard." (Acts 4:13–20)

The exalted name of Jesus carries the full legal weight and authority of almighty God. His name is sovereign, and when it is invoked, the power of heaven is unleashed. The Devil trembles at His name and will do anything to prevent you from using it. In our warfare against the Devil, we have three mighty weapons for our dispensation: the name of Jesus, the blood of Jesus, and the Word of God. When these three are combined together and mixed with faith, mountains will be cast into the sea, the dead will rise, and the power of darkness over you will be broken forever. Amen.

Now that we've covered the four elements necessary for answered prayer, we can resume our story. The water was off for hours, and my cellie had to answer the call of nature. I'm not trying to be disrespectful or vulgar, but the story must be told in its entirety. As you well know, bodily waste is accompanied by an unpleasant odor. Well, this particular odor was beyond unpleasant. It was downright noxious, fetid, unbearable, like raw sewage confined to an eight-by-ten cell with no windows and no way out. My cellie had a special diet, and when his meal trays came, they were covered in a sheet of cellophane—you know, plastic wrap. After a while, he remembered that he'd saved sheets and decided to cover the steel toilet with the plastic wrap in hopes of preventing any further contamination, but alas, the damage was done.

I silently cried out to God, "Please God, turn the water back on!" No answer ... Hours went by, and I frantically tried to formulate a prayer that would work. Up until then, I wasn't having much success. Then a still, small voice said, "Use His name." I was mortified. I wasn't about to invoke the holy name of Jesus for such a request. I was afraid that the roof would open up and the hand of God would snatch me out of my bed and body slam me for daring to tarnish His Son's name, so I dismissed it.

A while more passed, and the voice returned: "Today is the Sabbath. Use His name."

Go away, voice. I am not going to do it. I am too scared to make God mad. No way! I said to myself. So I started formulating again: God, I know it's a trivial matter and that You're probably busy holding up the universe or something, but if it be within Your will, could You please turn the water back on?"

Nothing ... The voice returned. "Quit fearing and doubting and use His name." Well, needless to say, I was in some serious turmoil. As I saw it, I had to do something. I had to try. So I remember that I spoke ever so slowly and reluctantly: "God, please, if it is within Your will, and please don't be mad, please turn the water back on." Then painfully slow, I added, "I ... n ... J ... E ... S ... U ... S' ... S ... N ... A ... M ... E ... Amen." As soon as His name left my reluctant lips, there was the faint yet unmistakable sound of water pipes banging. I had been in the plumbing industry for a while, so I knew what I heard, but it was faint. Maybe I was hearing things. I was just being too hopeful, silly. I waited to see movement outside in the hall ... Nothing. Then an officer walked by. He was messing around in the service doors outside every cell. I pushed the water button ... Nothing. *What's going on?* I thought. *I know I heard the pipes charge with water, but there was none at the tap.*

The officer returned our way, and I asked him what he was doing, and he said, "The water is back on, and I am turning all of your supplies back on."

"But ours is off," I said.

He said, "Oh, let me see." He checked, and sure enough, he hadn't flipped the handle all the way. I checked the faucet and ... rush. Here came the water. I immediately flushed the toilet. *Away with you, you foul stench*, I thought.

Our toilet had been acting up. The vacuum breaker in the flush valve was failing, so on occasion, when you flushed the toilet, it would continue running … *whooooosh, guuuurgle … whooooosh*. It would just keep going until the vacuum breaker fell back into place. As you all know, those steel toilets are obnoxiously loud, especially in a confined space with concrete walls and floor.

I looked in the toilet, and there was a straggler mocking me. *Yuck*, I thought. Without a second thought, I flushed again with the confidence of victory. But my joy was interrupted with my cellie's cry, "No, it might stay on!" Too late … *whoosh, gurgle, whoosh. Oh no*, I thought. I should have been satisfied with most of it gone. Now I got this institutionalized convict all upset and ready to go off any second. Now what was I going to do?

The still, small voice returned: "Use His name," it said. *No way, no how, am I going to use His name to answer my toilet problems! The water was bad enough but* not *the toilet, no way … whoosh, gurgle, whoosh!* This was a bad situation. I was resigned to the fact that I was seconds away from getting a pencil in the neck, so I said the words, this time even more excruciatingly slow. When I got to the part where I needed to invoke His name, I stopped for an eternity, it seemed. I finally said it even slower than before. "I … N … J … E … S … U … S' … S … N … A … M … E." And again, as soon as His name left my lips … *Wham!* The water stopped with authority, not like all the other times when it just slowly whooshed quiet, but *wham!* The whole place shook and vibrated. It was at that moment that I understood that no problem was too small or even too gross for Jesus. He was willing and able to answer. *It was more than that*, the still, small voice said. *It is your obligation to pray. I want you to pray.* He had answered my prayer and then confirmed it with a second, back to back. That day my faith grew. It was still a little seed, but it now had water on it. The water problem was my mulberry bush, and God commanded me to pray it back on. And so I did in Jesus's name.

149

The reason God answered that prayer wasn't so my head would swell. It wasn't so I could walk around, snapping my fingers in Jesus's name, and a miracle would result. It was to teach me to use my faith in the face of a great need and not to be afraid to invoke the holy name of Jesus. He wanted me to pray for the great need of humanity and to do it liberally without fear or reservation. He taught me that prayer was an essential and integral part of my new life in Jesus. Every single prominent figure in the Bible, including and especially Jesus, had a prayer life. All of them took time, usually a specific time, to engage God in prayer. This allowed them to hear from God while bringing their petitions before Him.

CHAPTER 21

PRAYER FORMULAS

There are two model prayers I want to show you, one from the Old Testament and one from the New Testament. The first one comes from the book of Daniel. It is important to understand the historical context of the book so we can see its relevance in today's life application. During Israel's history, from the time of the exodus on, they were witnesses to God's magnificent power and enjoyed monumental victories while conquering the Promised Land. But because of their disobedience, they also suffered equally great disasters. But God always sent a messenger to warn them ahead of time. He even promised that if they turned away from their idolatrous ways and went back to Him, He would relent, stay the coming judgment, and even grant a time of refreshing. Tragically, most times they not only didn't heed the warning but also often killed the messengers. These messengers were called "the prophets."

One such prophet was Daniel. He was alive during a period when Judah was serving out a seventy-year sentence of exile and captivity another prophet by the name of Jeremiah had prophesied. The history is long and detailed. Ancient cultures rose against each other in power struggles designed to increase territory and subject the conquered people into slavery, a monetary tribute (a kind of tax), or both. Also, to ensure that the conquered people would remain passive, the conquering nation often dispersed great numbers of the conquered people throughout the empire. One such dispersion took place around 722 BC when the Assyrians conquered the northern half of Israel, thereby executing God's judgment on their gross idolatry. One must understand that the use of violence against Israel wasn't God's first choice of correction. He sent messenger after messenger to warn them to stop their idolatry, but they refused. It had gotten so bad that the northern tribes had completely turned from serving the living God and had erected their own images under every tree, even right in the very places God had chosen for His worship. Statues and graven images stood side by side near the altar of the Most High. They even resorted to human sacrifice, throwing their own children into the fire.

The idolatry that consumed northern Israel would soon sweep across Judah to the south. While Jeremiah was consigned to prophesy of the coming judgment of Judah's seventy-year exile into Babylon, Daniel actually lived it.

Wise conquerors often took the nobles and upper class of those being conquered and made them serve in the courts of their new masters. This kind of servitude served two purposes: (1) it allowed the nobles to maintain their princely estates and places of honor while still subject to their new king; and (2) it afforded the conquering king to pick and choose from the brightest and smartest of his new subjects, thereby gaining wise counsel on local and cultural matters. Most conquerors weren't trying to wipe out a people but rather subjugate them while acquiring their land for their own.

One such conqueror was a Babylonian king named Nebuchadnezzar. He besieged Jerusalem around 605–606 BC after successfully defeating the Egyptians. At that time Judah had an alliance with Egypt. Egypt's defeat would sever any military support for Judah and swing the door wide open for Nebuchadnezzar to invade Judah, which he did, but that was all part of God's judgment and plan.

In the midst of judgment, God always leaves for Himself a faithful remnant. In this remnant are the ones who cry out to God for deliverance. The purpose of this remnant is to establish God's sovereignty in the midst of the judgment through repentant people. The humble actions of this remnant affected even the conquering nations. Beyond the obvious consequences of idolatry, the fleeting governments of the earth stand in contraposition to the constant presence of God, the true King, through the voice of the prophet.

The reason I chose Daniel's prayer as a model is because it reveals a formula for prayer. The formula or pattern isn't a technique guaranteed to get results, but it reveals something far more important than the mechanics of prayer. It reveals the condition of the heart. God is far more interested in producing His character in you than in producing instantaneous answers, although He can and often does. He uses circumstances to produce His character in us, such as patience, faith, hope, love, and so forth. Daniel's prayer reveals the condition of a heart who understands his own faults and shortcomings yet puts his trust in God in the face of severe circumstances. Let us study Daniel's prayer in detail.

A Prayer of Repentance and Restoration

Then I set my face toward the Lord God to make request by prayer and supplications, with fasting, sackcloth, and ashes. And I prayed to the Lord my God, and made confession, and said, "O Lord, great and awesome God, who keeps His covenant and mercy with those who love Him, and with those who keep His commandments, we have sinned and committed iniquity, we have done wickedly and rebelled, even by departing from Your precepts and Your judgments. Neither have we heeded Your servants the prophets, who spoke in Your name to our kings and our princes, to our fathers and all the people of the land. O Lord, righteousness belongs to You, but to us shame of face, as it is this day—to the men of Judah, to the inhabitants of Jerusalem and all Israel, those near and those far off in all the countries to which You have driven them, because of the unfaithfulness which they have committed against You.

"O Lord, to us belongs shame of face, to our kings, our princes, and our fathers, because we have sinned against You. To the Lord our God belong mercy and forgiveness, though we have rebelled against Him. We have not obeyed the voice of the Lord our God, to walk in His laws, which He set before us by His servants the prophets. Yes, all Israel has transgressed Your law, and has departed so as not to obey Your voice; therefore the curse and the oath written in the Law of Moses the servant of God have been poured out on us, because we have sinned against Him. And He has confirmed His words, which He spoke against us and against our judges who judged us, by bringing upon us a great disaster; for under the whole heaven such has never been done as what has been done to Jerusalem.

"As it is written in the Law of Moses, all this disaster has come upon us; yet we have not made our prayer before the Lord our God, that we might turn from our iniquities and understand Your truth. Therefore the Lord has kept the disaster in mind, and brought it upon us; for the Lord our God is righteous in all the works which He does, though we have not obeyed His voice. And now, O Lord our God, who brought Your people out of the land of Egypt with a mighty hand, and made Yourself a name, as it is this day—we have sinned, we have done wickedly!

"O Lord, according to all Your righteousness, I pray, let Your anger and Your fury be turned away from Your city Jerusalem, Your holy mountain; because for our sins, and for the iniquities of our fathers, Jerusalem and Your people are a reproach to all those around us. Now therefore, our God, hear the prayer of Your servant, and his supplications, and for the Lord's sake cause Your face to shine on Your sanctuary, which is desolate. O my God, incline Your ear and hear; open Your eyes and see our desolations, and the city which is called by Your

name; for we do not present our supplications before
You because of our righteous deeds, but because of Your
great mercies. O Lord, hear! O Lord, forgive! O Lord,
listen and act! Do not delay for Your own sake, my God,
for Your city and Your people are called by Your name."
(Dan. 9:3–19)

Keywords reveal to us a formula for effective prayer, but bear in
mind that it was the condition of Daniel's heart that brought him to the
place of prayer to begin with. Daniel's circumstances required that he
turn to the only place he could for help: God. Verse three says, "Then I
set my face toward the Lord God." The phrase "set my face" indicates a
determined purpose. "Toward the Lord" indicates where Daniel's trust
was being placed. Therefore, Daniel's heart was determined to put his
trust in God.

Next, how did he determine to place his trust? He did this by
making "prayer and supplication." Since prayer and supplication are so
closely related, the concept we're looking for may be better understood
as "prayer of supplication." Supplication isn't another form of prayer but
rather the condition of the heart the prayer comes from. The phrase
"with fasting, sackcloth and ashes" means an urgent humility. Fasting
will be covered more thoroughly in another chapter, but basically it
means to abstain from food and/or water for a determined amount
of time to consecrate oneself to prayer. *Consecrate* means to "set apart
for a purpose";[16] usually it's specific to God and His service. Wearing
sackcloth refers to the removing of the better outer garments, which
are usually worn, and replacing them with something plain and crude.
Ashes mean a sorrowful condition so low that they reflect the dust
of something consumed by fire. In Old Testament times, people in
mourning would pour or rub ashes on their heads to symbolize their
broken spirits. All three—fasting, sackcloth, and ashes—are forms of
humility and reflect a broken spirit and urgent need only God can meet.

Of course, since you're locked up, you won't have access to ashes,
but I would say that what you're wearing now could be considered
sackcloth. So what remains to be done is fasting. Fasting removes the

flesh out of the way and presents a willingness to yield; this is a humble attitude that is earnestly seeking God and His will. One thing that you can do to represent ashes is to pray on your knees as a sign of humility before the living God. If you can't do this one thing, whether you have a cellie or not, then you're stuck. God demands a humble heart, and it may be that pride is the very thing God seeks to address in your life so He can bless you.

Now, in verses 4–7 we see the formula take shape. Verse 4 announces, "O Lord, great and awesome God, who keeps His covenant and mercy with those who love Him, and with those who keep His commandments." The first step Daniel took was to declare the majesty and eminence of God: "O Lord, great and awesome." By this declaration, Daniel humbled himself and proclaimed that there is none other in whom help can be found. He vocally placed God in His rightful place as King of the universe; all creation is subject to His will. The second part of verse 4 states, "Who keeps His covenant and mercy." Daniel was, in one sense, reminding God that He is a God of mercy and truth. It isn't that God is forgetful. What Daniel was actually doing was praising God for His attributes and incorporating them into his prayer formula.

Next, in verses 5–6, Daniel made confession for the people and even included himself because we all sin and fall short. In verses 7–8, he reiterated God's attributes: "O Lord, righteousness belongs to You." And immediately Daniel followed up with another confession: "But to us shame of face." Verse 9, a key point, says, "To the Lord our God belong mercy and forgiveness, though we have rebelled against Him." Again, Daniel called attention to the character of God but added forgiveness to counter the charge of rebellion. But it is more than that; Daniel acknowledged that forgiveness of sins can come only from God Himself.

In verses 10–12, confession is continued followed by acknowledgment that God's judgment was true and just. Daniel said, "We deserve this punishment. We got what we had coming because God warned us, and we didn't listen but did our own thing anyway, even though we knew what would happen." Does that sound strangely familiar, folks? Well, it should because this is where you are in Daniel's prayer.

Then in verses 13–15, Daniel connected the condition of the heart with God's response. Daniel said, "Yet we have *not* made our prayer before the Lord our God." This verse shows the stubborn nature and condition of the human heart. God is waiting—in fact, longing—for us to come to Him and confess our selfishness and rebellion against Him so we can be healed and brought back into a place of blessing, peace, and normalcy. But He can't until we do that. Verse 14 says, "Therefore the Lord has kept the disaster in mind." This isn't because He is being vindictive toward us but because He is bound by His own words to maintain a posture of correction until a change of heart is accomplished in us.

Look at these examples of repentant hearts and subsequent deliverances by God. God doesn't change His mind, but He does change His posture toward us, from one of correction to one of healing, deliverance, and restoration. Observe the following:

FORSAKE UNRIGHTEOUS WAYS AND THOUGHTS

Isaiah 55:6–7 says,

> Seek the Lord while He may be found,
> Call upon Him while He is near.
> Let the wicked forsake his way,
> And the unrighteous man his thoughts;
> Let him return to the Lord,
> And He will have mercy on him;
> And to our God,
> For He will abundantly pardon.

ACKNOWLEDGE YOUR GUILT AND REBELLION

Jeremiah 3:12–14 says,

> Go and proclaim these words toward the north, and say:
> "Return, backsliding Israel," says the Lord;
> "I will not cause My anger to fall on you.
> For I am merciful," says the Lord;
> "I will not remain angry forever.
> Only acknowledge your iniquity,
> That you have transgressed against the Lord your God,
> And have scattered your charms
> To alien deities under every green tree,
> And you have not obeyed My voice," says the Lord.
> "Return, O backsliding children," says the Lord; "for I
> am married to you. I will take you, one from a city and
> two from a family, and I will bring you to Zion."

REMEMBER THE WARNING: RETURN TO THE LORD, AND HE WILL RESTORE

Deuteronomy 30:1–3 says,

> Now it shall come to pass, when all these things come
> upon you, the blessing and the curse which I have
> set before you, and you call them to mind among all
> the nations where the Lord your God drives you, and
> you return to the Lord your God and obey His voice,
> according to all that I command you today, you and
> your children, with all your heart and with all your
> soul, that the Lord your God will bring you back from
> captivity, and have compassion on you, and gather you
> again from all the nations where the Lord your God has
> scattered you.

Now we see the crescendo of Daniel's prayer in verses 16–19. In verse 16, Daniel asked God to change His corrective posture and turn His fury and anger away because a change of heart had taken place. Keep in mind that Daniel too was a prophet and had been keeping a close watch on Jeremiah's prophecy; he knew the time was drawing near for the captivity and exile to be over. God's corrective posture had done its work in the hearts of the people, and Daniel cried out to God to bring restoration. Not everyone needs a seventy-year correction period. Jeremiah's prophecy was on a national level. God had chased after Israel and Judah for years and finally did what it took to bring correction so He could once again bring healing, deliverance, and restoration to the group of people He chose to reveal Himself through. Also, the Messiah had to come through their lineage. God did what was necessary to fulfill His purpose.

Those of us who believe in God are also chosen in Christ, and God will certainly do what it takes, what is necessary, to bring about correction in our lives because He loves us so much.

In verses 17–19 Daniel asked God to hear his prayer, to hear and forgive, to listen, and to act. Daniel then brought in the "big guns" and said to God, "For Your own sake" and "The people called by Your Name." Daniel's formula for prayer came to an end. He had begun with a determined purpose to seek God's help. Then he completely placed his trust in someone he couldn't even see. He began his communication with God in humility, expressed by the intent of his heart and his action (ashes, sackcloth, and fasting). He then declared God's sovereignty over all things and praised Him for His attributes. Then came confession followed by more praise. Then he humbled himself again as he acknowledged that he needed forgiveness and that forgiveness of sins comes only from God. He then agreed that their sin was rebellion against God and that God's ways and corrective posture were valid. Also, they maintained a rebellious attitude and for a time refused to ask God for help. They wanted to continue doing their own thing, even though they knew they were being corrected. Daniel admitted that their punishment was justified. Finally, he in a sense reminded God (or rather praised God's attributes) of mercy and righteousness. You see, by God's own mouth, He said that correction would come, and once a change of heart took place, so would come deliverance, healing, and restoration. So Daniel called on God's honor to keep His Word and rescue the remnant of repentant hearts.

It's the same thing for us today. We all think our way is best. The Bible says in Proverbs 14:12, "There is a way that seems right to a man, but its end is the way of death." The death spoken of here is both physical and spiritual. A man and woman, whose lives seem bleak, steeped in poverty or addiction, may conclude that they have nothing to lose but everything to gain by robbing a bank or store. The alarm is sounded, and the police come. They are cornered and scared with no way out. Shots are fired, one is injured, and one is killed. The decision to rob the bank to give them what they thought they needed to make a better life ends in physical death. The other who faces life in prison and thought they had nothing to lose soon realizes they have now truly lost everything: their lover and best friend, and freedom. Only a shell of the person remains. He or she is completely without hope as darkness closes in. You see, hope is born of the spirit, and if the spirit is dead, then there is no hope.

Our prayer for deliverance must be like Daniel's: one of purpose, clothed in humility and a genuine desire to change. There is a desire to do whatever it takes, including letting God have your heart and complete control over your life. Then the spirit is awakened, and hope soars on the wings of eagles. Amen.

> Trust in the Lord with all your heart,
> And lean not on your own understanding;
> In all your ways acknowledge Him,
> And He shall direct your paths. (Prov. 3:5–6)

The second model for prayer comes from Jesus Himself. Commonly called the Lord's Prayer, it can be found in Matthew 6:5–14 or Luke 11:1–4. Unlike Daniel's prayer of repentance, Jesus's prayer comes from an already existing, established relationship with God the Father. The prayer of repentance is designed to bring one back into or restore a relationship. Jesus's prayer is a prayer of faith; it simply puts its trust in God to provide for daily needs and guidance. This prayer seeks the will of God to be done in the life of the one praying but also asks that God's presence would affect the whole earth. Let's take a closer look at the Lord's model for prayer in Matthew 6.

> And when you pray, you shall not be like the hypocrites. For they love to pray standing in the synagogues and on the corners of the streets, that they may be seen by men. Assuredly, I say to you, they have their reward. But you, when you pray, go into your room, and when you have shut your door, pray to your Father who is in the secret place; and your Father who sees in secret will reward you openly. And when you pray, do not use vain repetitions as the heathen do. For they think that they will be heard for their many words.
>
> Therefore do not be like them. For your Father knows the things you have need of before you ask Him. In this manner, therefore, pray:
>
> Our Father in heaven,
> Hallowed be Your name.
> Your kingdom come.
> Your will be done
> On earth as it is in heaven.
> Give us this day our daily bread.
> And forgive us our debts,
> As we forgive our debtors.
> And do not lead us into temptation,
> But deliver us from the evil one.
> For Yours is the kingdom and the power and the glory forever. Amen.
> (Matt. 6:5–13)

Verse 5 begins as Daniel's did, with the intent, attitude, or condition of the heart. The people praying in verse 5 are called "hypocrites," because their hearts betray their actions; they want to be seen as very religious men. There is a difference between religion and relationship. Jesus wants you to have a dynamic, living relationship with Him.

Verse 6 says, "But you, when you pray." Who is the "you" Jesus referred to? Well, historically and contextually, He spoke to His disciples, as revealed in Luke 11:1: "Now it came to pass, as He was praying in a certain place, when He ceased, that one of His disciples said to Him, 'Lord, teach us to pray, as John also taught his disciples.'" They had asked Jesus to teach them how to pray because they saw Jesus praying and wanted to learn how He did it. By contrasting the prayer life of the hypocrites to His disciples, Jesus signified that His disciples were working out of a relationship rather than religion. You see, the disciples had a relationship with Jesus, and Jesus had a relationship with the Father. They walked with Him, they talked with Him, they sat down and ate together, and they were friends. They had a direct link to God the Father through Jesus, and so do we! Observe and see how these Scriptures apply the relationship principle to us today.

> Thomas said to Him, "Lord, we do not know where You are going, and how can we know the way?" Jesus said to him, "I am the way, the truth, and the life. No one comes to the Father except through Me. If you had known Me, you would have known My Father also; and from now on you know Him and have seen Him." (John 14:5–7)

> Abide in Me, and I in you. As the branch cannot bear fruit of itself, unless it abides in the vine, neither can you, unless you abide in Me. I am the vine, you are the branches. He who abides in Me, and I in him, bears much fruit; for without Me you can do nothing. If anyone does not abide in Me, he is cast out as a branch and is withered; and they gather them and throw them into

the fire, and they are burned. If you abide in Me, and My words abide in you, you will ask what you desire, and it shall be done for you. (John 15:4–7)

May be able to comprehend with all the saints what is the width and length and depth and height. (Eph. 3:18)

He who did not spare His own Son, but delivered Him up for us all, how shall He not with Him also freely give us all things? Who shall bring a charge against God's elect? It is God who justifies. Who is he who condemns? It is Christ who died, and furthermore is also risen, who is even at the right hand of God, who also makes intercession for us. (Rom. 8:32–34)

So the "you" in Matthew 6:6 is practically transferred and applied to contemporary disciples (us). By entering into a relationship with Jesus, we entered into a relationship with the Godhead: the Father, the Son, and the Holy Spirit.

The middle part of verse 6 says, "Go into your room and when you have shut the door." This is Jesus's way of telling His disciples to start cultivating a prayer life. *Go* means "initiate," *into* means "enter into," and *your room* means "a personal place." Jesus wanted them to start making and taking time to talk to God on a personal level. The kind of prayer Jesus talked about isn't just a feeble attempt to reach some ambiguous deity that may or may not hear or respond, but it's the kind that joyfully expects an answer from a loving father or close friend.

The last part of verse 6 says to "pray to your Father who is in the secret place; and your Father who sees in secret will reward you openly." The "secret place" is a direct reference to the inner chambers of the heart and a deep, immoveable trust in someone or something you cannot see but are convinced certainly exists, just like the atom that makes up mass you cannot see. Our reward for pouring our hearts out in faith is manifested in public sight or all to see. This is how God proves His existence to us and His ultimate control over all things. God asks us to have simple faith in something we can't see and rewards us by pouring out His response on the five senses so no one can deny it came from God.

The Greek word for "pray" in this verse is actually a combination of two words: *pros* meaning "toward" and "to exchange," and *euxoma* meaning "to wish." *Proseuxoma* literally translates "to interact with the Lord" by switching human wishes or ideas for His wishes as He imparts faith (divine persuasion).[17] Praying is so much more than begging God to get us out of trouble. It's trusting Him to make the changes necessary to lead us in a victorious life as we can step into a place where we're ready to let God do what it takes to make us whole again.

Verse 7 warns us of a stagnant prayer life born out of obligation, but it encourages us to keep our prayers fresh and joyful as we seek God's guidance. Chanting words or phrases over and over again is no longer prayer, but it becomes human effort to force God into a response. This type of prayer is completely useless and will breed only frustration and possibly bring forth a negative result by bombarding heaven with an insolent, self-willed approach. The condition of the heart is what matters to God. This is what He responds to, and this is what moves Him.

Verse 8 reminds us that God knows we have needs just like our own parents did when we were babies. Any halfway decent parent knows his or her infant needs clean diapers and formula. How much more does the living God know our needs?

Verse 9 opens with a revelation. Jesus said, "In this manner therefore pray" ... (our Father in heaven). The designation of "Father" for God is of grand significance. This designation has a pure relational value and carries with it the full legal weight and responsibilities associated with being a father. A father protects, provides, and progenerates his own likeness through his seed. In other words, God takes His responsibilities very seriously. And since we were created in His likeness through His creative power, we are His children. And just like human children grow up to resemble the likeness of their earthly fathers, so are we to resemble our father in heaven through the sanctification of our entire being— spirit, soul, and body. Our prayer to God should be approached and steeped in the same trust and reverence we have for our earthly fathers.

It's as simple as "Hey, Dad, what do You think I should do about this or that?"

I understand that some of you may have never known your earthly father, and for this I'm truly sorry. The difficulties and sense of loss associated with one or both parents being absent are beyond description. The effects of not having an identity or someone to guide us through this painful process are evidenced by where we end up in life. But there's hope, and it's not too late to form a relationship with your heavenly Father. Look at what the Bible has to say about this and take great comfort.

> Have I not commanded you? Be strong and of good courage; do not be afraid, nor be dismayed, for the Lord your God is with you wherever you go. (Josh. 1:9)

> (For the Lord your God is a merciful God), He will not forsake you nor destroy you, nor forget the covenant of your fathers which He swore to them. (Deut. 4:31)

> Be strong and of good courage, do not fear nor be afraid of them; for the Lord your God, He is the One who goes with you. He will not leave you nor forsake you." (Deut. 31:6)

> Let your conduct be without covetousness; be content with such things as you have. For He Himself has said, "I will never leave you nor forsake you." (Heb. 13:5)

> And I give them eternal life, and they shall never perish; neither shall anyone snatch them out of My hand. My Father, who has given them to Me, is greater than all; and no one is able to snatch them out of My Father's hand. I and My Father are one." (John 10:28–30)

The second part of Matthew 6:9 says, "Hallowed be Your Name." This could be construed as an ascription to praise as the person praying prepares the condition of the heart for prayer. But the verb is an imperative. An imperative verb is called a "bossy verb." It tells us what to do. For example, "Clean your room!" So, in a sense, Jesus asked the Father to hallow His own name. *Hallow* means "to make holy, consecrate, sanctify." The Greek word for "name" is *onoma*, which means "a name, authority and cause." So Jesus said, "Father, bring forth Your holy cause with authority." Verse 9 is directly tied to verse 10. "Your kingdom come, Your will be done." The holy cause Jesus spoke of was the coming of the kingdom of God. Moreover, it was the arrival of the kingdom, as the rule of God reigns in the hearts of men and women through their faith and belief in Jesus as the Messiah.

You see, God spent thousands of years establishing Israel as the nation He would reveal Himself through. They were entrusted with the oracles of God and the responsibility of representing God and bringing light to the world through that revelation. But Israel was stubborn, disobedient, and idolatrous, thereby stifling the cause of God. Observe Ezekiel 36:21–23.

> "But I had concern for My holy name, which the house of Israel had profaned among the nations wherever they went. Therefore say to the house of Israel, 'Thus says the Lord God: "I do not do this for your sake, O house of Israel, but for My holy name's sake, which you have profaned among the nations wherever you went. And I will sanctify My great name, which has been profaned among the nations, which you have profaned in their midst; and the nations shall know that I am the Lord,' says the Lord God, 'when I am hallowed in you before their eyes.'"

You see, Jesus recalled this prophecy of Ezekiel and agreed with the Father that the appointed time had come for the kingdom of God to arrive in the hearts of His choice creation. The Devil's rule of lies was coming to an end, and God would once again establish His rightful place in the hearts and minds of men and women. Observe Ezekiel 36:24–27.

> For I will take you from among the nations, gather you out of all countries, and bring you into your own land. Then I will sprinkle clean water on you, and you shall be clean; I will cleanse you from all your filthiness and from all your idols. I will give you a new heart and put a new spirit within you; I will take the heart of stone out of your flesh and give you a heart of flesh. I will put My Spirit within you and cause you to walk in My statutes, and you will keep My judgments and do them.

Jesus knew the time for the Holy Spirit to be poured out on the earth was at hand, but for the Holy Spirit to come, Jesus first had to suffer, die, be buried, resurrect, and ascend back to the Father. Observe John 14:15–18. "If you love Me, keep My commandments. And I will pray the Father, and He will give you another Helper, that He may abide with you forever—the Spirit of truth, whom the world cannot receive, because it neither sees Him nor knows Him; but you know Him, for He dwells with you and will be in you. I will not leave you orphans; I will come to you." And also observe John 16:5–15.

> But now I go away to Him who sent Me, and none of you asks Me, "Where are You going?" But because I have said these things to you, sorrow has filled your heart. Nevertheless I tell you the truth. It is to your advantage that I go away; for if I do not go away, the Helper will not come to you; but if I depart, I will send Him to you. And when He has come, He will convict the world of sin, and of righteousness, and of judgment: of sin, because they do not believe in Me; of righteousness, because I go to My Father and you see Me no more; of judgment, because the ruler of this

world is judged. I still have many things to say to you, but you cannot bear them now. However, when He, the Spirit of truth, has come, He will guide you into all truth; for He will not speak on His own authority, but whatever He hears He will speak; and He will tell you things to come. He will glorify Me, for He will take of what is Mine and declare it to you. All things that the Father has are Mine. Therefore I said that He will take of Mine and declare it to you.

Part of the Holy Spirit work is to make Jesus alive to us. He is called the Spirit of truth. As the spirit of truth bears witness with our spirit, we realize the kingdom power and authority available to us. Furthermore, as we pray for the perfect will of God to be done "on earth as it is in heaven," we partake in the divine nature, allowing God's character, purpose, and love to flow through us. The will of God thereby affects the whole earth. God doesn't need us to affect His will. He allows us the privilege to enter into His work and reflect His holy attributes.

God can and does orchestrate circumstances for our benefit, but it's up to us to enter into them. Nothing will change our lives if we don't let that change take place. Change comes from learning from our mistakes and applying that new knowledge into making different choices for the betterment of our future.

Verse 11 states, "Give us this day our daily bread." Because tomorrow isn't promised or guaranteed to anyone, our focus should be on the here and now. That doesn't mean we don't make plans for the future, such as school, retirement, or completing projects but rather that we aren't consumed by worrying about tomorrow, which is saying that we don't trust God. Also, being consumed by accumulating treasures rather than being content with what you already have is dangerous. Anything that takes your focus off God is idolatrous. I'm as guilty of this as anyone. My wife just recently had to put me in check over an object I was fixating on, which would cost us money. Thanks be to God for His faithfulness and wisdom He speaks to us through our wives. Mine truly is a blessing from God and exemplifies the virtuous wife outlined in Proverbs 31:10–31.

The second part of verse 11, "our daily bread," recalls Israel's days in the wilderness during the exodus from Egypt, when God fed them with manna from heaven. The manna provided sustenance in their lives and gave them strength. Moreover, it supernaturally provided for representing God's constant presence and care for His people. Also, God instructed them to collect the manna and share it with others around them, thereby teaching them unity and the principle of equity through charity. God freely gave to them to eat out of His great abundance. So should we give out of our abundance to those in need as opportunity arises.

See verse 12. When we read it side by side with Luke 11:4, we see that the words *debt* and *sin* are interchangeable. The definition of the Greek word *hamartia*—sin—is to miss the mark like missing a bull's-eye in darts or archery. God's character is the bull's-eye, and our lives are the arrows. When we fail to hit the bull's-eye of God's character with our lives, we completely miss the mark God has set of us.[18] Observe Romans 3:23. "For all have sinned and fall short of the glory of God." We cannot escape the presence of sin, but we may overcome it as the character of God is perfected in us. Observe Romans 7:18–25.

> For I know that in me (that is, in my flesh) nothing good dwells; for to will is present with me, but how to perform what is good I do not find. For the good that I will to do, I do not do; but the evil I will not to do, that I practice. Now if I do what I will not to do, it is no longer I who do it, but sin that dwells in me. I find then a law, that evil is present with me, the one who wills to do good. For I delight in the law of God according to the inward man. But I see another law in my members, warring against the law of my mind, and bringing me into captivity to the law of sin which is in my members. O wretched man that I am! Who will deliver me from this body of death? I thank God—through

> Jesus Christ our Lord! So then, with the mind I myself
> serve the law of God, but with the flesh the law of sin.

This may appear as a bleak situation, and undoubtedly without Jesus, it most certainly is. As we've stated before, our best intentions are steeped in selfish ambition. Imagine, if you will, a great expanse between two points of land like the Grand Canyon perhaps. On one side, there is you; on the other side is God. Your side is dark, cold, and scary; but God's side is full of brilliant light and color. You can see warmth radiating from it, but you cannot feel it on your face. Your heart yearns to be in that light and to be comforted by its warmth and security. You try to replicate what you see there where you are, but no matter how hard you try, it's still dark and cold and scary. You try to build a fire for warmth but only end up burning your fingers and singeing your hair off. You look funny, your fingers throb, and the fire goes out every time.

Somehow you have to bridge the gap between that beautiful warm place and the dark, lonely one you live in. That is where Jesus comes in. He came specifically to span that gap. He is the bridge between heaven and earth, between God and man. Observe Romans 8:1–2. "There is therefore now no condemnation to those who are in Christ Jesus, who do not walk according to the flesh, but according to the Spirit. For the law of the Spirit of life in Christ Jesus has made me free from the law of sin and death."

Now watch this: Jesus is that bridge, and the Holy Spirit is the contractor who builds that bridge. Every bridge begins with a foundation, which has a footing all the way down to the bedrock of the earth. Your heart is that bedrock. When the Holy Spirit begins building on your heart, your heart is changed and transformed forever. The Holy Spirit builds a living bridge, the bridge of Jesus on your heart, back to God. That is how close you are to God. With each beat, another rivet is set, another cable is stretched, and another guardrail is placed. Soon safe passage to that beautiful, warm, light-filled place is built and ready for use; this bridge can be used to take other people to that place to meet Jesus.

Romans 12:12–16 says, "Rejoicing in hope, patient in tribulation, continuing steadfastly in prayer; distributing to the needs of the saints, given to hospitality. Bless those who persecute you; bless and do not curse. Rejoice with those who rejoice, and weep with those who weep. Be of the same mind toward one another. Do not set your mind on high things, but associate with the humble. Do not be wise in your own opinion."

The first attributed characteristic of God, which He begins to restore in us, is faith. This is how we overcome the presence of sin in our lives. Faith leads us to repentance, which leads us to salvation, which leads us to sanctification, which leads us to holiness. And holiness, my friends, is where we walk in victory over the sins that enslaved us, where the chains of addiction are broken, where the character of God is revealed in the earth through us.

In the inclusion of Romans 12:12–16, which we just read, you will see that verses 15 and 16 are directly related to the beginning of the Lord's Prayer: "Our Father." It is so important for us to really grasp and understand that our God, our Creator and Father, is not unreachable but is as close as our own heartbeat. We aren't orphans. We haven't been abandoned. Even if our own parents have abandoned us, God our Father hasn't, nor will He ever.

> The Lord is my strength and my shield;
> My heart trusted in Him, and I am helped;
> Therefore my heart greatly rejoices,
> And with my song I will praise Him.
> The Lord is their strength,
> And He is the saving refuge of His anointed.
> Save Your people,
> And bless Your inheritance;
> Shepherd them also,
> And bear them up forever. (Ps. 28:7–9)

We see a relationship between God and ourselves as it relates to forgiveness when we take a closer look at Matthew 6:12 and Luke

11:4. Only God can pardon the actual penalty of sin, which is death. Jesus paid for that penalty in full at the cross, once and for all. But the principle of forgiveness must be an ongoing condition of our hearts. The willingness to forgive others for what they have done proves that the heart of God beats in us. Moreover, though our salvation is secured at the cross, unforgiveness breeds a root of bitterness, which automatically excludes us from answered petitions. It is a good indicator of whether we're walking in the light of the truth. One could even conclude that salvation hasn't yet been realized for the entrenched in unforgiveness.

> And whenever you stand praying, if you have anything against anyone, forgive him, that your Father in heaven may also forgive you your trespasses. But if you do not forgive, neither will your Father in heaven forgive your trespasses. (Mark 11:25–26)

> For if you forgive men their trespasses, your heavenly Father will also forgive you. But if you do not forgive men their trespasses, neither will your Father forgive your trespasses. (Matt. 6:14–15)

Again, forgiveness allows us to partake in the divine nature and does more than release the guilty party from his or her obligation. It releases *you* from the bondage of bitterness and hatred. By letting go of the wrong done to you, you remove the poison of bitterness from your own being. Bitterness affects the entire being—spirit, soul, and body. You cannot make one feel guilt or remorse, and in trying to do so, you will only further your own aggravation. Guilt is the work of the Holy Spirit as He convicts the offender of his or her unrighteous acts. Perhaps if we consider that our act of forgiveness might be the catalyst by which the Holy Spirit begins His work in the heart of the one who hurt us, we would be more inclined to enter into God's divine nature through the act of forgiveness.

To further expand this thought, let us consider this observation from Matthew 9:1–8:

So He got into a boat, crossed over, and came to His own city. Then behold, they brought to Him a paralytic lying on a bed. When Jesus saw their faith, He said to the paralytic, "Son, be of good cheer; your sins are forgiven you." And at once some of the scribes said within themselves, "This Man blasphemes!" But Jesus, knowing their thoughts, said, "Why do you think evil in your hearts? For which is easier, to say, 'Your sins are forgiven you,' or to say, 'Arise and walk'? But that you may know that the Son of Man has power on earth to forgive sins"—then He said to the paralytic, "Arise, take up your bed, and go to your house." And he arose and departed to his house. Now when the multitudes saw it, they marveled and glorified God, who had given such power to men.

The healing the man received was directly related to whatever sin he'd carried with him. When the sin was exposed and dealt with, the miracle of his healing manifested. But our focus is on verses 6 and 8. In verse 6, it is Jesus who is revealed as the One who has the power to forgive the penalty of sin through His own substitutionary death. But verse 8 says, "They marveled and glorified God who gave such power to men." It doesn't say "a" man, but "men." Although only God can forgive sin's actual penalty, we as men and women have the power to unleash the character of God in the earthly realm through the act of forgiveness as we partake in the divine nature. God gave "us" the power to overcome the effects of bitterness bred by unforgiveness.

To conclude this subject of forgiveness, understand that evil is present wherever unforgiveness lives. There are actual demons and every sort of evil spirit present wherever bitterness and unforgiveness are. When you choose to forgive, you actually force the presence of evil to flee. Observe Ephesians 4:26–27, 29–32:

Be angry, and do not sin: do not let the sun go down on your wrath, nor give place to the devil … Let no corrupt word proceed out of your mouth, but what is good for necessary edification, that it may impart grace to the hearers. And do not grieve the Holy Spirit of God, by whom you were sealed for the day of redemption. Let all bitterness, wrath, anger, clamor, and evil speaking be put away from you, with all malice. And be kind to one another, tenderhearted, forgiving one another, even as God in Christ forgave you.

Righteous indignation is okay. To be angry when an injustice occurs is natural, but that anger should lead us to restore both the offended and the offender and not lead to bitterness. Remember that only God can soften somebody's heart, but your act of forgiveness may be the vehicle He uses to show His mercy. James 4:7–8 says, "Therefore submit to God. Resist the devil and he will flee from you. Draw near to God and He will draw near to you. Cleanse your hands, you sinners; and purify your hearts, you double-minded."

This verse clearly shows that in the pressure of a yielding heart to God, a simple "No, Devil" will send the Devil "fleeing"! First Peter 5:5–11 says,

Likewise you younger people, submit yourselves to your elders. Yes, all of you be submissive to one another, and be clothed with humility, for "God resists the proud, But gives grace to the humble."

Therefore humble yourselves under the mighty hand of God, that He may exalt you in due time, casting all your care upon Him, for He cares for you.

Be sober, be vigilant; because your adversary the devil walks about like a roaring lion, seeking whom he may devour. Resist him, steadfast in the faith, knowing that the same sufferings are experienced by your brotherhood in the world. But may the God of all grace, who called

us to His eternal glory by Christ Jesus, after you have
suffered a while, perfect, establish, strengthen, and
settle you. To Him be the glory and the dominion
forever and ever. Amen.

Submitting to God means we have a humble heart that is ready to
forgive. These verses teach us that resisting the Devil takes constant
diligence. The Devil doesn't stop trying to make us fall and ultimately
destroy us. We have to be on the offensive, not just the defensive.
When situations arise that hurt us, we must be ready to forgive. Painful
situations rarely give advance notice but rather sideswipe us out of
nowhere. A heart that has been trained and prepared to love in the face
of adversity is the heart that will overcome and heal quickly. Suffering
is common to all of humanity, and we will all at some point feel the
sharp, painful hurt of betrayal. Forgiveness proves that the heart of God
is beating within us.

The end of the Lord's Prayer in both Matthew and Luke is called
"a doxology." A doxology is a form of praise to God, from whom all
things flow. It is a public announcement of both God's sovereignty and
mercy.[19] We shouldn't misconstrue that God could somehow lead us
into any temptation but rather understand that when the Spirit of God
leads us and His Word governs us, we are delivered and kept from the
temptations that lead us into sin.

> Blessed is the man
> Who walks not in the counsel of the ungodly,
> Nor stands in the path of sinners,
> Nor sits in the seat of the scornful;
> But his delight is in the law of the Lord,
> And in His law he meditates day and night.
> He shall be like a tree
> Planted by the rivers of water,
> That brings forth its fruit in its season,
> Whose leaf also shall not wither;
> And whatever he does shall prosper. (Ps. 1:1–3)

My son, do not forget my law,
But let your heart keep my commands;
For length of days and long life
And peace they will add to you.
Let not mercy and truth forsake you;
Bind them around your neck,
Write them on the tablet of your heart,
And so find favor and high esteem
In the sight of God and man.
Trust in the Lord with all your heart,
And lean not on your own understanding;
In all your ways acknowledge Him,
And He shall direct your paths.
Do not be wise in your own eyes;
Fear the Lord and depart from evil.
It will be health to your flesh,
And strength to your bones …
The Lord by wisdom founded the earth;
By understanding He established the heavens;
By His knowledge the depths were broken up,
And clouds drop down the dew.
My son, let them not depart from your eyes—
Keep sound wisdom and discretion;
So they will be life to your soul
And grace to your neck.
Then you will walk safely in your way,
And your foot will not stumble.
When you lie down, you will not be afraid;
Yes, you will lie down and your sleep will be sweet.
Do not be afraid of sudden terror,
Nor of trouble from the wicked when it comes;
For the Lord will be your confidence,
And will keep your foot from being caught. (Prov. 3:1–
8; 19–26)

God simply wants to rule our hearts, thoughts, and actions. And when He does, His abiding presence preserves us from the powers of darkness. Observe Ephesians 6:10–18.

> Finally, my brethren, be strong in the Lord and in the power of His might. Put on the whole armor of God, that you may be able to stand against the wiles of the devil. For we do not wrestle against flesh and blood, but against principalities, against powers, against the rulers of the darkness of this age, against spiritual hosts of wickedness in the heavenly places. Therefore take up the whole armor of God, that you may be able to withstand in the evil day, and having done all, to stand.
>
> Stand therefore, having girded your waist with truth, having put on the breastplate of righteousness, and having shod your feet with the preparation of the gospel of peace; above all, taking the shield of faith with which you will be able to quench all the fiery darts of the wicked one. And take the helmet of salvation, and the sword of the Spirit, which is the word of God; praying always with all prayer and supplication in the Spirit, being watchful to this end with all perseverance and supplication for all the saints—

:

> Shall the prey be taken from the mighty,
> Or the captives of the righteous be delivered?
> But thus says the Lord:
> "Even the captives of the mighty shall be taken away,
> And the prey of the terrible be delivered;
> For I will contend with him who contends with you,
> And I will save your children.
> I will feed those who oppress you with their own flesh,

And they shall be drunk with their own blood as with
sweet wine.
All flesh shall know
That I, the Lord, am your Savior,
And your Redeemer, the Mighty One of Jacob." (Isa.
49:24–26)

What then shall we say to these things? If God is for us,
who can be against us? … Who is he who condemns? It
is Christ who died, and furthermore is also risen, who
is even at the right hand of God, who also makes
intercession for us. Who shall separate us from the love
of Christ? Shall tribulation, or distress, or persecution,
or famine, or nakedness, or peril, or sword? … Yet in all
these things we are more than conquerors through Him
who loved us. For I am persuaded that neither death
nor life, nor angels nor principalities nor powers, nor
things present nor things to come, nor height nor depth,
nor any other created thing, shall be able to separate us
from the love of God which is in Christ Jesus our Lord.
(Rom. 8:31, 34–35, 37–39)

In summary, the Lord's Prayer, Jesus's model of prayer for us,
helps us to understand that we have an already-existing father-and-son
relationship with God the Father through His Son, Jesus, the Christ.
Our desire is to see the will and character of God permeate the whole
earth. We can most certainly trust in Him for provision and supply. We
are reminded to maintain and train a heart of forgiveness, and know
that God will preserve our lives and guide our steps so we don't stumble
and fall as we allow the Word and Spirit of God to govern our lives.

CHAPTER 22

THE APPOINTED TIMES AND THE CONDITION OF THE HEART

One night, while in prison and seeking God, He gave me a dream. The dream took place at the house I grew up in. My parents had divorced in my late thirties, so the news didn't affect me like it would have had I been a child or adolescent. They had honored my sister and me enough to stick it out until we were grown. Divorce wasn't the wish of either, but my father wouldn't stop drinking, and he was very verbally and mentally abusive. Finally, while he was on a hunting trip, she packed all her belongings and the two grandchildren she was raising and left. The divorce, like most, was ugly, drawn out, and painful. But we kids were old enough to handle it emotionally—my sister and me, that is. The grandchildren, my nephews, were very young at the time, so it didn't have much impact on them either.

As I stated earlier, my relationship with my father wasn't a good one. He was incapable of love because of his drinking. After years and years of abusive speech and lack of interest in me, I grew to resent him. Soon that resentment turned to hatred as the root of bitterness took hold of me. It got so bad that I would slander him in front of my friends. It was no secret that I disliked my father. I say this to my great shame today, but that is how it was then, and he pretty much felt the same way toward me. We couldn't be in the same room together, and if we were, we always exchanged sharp, hateful words.

I carried this burden with me all my life, and each year it got worse until finally only hatred remained. I was so angry at him for failing me. His disinterest in me hurt so badly. I just couldn't understand how a father could care so little about his own flesh and blood, even his firstborn, especially since we lived in the same house. Each time we passed each other, my little heart cried out for his attention, but he would never respond. It was like he couldn't stand me. It was like I was in the way. So over time that rejection and pain festered into hatred.

Once a person gets that far, that entrenched in bitterness, only God can break that yoke of bondage. No one can carry that much hatred around and have it not affect all other aspects of life. I felt worthless and useless. So I would just give up if something was hard. The root of bitterness affects every relationship. Even if things are going okay, as soon as any form of rejection surfaces, the root will spread. Soon it's all about payback. "I'll get even with so-and-so if it takes me forever." Pretty soon that's all that's left of a person. That is where the Devil wants us, with not even a shred of humanity left. The Devil wants us to resemble him, not our true Father, who is the blessed God of all creation. Amen.

And that is where I was: stuck in the miry clay of bitterness and hatred. But the Lord wanted me free, so He spoke to me in a dream. In the dream I was outdoors on the side of the house where I played as a child. A beautiful pine tree forest surrounded the house. I wasn't a child in the dream but an adult. Suddenly, my father came roaring out of the house. He bounded down the steps, gripping a letter in his hand. The letter was from my mother, and she had asked him to mail it. He was irate because it was to her lover. He couldn't believe that she had the nerve to ask him to mail a love letter to someone. I answered, "Maybe you should just mail it. You don't even know what's in it. You could be wrong. Stop accusing her and just mail it."

I awoke from the dream and lay there for a moment, zoning in and out of sleep. The dream had seemed so real, and at first I had trouble distinguishing between sleep and consciousness, but there was a reality connecting the two. Then the Lord gave me the meaning of the dream. The contentious attitude of my father was a manifestation of the embittered relationship we all shared. Jealousy, self-seeking, hatred, and anger were all present. He didn't want to mail the letter because he wanted to hold on to his misery. The letter was an actual love letter. *I* was the love letter between them, written on the tablet of flesh. She was asking him to reconcile with me, though he was stubborn. I had said, "Mail the letter." This signified my obedience to God and my own necessity to forgive and ask for forgiveness.

The Lord told me, "Son, I have brought you this far, but I can't take you any further until you obey this command to forgive." I shot straight up from my bed and knew exactly what I needed to do. I sat down and wrote a ten-page letter to my father, asking him to forgive me for all my bitterness toward him. I told him I loved him and that I knew and understood he loved me too in his own way, the only way he knew how, and that it was okay. He received the letter a short time later and responded in like manner, and so the Lord healed the broken relationship between father and son that had been lost so long ago.

That act of obedience catapulted me forward in my growth in Christ, and my understanding grew by leaps and bounds. I was turning into a man of God. And the things God was asking me to do became not only easier but a joy to complete. God was tearing down my wall of shame, which I'd hidden behind for so long. Brick by brick, He lovingly removed the pain and shame I felt and replaced it with love and purpose. I had finally found the acceptance and confirmation I had been looking for all my life in the eyes of my earthly father through the eyes of my heavenly Father. What a revelation!

It would be good if we could only understand that God has already answered all our prayers and that two keys to understanding answered prayer are the appointed time and the condition of the heart. Observe Daniel 9:23. "At the beginning of your supplications the command went out, and I have come to tell you, for you are greatly beloved."

It shall come to pass
That before they call, I will answer;
And while they are still speaking, I will hear. (Isa. 65:24)

But from there you will seek the Lord your God, and you will find Him if you seek Him with all your heart and with all your soul. When you are in distress, and all these things come upon you in the latter days, when you turn to the Lord your God and obey His voice. (Deut. 4:29–30)

CHAPTER 23

DEALING WITH FEAR AND GOD'S CORRECTIVE POSTURE

Ultimately, the Holy Spirit begins to lead us in prayer as He reveals the truly important needs of the heart as they align with God's will. Soon we are praying effectual prayer that benefits the kingdom of God, which benefits us in return.

The answered prayers for the *Kenneth Copeland Bible* I had specifically requested and the miracle of the water had begun to build my faith, but I was still walking in fear. Fear is insidious and won't go away on its own. It has to be forced out. My time in the hole was coming to an end, and my reclassification papers came. My heart sank when I read them. They were sending me to the worst yard in the system. Fear poured into my whole being, leaving me sick to my stomach. In those days, my hair fell out by the handfuls with worry, but this was really bad. I just felt that the cops were going to set me up to get killed. Of course, this was all in my mind, caused by years of experiencing drug abuse, going through sleep deprivation, and living a dirty life, but it seemed very real to me.

God had allowed all the events leading up to that moment to teach me a lesson. Circumstances and experience had to shape the call He had on my life and the vow I had made. All my shortcomings and fears had to be dealt with by the hand of God so I could share my testimony of deliverance and proclaim the life-transforming power of God by my own witness.

So the morning arrived, and transportation came for me early, as it always does. I was a nervous wreck. I just couldn't shake that horrible paralyzing fear. I wanted to trust God so much. I was in such turmoil inside that it physically hurt. So they shackled me hand and foot, and led me out to the awaiting van. The guard asked with a chipper smile, "Where are you heading?"

I was immediately suspicious and thought, *Yeah, like you're not in on it.* But he really seemed genuinely nice and was just trying to make conversation. Not wanting to admit to where I was going or take part in any foreknowledge of my destination, I just shrugged and said, "I don't know." I guess it was my way of being in denial and trying not to think about it. Maybe I would just wake up, and it would all be a bad dream. Maybe the sun would kiss my face through a pane of glass in some nice house. Maybe I would stretch, yawn, and shake off the effects of that bad dream and get up and enjoy a cup of coffee on my porch as the birds sang me a pleasant melody. *Yeah, right.*

A blast of cold air swept across the back of my bare neck and snapped me out of my ridiculous fantasy. There were no sun, no house, no coffee, and certainly no harmonious quintet to greet the morning. Nope, there were just cold wind and shackles ... and fear.

The guard said with a smile, "Here, let me look. I got your paper right here." He stopped us right in the middle of the yard, setting my personal belongings on the ground. He reached into his breast pocket and pulled out a folded piece of paper.

I felt foolish. All I had to do was say, "Yeah, I know where I'm going." But now I was halted, standing in the howling cold wind, shackled both hand and foot, just to wait and hear him tell me some horrible news I already knew. How much more cruel could this get?

He fumbled with the paper, trying not to lose it in the wind and read aloud the destination. At first, it didn't register. He must have been reading a prior stop or someone else's destination but not mine. I kept listening and shivering. But that was the only one he read.

I looked up from the ground toward him. He looked at the paper, looked at me, and looked back at the paper. "Yep, that's it all right," he said and bent over to get my property, returning the paper to his pocket on the way down.

I was utterly stunned and in disbelief. I was going to the best yard in the system. Sure, politics existed on every yard, but I was going to live, and I knew it. I was going to make it. God had shown up right on time. There was no denying that it was an act of God. I'm pretty sure that no one else has the authority to indiscriminately alter a direct decision made by the central office of the Arizona State Department of Corrections. Nope. It was God all right.

You see, He knew my heart, and He knew how much pain and anguish I was in, and He knew exactly how much hair had fallen out of my head and how much I could stand. My exile was over; my chastening period had come to an end. God knew I had learned my lesson and was ready to change His corrective posture to one of healing and restoration.

Let's take some time and look over God's corrective posture with me as an example:

First, I (as we all are) was created in God's image, so His image had to be restored.

Second, my name means "God will establish," so His name's sake was in jeopardy. It had to be rescued and its honor kept intact; moreover there is a command and promise in the meaning of my name. "God will establish!" So God had to honor the meaning of my name and establish me.

Third, I had made a vow to the Lord, and it had to be honored.

> When you make a vow to God, do not delay to pay it; For He has no pleasure in fools. Pay what you have vowed. (Eccl. 5:4)

> If a man makes a vow to the Lord, or swears an oath to bind himself by some agreement, he shall not break his word; he shall do according to all that proceeds out of his mouth. (Num. 30:2)

When you make a vow to the Lord your God, you shall not delay to pay it; for the Lord your God will surely require it of you, and it would be sin to you. (Deut. 23:21)

Fourth, I turned my back on God and didn't keep my vow, so God allowed me enough rope to hang myself, and then He allowed fear to overcome me.

> Just as they have chosen their own ways,
> And their soul delights in their abominations,
> So will I choose their delusions,
> And bring their fears on them;
> Because, when I called, no one answered,
> When I spoke they did not hear;
> But they did evil before My eyes,
> And chose that in which I do not delight. (Isa. 66:3–4)

Fifth, God began the final stages of chastening and correction, leading to restoration.

For consider Him who endured such hostility from sinners against Himself, lest you become weary and discouraged in your souls. You have not yet resisted to bloodshed, striving against sin. And you have forgotten the exhortation which speaks to you as to sons:

"My son, do not despise the chastening of the Lord,

Nor be discouraged when you are rebuked by Him;

For whom the Lord loves He chastens,

And scourges every son whom He receives." If you endure chastening, God deals with you as with sons; for what son is there whom a father does not chasten? But if you are without chastening, of which all have become partakers, then you are illegitimate and not sons. Furthermore, we have had human fathers who corrected us, and we paid them respect. Shall we not much more readily be in subjection to the Father of spirits and live? For they indeed for a few days chastened us as seemed best to them, but He for our profit, that we may be partakers of His holiness. Now no chastening seems to be joyful for the present, but painful; nevertheless, afterward it yields the peaceable fruit of righteousness to those who have been trained by it. (Heb. 12:3–11)

No temptation has overtaken you except such as is common to man; but God is faithful, who will not allow you to be tempted beyond what you are able, but with the temptation will also make the way of escape, that you may be able to bear it. (1 Cor. 10:13)

Before I was afflicted I went astray,

But now I keep Your word. (Ps. 119:67)

CHAPTER 24

THE CALL OF GOD

From the time we are conceived, we have a call on our lives to seek out God and serve Him. We either answer this call or reject it, but all feel and know the voice of God. It is that deep inclination that there is something more to life. As we progress in life, God sets before us opportunities to answer His call. The circumstances of my life shaped my willingness to answer God's call. I had made such a mess of my life and the lives of those around me that it took God to straighten it all back out. But God loved me enough to let me make all the mistakes necessary that would lead me back to Him. But like a good Father, He also loved me enough to maintain a corrective posture with me until I learned my lesson and stopped running from Him and being self-willed. Trust me when I say, "You don't want to have to receive 'tough love' from the living God."

Answering God's call isn't just beneficial; it is honor. Our lives start to take shape and have real purpose as we put on the character of our Creator, God and Father. The call of God is manifold and transcends time and space because God is eternal. We will get back to the restoration and healing process of my life shortly, but I would like to take some time to address the call of God and how that call is sent out and answered. The call has everything to do with healing and restoration, so I think it fits here, and we'll cover it before we move on to the next exciting part of our story. Shall we proceed? The call of God begins in eternity past. For better perspectives of the concept of eternity, the publisher has been gracious enough to include this illustration:

Eternity Past   Eternity Present   Eternity Future

Time

The Origin and End of Time

God is eternal and therefore always has and always will exist outside the constraints of time and space. Time entered the earthly realm when man fell in the garden and will continue marching on until the Lord culminates the end of time with His second coming. Don't be alarmed or confused by the term "end of time" or "end of days," for this only signifies the end of time being marked. When we step into eternity with God, time will cease to exist. So from God's perspective in eternity past, He called us into existence so that in the fullness of time as we know it, we were brought forth in the flesh. Observe Isaiah 49:1: "Listen, O coastlands, to Me, and take heed, you peoples from afar! The Lord has called Me from the womb; From the matrix of My mother He has made mention of My name. Also observe Jeremiah 1:5: "Before I formed you in the womb I knew you; Before you were born I sanctified you; I ordained you a prophet to the nations." And also observe Psalm 139:13–16:

> For You formed my inward parts;
> You covered me in my mother's womb.
> I will praise You, for I am fearfully and wonderfully made
> Marvelous are Your works,
> And that my soul knows very well.
> My frame was not hidden from You,
> When I was made in secret,
> And skillfully wrought in the lowest parts of the earth.
> Your eyes saw my substance, being yet unformed.

> And in Your book they all were written,
> The days fashioned for me,
> When as yet there were none of them.

Contextually speaking, both Isaiah and Jeremiah recount the legitimacy of their prophetic calling, but when they are coupled with Psalm 139:13–16, we see that all people who have ever been born (or ever will be born) are brought forth by God's command. Not one human being goes without this divine signature. So the call of God unto life began in eternity past but wasn't made manifest in the earthly realm until we were conceived.

There are no mistakes in the kingdom of God. However, one's conception has come into being; God has ordained and sanctified that life. Each life is precious in the sight of God, and to Jesus they were worth dying for. Don't let anyone tell you that you are insignificant, unwanted, or a mistake. God doesn't make mistakes. Period.

As we've discussed earlier, all have sinned and have been born into sin. Our greatest need is salvation, and God has revealed Himself as our God and Savior. So the next part of God's call is the call to repentance. Repentance is necessary because man's current condition apart from Christ is fallen and degenerate. The Scriptures confine all of mankind under sin and its penalty: death.

> For all have sinned and fall short of the glory of God. (Rom. 3:23)

> For the wages of sin is death, but the gift of God is eternal life in Christ Jesus our Lord. (Rom. 6:23)

> I have not come to call the righteous, but sinners, to repentance. (Luke 5:32)

God leads us by the hand like a good father into the knowledge of Him. It is He who, through the Scriptures, teaches us all we need to know about ourselves, Him, and our eternal destiny. Armed with the truth of who we are and where we came from, we can choose to trust God for His mercy and grace, which lead us into a victorious life free of drugs, alcohol, crime, and the corrupt lifestyle that accompanies those things. All those things are temporal, but our spirits and souls are eternal. They will eventually end up in one of two places, either in the presence of the Almighty or eternally separated from Him in hell. That's why God has called us to repentance. Repentance is the first step in acknowledging that we're sinful by nature and hell bound without Jesus.

Jesus said in Luke 5:23, "I have not come to call the righteous but sinners to repentance." Even on our best days, we are corrupt and selfish.

As it is written:

"There is none righteous, no, not one;
There is none who understands;
There is none who seeks after God.
They have all turned aside;
They have together become unprofitable;
There is none who does good, no, not one.
Their throat is an open tomb;
With their tongues they have practiced deceit;
The poison of asps is under their lips;
Whose mouth is full of cursing and bitterness.
Their feet are swift to shed blood;
Destruction and misery are in their ways;
And the way of peace they have not known.
There is no fear of God before their eyes. (Rom. 3:10–18)

This is why we need the mercy and grace of God gained at the cross. When we understand the vested interest God has in us through the ultimate sacrifice of Himself through Jesus, our hearts are humbled, and we can easily come to God for forgiveness for our daily shortcomings. Repentance is more than confessing our mistakes. It is turning from them and toward God. We turn from our own way of thinking and turn toward God's way. His way is best. His way brings life, peace, and prosperity. There is no more shame, no more pain from a failed life, only hope and power to overcome because God is at the helm, steering our life in all the right directions. Victory is up ahead. It is within your reach. When you surrender to God and let Him take control, you will be amazed by how much is available to you. God wants you to prosper, and you will. Repentance is the doorway to restoration and the next part of God's call.

Salvation:

As we've mentioned earlier, salvation is the all-inclusive word describing the rescuing of man from his fallen condition. Within the description of salvation, there are four aspects belonging to it: justification, redemption, forgiveness, and sanctification. For the simplicity of this text, we won't include an extensive doctrinal narrative, but to preserve and complete the thought, we add a short description of each aspect.

Justification means to be in a right standing. It carries with it a legal weight that gives the believer full rights as an heir of the kingdom of God. It also means to be declared righteous, acquitted, and freed. By Jesus's dying on the cross for us, the righteous requirement of God's law was fulfilled, and by our faith through His act of obedience, we are found guiltless before God the Father. We are acquitted of all charges and found to be in a right standing, thereby receiving the inheritance of eternal life under the lordship of Jesus, the one true King.

> For you did not receive the spirit of bondage again to fear, but you received the Spirit of adoption by whom we cry out, "Abba, Father." The Spirit Himself bears witness with our spirit that we are children of God, and if children, then heirs—heirs of God and joint heirs with Christ ... And we know that all things work together for good to those who love God, to those who are the called according to His purpose. For whom He foreknew, He also predestined to be conformed to the

image of His Son, that He might be the firstborn among many brethren. Moreover whom He predestined, these He also called; whom He called, these He also justified; and whom He justified, these He also glorified. (Rom. 8:15–17, 28–30)

For you are all sons of God through faith in Christ Jesus. For as many of you as were baptized into Christ have put on Christ. There is neither Jew nor Greek, there is neither slave nor free, there is neither male nor female; for you are all one in Christ Jesus. And if you are Christ's, then you are Abraham's seed, and heirs according to the promise ... And because you are sons, God has sent forth the Spirit of His Son into your hearts, crying out, "Abba, Father!" Therefore you are no longer a slave but a son, and if a son, then an heir of God through Christ. (Gal. 3:26–29; 4:6–7)

The concept of redemption is a main biblical theme expressing humanity's need to be delivered from a condition of enslavement and the price paid for that deliverance. The book of Exodus is a beautiful and powerful illustration of man's redemption. Israel was enslaved in Egypt for 430 some years, and God raised up Moses to help deliver Israel out of that slavery. But it was God who orchestrated all the events in history up to that moment to reveal Himself and show His sovereign power and ability to deliver out of slavery. Egypt was raised up as the most powerful and influential nation on earth at that time, specifically to illustrate a world system steeped in idolatry and the power idolatry has to enslave.

Militarily speaking, there was no greater army on earth, so there was no military might available from any other nation to deliver Israel. Spiritually speaking, the worshipping of false gods and the deifying of man, as they did the pharaohs, reflects the world order of today. Israel's exposure to these two elements formed a lost and distant condition of their hearts. For over four hundred plus years, they had lost sight of their true identity, and that is how we are as well until we accept Jesus into our hearts as Lord and Savior. He then opens our understanding to grasp the slavery we are in and the ultimate price He paid to buy us back and set us free.

> Therefore say to the children of Israel: "I am the Lord; I will bring you out from under the burdens of the Egyptians, I will rescue you from their bondage." (Ex. 6:6)

> For I brought you up from the land of Egypt, I redeemed you from the house of bondage. (Mic. 6:4)

> For the grace of God that brings salvation has appeared to all men, teaching us that, denying ungodliness and worldly lusts, we should live soberly, righteously, and godly in the present age, looking for the blessed hope and glorious appearing of our great God and Savior Jesus Christ, who gave Himself for us, that He might redeem us from every lawless deed and purify for Himself His own special people, zealous for good works. (Titus 2:11–14)

In summary, redemption means to buy back at a certain price. In our case, the price to buy us back from the power of sin and death was the life of the Son of God, who is God, Jesus the Christ.

Forgiveness, the third aspect of salvation, means to pardon. Since man's sins are against God, it is God who does the pardoning. We, of course, can sin against one another as human beings, but ultimately those sins are against God as well, since we're all created in His image. We can forgive one another for their sins against us, but all that does is release them of any obligation and us from the bondage of unforgiveness, which leads to bitterness. Only God can forgive and pardon the penalty of sin, which is death.

Have mercy upon me, O God,
According to Your lovingkindness;
According to the multitude of Your tender mercies,
Blot out my transgressions.
Wash me thoroughly from my iniquity,
And cleanse me from my sin.
For I acknowledge my transgressions,
And my sin is always before me.
Against You, You only, have I sinned. (Ps. 51:1–4)

For as the heavens are high above the earth,
So great is His mercy toward those who fear Him;
As far as the east is from the west,
So far has He removed our transgressions from us.
As a father pities his children,
So the Lord pities those who fear Him. (Ps. 103:11–13)

God's forgiveness of sin is contingent upon two requisites. First is the proprietary sacrifice of an innocent life as substitute for the life of the sinner.

> "For the life of the flesh is in the blood, and I have given it to you upon the altar to make atonement for your souls; for it is the blood that makes atonement for the soul." For it is the life of all flesh. Its blood sustains its life. Therefore I said to the children of Israel, "You shall not eat the blood of any flesh, for the life of all flesh is its blood. Whoever eats it shall be cut off." (Lev. 17:11,... 14)

> And according to the law almost all things are purified with blood, and without shedding of blood there is no remission. (Heb. 9:22)

Second, the sinner must accept God's own sacrifice of His Son on man's behalf in a spirit of true repentance and faith.

> John came baptizing in the wilderness and preaching a baptism of repentance for the remission of sins. (Mark 1:4)

> To Him all the prophets witness that, through His name, whoever believes in Him will receive remission of sins. (Acts 10:43)

> And the prayer of faith will save the sick, and the Lord will raise him up. And if he has committed sins, he will be forgiven. (James 5:15)

Our forgiveness is absolute and ratified by the resurrection of Jesus from the dead. Jesus's resurrection is proof that God the Father wholly accepted Jesus's sacrifice, thereby declaring not only Jesus's innocence of all accusations against Him but also the perfect standard required by God's law to be that acceptable substitute.

The fourth aspect of salvation is sanctification. The work of sanctification is multilayered. Primarily the word means "to be set apart." As it relates to God, it means "to be made holy and set apart for God's work." Sanctification, being the fourth aspect of salvation, overlaps and becomes the fourth aspect of "the call of God," which is holiness. We are sanctified by faith the moment we believe in the atoning sacrifice of Jesus, our Lord.

Acts 26:18 says, "To open their eyes, in order to turn them from darkness to light, and from the power of Satan to God, that they may receive forgiveness of sins and an inheritance among those who are sanctified by faith in Me."

But that is only where sanctification begins. It is a lifelong process accomplished by The Word of God, and by the indwelling of The Holy Spirit.

Sanctify them by Your truth. Your word is truth. (John 17:17)

For what the law could not do in that it was weak through the flesh, God did by sending His own Son in the likeness of sinful flesh, on account of sin: He condemned sin in the flesh, that the righteous requirement of the law might be fulfilled in us who do not walk according to the flesh but according to the Spirit. (Rom. 8:3–4)

But we are bound to give thanks to God always for you, brethren beloved by the Lord, because God from the beginning chose you for salvation through sanctification by the Spirit and belief in the truth. (2 Thess. 2:13)

Elect according to the foreknowledge of God the Father, in sanctification of the Spirit, for obedience and sprinkling of the blood of Jesus Christ (1 Peter 1:2)

The Holy Spirit sanctifies us in two ways. First, we are marked in both the earth and spirit realms by a special seal, like the seal of a king or even a state. That seal signifies that the object bearing the seal belongs to the king or state. It has the rights, provision, and protection of the king or state.

Who also has sealed us and given us the Spirit in our hearts as a guarantee. (2 Cor. 1:22)

And do not grieve the Holy Spirit of God, by whom you were sealed for the day of redemption. (Eph. 4:30)

This seal that is the Holy Spirit is set upon us for all the spirit world to see, and we are known as the "redeemed of the Lord." This seal also lives in our hearts and bears witness with our entire being—spirit, soul, and body—convincing us of our salvation in Christ and eternal destiny with God.

Second, the second work of sanctification by the Holy Spirit is an ongoing, lifelong tutelage. This Holy Spirit–led instruction leads us in a victorious life over sin and the temptations of this world, the Devil, and our selfish ambitions.

> For this is the will of God, your sanctification: that you should abstain from sexual immorality; that each of you should know how to possess his own vessel in sanctification and honor, not in passion of lust, like the Gentiles who do not know God; that no one should take advantage of and defraud his brother in this matter, because the Lord is the avenger of all such, as we also forewarned you and testified. For God did not call us to uncleanness, but in holiness. Therefore he who rejects this does not reject man, but God, who has also given us His Holy Spirit. (1 Thess. 4:3–8)

> I say then: Walk in the Spirit, and you shall not fulfill the lust of the flesh. For the flesh lusts against the Spirit, and the Spirit against the flesh; and these are contrary to one another, so that you do not do the things that you wish. But if you are led by the Spirit, you are not under the law. Now the works of the flesh are evident, which are: adultery fornication, uncleanness, lewdness, idolatry, sorcery, hatred, contentions, jealousies, outbursts of wrath, selfish ambitions, dissensions, heresies, envy, murders, drunkenness, revelries, and the like; of which I tell you beforehand, just as I also told you in time past, that those who practice such things will not inherit the kingdom of God. But the fruit of the Spirit is love, joy, peace, longsuffering, kindness, goodness, faithfulness, gentleness, self-control. Against such there is no law. And those who are Christ's have crucified

the flesh with its passions and desires. If we live in the
Spirit, let us also walk in the Spirit. (Gal. 5:16–25)

The objective of this sanctifying work is to transform us into the
image of Christ, who is God's obedient example for us. As the Holy
Spirit begins to make the Word of God alive to us, our lives take on
new meaning as that Word is practically applied. We no longer just
read the words of the Bible but live them. We act out the character of
God on earth so that the whole of creation can see that the Word of
God is written on our hearts as well as on the pages of a Bible. This
is the transforming power of the Word of God and the lamp of the
Holy Spirit working together as He shines His light on that Word. So
the fourth aspect of salvation (sanctification) and the fourth aspect of
the call of God (holiness) lie hand in hand. Sanctification is the act of
God separating us unto Himself for His purpose through our act of
faith in his Son, Jesus the Christ, and His sacrificial atonement on the
cross. And it is also the work of the Holy Spirit that leads us to holiness
through the practical application of the Word of God in our daily lives.

And you shall be holy to Me, for I the Lord am holy, and
have separated you from the peoples, that you should be
Mine. (Lev. 20:26)

To the pilgrims of the Dispersion in Pontus, Galatia,
Cappadocia, Asia, and Bithynia, elect according to the
foreknowledge of God the Father, in sanctification of
the Spirit, for obedience and sprinkling of the blood
of Jesus Christ … Therefore gird up the loins of your
mind, be sober, and rest your hope fully upon the grace
that is to be brought to you at the revelation of Jesus
Christ; as obedient children, not conforming yourselves
to the former lusts, as in your ignorance; but as He
who called you is holy, you also be holy in all your
conduct, because it is written, "Be holy, for I am holy."
(1 Peter 1:1–2, 13–16)

Though this is not an exhaustive study on every single call God makes in the universe, for this application, it is the author's view that there are five core calls. The final and fifth call is ministry. Since all believers are called to be a voice to the lost, we all enter into a form of ministry according to 2 Corinthians 5:17–21.

> Therefore, if anyone is in Christ, he is a new creation; old things have passed away; behold, all things have become new. Now all things are of God, who has reconciled us to Himself through Jesus Christ, and has given us the ministry of reconciliation, that is, that God was in Christ reconciling the world to Himself, not imputing their trespasses to them, and has committed to us the word of reconciliation. Now then, we are ambassadors for Christ, as though God were pleading through us: we implore you on Christ's behalf, be reconciled to God. For He made Him who knew no sin to be sin for us, that we might become the righteousness of God in Him.

By definition, a minister is one who performs the functions of a religion or government. Since believers belong to the kingdom of God, ministers of that kingdom perform the functions of that kingdom government. The short definition means to serve. Being or becoming a servant may seem undignified to some, and of course the ego bristles against it. But the greatest leaders are servants attending to the needs of their people. Jesus was and is the greatest minister of all time. Mark 10:44–45 says, "And whoever of you desires to be first shall be slave of all. For even the Son of Man did not come to be served, but to serve, and to give His life a ransom for many." As always, Jesus exemplifies the perfect condition of the heart—always ready, willing, and able to do the will of the Father.

As ministers of God's people, those of us who answer the call to ministry must become servants. When we serve others, we are actually serving God. Always remember that man is created in the image of

God, and when we choose to partake in the restoration of God's image in us, we answer life's highest call. The call to ministry doesn't come lightly and is filled with burden and promise. The burden is one of the heart. An urgent fervency to win the lost for Christ burns from within. Once one has tasted the goodness of God, he or she is never the same. One has to share the glory of Jesus and the freedom that comes from a resurrected spirit. Once Jesus gets inside us, we are compelled to let Him back out by sharing Him with others. He never leaves us and is the source of our strength in times of need.

The ultimate expression of ministry is Jesus living through us. And since Jesus is the perfect expression of love, we are called to let Jesus love through us. It's impossible for us to produce this level of love on our own. It must come from Jesus. When Jesus walked the earth as a man, He characterized the love of God through acts of compassion, miracles, power over nature, and an understanding of human nature that always led those He spoke to to a greater depth of God consciousness. He was able to expose the intents of the heart and reveal man's greatest need of salvation.

CHAPTER 25

THE GIFTS OF THE GODHEAD[20]

(The title "The Gifts of the Godhead," its outline, and its general theme were expounded on and taken from the *New Spirit Filled Life Bible* by Thomas Nelson [2002].)

So how do we walk in Jesus's footsteps? There is a saying in Christendom that says, "God rarely calls the equipped but is always faithful to equip the called." This is because man's propensity to revel in his own self-sufficiency is contrary to the workings that bring God glory. In other words, man gets a big ol' swollen head and starts to say, "Look what *I* have done!" So God resists the proud but gives grace to the humble. God wants the world to know that it's by His power and providence that man is able to perform miracles and operate in the supernatural realm.

The equipping of God's people is manifest in what is referred to as "the gifts of the Godhead." There are twenty-one documented gifts in all. Each person of the Godhead renders to the believer a measure of a gift or gifts proportionate to his or her faith. The reason for the gifts is to edify and empower the body of Christ as a whole. All the known gifts can and often do overlap with the other gifts so that any particular believer may operate in multiple gifts. Or rather there may be multiple manifestations of those gifts in operation through one person, but they aren't limited to just one person. Every single believer has a gift waiting to be released. Moreover, though one gift may be more prominent, usually there will be a combination of gifts operating at the same time.

The first sets of gifts we'll discuss are foundational and given at the moment of creation for a basic motivation and life in general. These foundational gifts increase incrementally as we mature. But when we realize our point of creation, who our Creator is, their potential explodes with purpose. These first seven gifts are directly tied to the character of God the Father and typify exactly how one would expect our heavenly Father to conduct Himself. Furthermore, a good Father teaches His children the way they should go by transferring His good character to His children. Let's examine them one by one, according to Romans 12:3–8:

> For I say, through the grace given to me, to everyone who is among you, not to think of himself more highly than he ought to think, but to think soberly, as God has dealt to each one a measure of faith. For as we have many members in one body, but all the members do not have the same function, so we, being many, are one body in Christ, and individually members of one another. Having then gifts differing according to the grace that is given to us, let us use them: if prophecy, let us prophesy in proportion to our faith; or ministry, let us use it in our ministering; he who teaches, in teaching; he who exhorts, in exhortation; he who gives, with liberality; he who leads, with diligence; he who shows mercy, with cheerfulness.

Prophecy

Each group of gifts, respective to each member or person of the Godhead, involves some interpretation of prophecy. As we've stated before, the gifts tend to overlap for the betterment and benefit of all, but the offices they operate under are specific and manifest at different levels of need and maturity according to the will of God. Each believer has the ability to speak prophetically in its most general sense, but being prophetic means to walk in the supernatural. The conduct of an individual is just as important as what comes out of his or her mouth. When you put these two together, you have someone who is willing and able to boldly stand up for his or her moral values as revealed in the Scriptures and now living in the heart of that person. The influence generated by this Holy Spirit–driven conduct has the power to redirect the hearts and minds of those you come in contact with, including friends and family, thereby multiplying God's moral values.

To further expound on this general sense of prophecy, we will look at a very relevant Scripture verse that should put this in a clear, concise context. Revelation 19:10 says, "And I fell at his feet to worship him. But he said to me, 'See that you do not do that! I am your fellow servant, and of your brethren who have the testimony of Jesus. Worship God! For the testimony of Jesus is the spirit of prophecy.'" Here we see the last living apostle, Saint John, receiving revelation from an angel on the Isle of Patmos. Upon the words of the angel, John was overwhelmed and fell to his face to worship the messenger sent from God. But the angel quickly ascribed all praise to Him who alone is worthy: God. The angel called himself a "brethren," who had the testimony of Jesus in his mouth.

The entire Bible is prophetic in its purest sense, telling the future before it happens. Not only that, but the message of moral excellence in the face of corrupt humanity exemplifies the voice of the prophet. Almighty God is the great prophet telling the end from the beginning for all to see and know, with no doubt that He is who He says He is. So when we speak the truth of God's Word in a bold, uncompromising fashion in the face of adversity and corruption, we speak in a prophetic voice under the authority of the Holy Scriptures.

Ministry

As we've stated, the short-term definition of a *minister* is "servant," so the general well-being of a local assembly is the concern of the ministry, meeting the needs of God's people in spiritual, mental, and physical realms. An excellent example of ministry in action can be taken from Matthew 20:24–28:

> And when the ten heard it, they were greatly displeased with the two brothers. But Jesus called them to Himself and said, "You know that the rulers of the Gentiles lord it over them, and those who are great exercise authority over them. Yet it shall not be so among you; but whoever desires to become great among you, let him be your servant. And whoever desires to be first among you, let him be your slave—just as the Son of Man did not come to be served, but to serve, and to give His life a ransom for many."

Another example is in Acts 6:1–8.

> Now in those days, when the number of the disciples was multiplying, there arose a complaint against the Hebrews by the Hellenists because their widows were neglected in the daily distribution. Then the twelve summoned the multitude of the disciples and said, "It is not desirable that we should leave the word of God and serve tables. Therefore, brethren, seek out from among you seven men of good reputation, full of the Holy Spirit and wisdom, whom we may appoint over this business; but we will give ourselves continually to prayer and to the ministry of the word." And the saying pleased the whole multitude. And they chose Stephen, a man full of faith and the Holy Spirit, and Philip, Prochorus, Nicanor, Timon, Parmenas, and Nicolas, a proselyte from Antioch, whom they set before the apostles; and when they had prayed, they laid hands on them. Then the word of God spread, and the number of the disciples multiplied greatly in Jerusalem, and a great many of the priests were obedient to the faith.

This principle of servitude Jesus set before His disciples was ultimately played out on the cross, but that same yielding spirit was transferred to all those who would follow in His footsteps. The account in Acts shows perfectly how ministry is supposed to be administrated. The original twelve apostles were busy in their own ministry positions of leadership under Jesus for the newly birthed church or body of Christ. The situation grew contentious when the two groups of Jewish believers had culturally different views and expectations. Both, whom the Bible refers to as Hebrews and Hellenists, are in fact Jewish. The group, identified as Hebrews, was composed of those Jews who were born and lived in Palestine. Palestine was the land mass connecting the continents of Asia, Africa, and Europe. It was the land area God promised to Abraham as an inheritance to his descendants forever, the land of Canaan.

The Jews of Palestine were orthodox Jews who spoke Aramaic and used the Hebrew Old Testament. In Jesus's day, the Jews of Palestine had become strict adherents to the Law of Moses. In ancient Jewish law and custom, the woman received no inheritance. She was dependent solely on her husband or relatives for support. The Hebrews or orthodox Jews viewed all those Jews outside Palestine as suspect and ritually polluted. Since Hellenism by definition is the elevation of Greek thought, life, and philosophy, it clashed with the monotheistic rule of faith the orthodox Jews enjoyed. The Hellenistic Jews read and spoke Greek. They had a Greek version of the Old Testament called the "Septuagint."

Undoubtedly, the influence of Greek culture left its residue on the Hellenists and posed an invisible barrier between the two Jewish groups. Both groups knew and followed the Law of Moses concerning widows. The Hellenists complained that the bias felt against them by the Hebrews was spilling over into their widows being neglected in the daily distribution of food and daily essentials. According to Acts 2:40–47,

> And with many other words he testified and exhorted them, saying, "Be saved from this perverse generation." Then those who gladly received his word

were baptized; and that day about three thousand souls were added to them. And they continued steadfastly in the apostles' doctrine and fellowship, in the breaking of bread, and in prayers. Then fear came upon every soul, and many wonders and signs were done through the apostles. Now all who believed were together, and had all things in common, and sold their possessions and goods, and divided them among all, as anyone had need. So continuing daily with one accord in the temple, and breaking bread from house to house, they ate their food with gladness and simplicity of heart, praising God and having favor with all the people. And the Lord added to the church daily those who were being saved we see that the church or body was growing.

The church was being made up of all who would believe in Jesus as the Messiah. Both groups of Jews were included, and soon the Gentiles would be added as well. This merging posed great conflict with the orthodox Jews who believed that, because they didn't yet fully understand that salvation had now come to all humanity, Jesus was the end of the Law or rather its fulfillment. The joy, fellowship, and sharing of goods brought on by church growth was now being tested by that very growth. Jesus's finished works at the cross had torn down the wall of separation between different Jewish groups and Gentiles. All believers were now fit for kingdom duty through the shed blood of Jesus, but the orthodox Jews who believed (we will call them messianic Jews from now on) had trouble grasping this concept mainly because of their past failed history of idolatry, exile. and restoration. Their view was, Yes, Jesus is the Messiah, but ... and this is where their history and understanding of the Law muddled their relationships with other believers. It would take strong leadership to sort things out and bring a spirit of unity to the newly birthed and fast-growing church.

The twelve apostles needed to act fast, so they summoned the multitude of disciples and chose seven men to be ministers to the people. Among these seven were two men by the names of Stephen and

Philip. The word used to describe these newly appointed positions can be found only twice; in the New King James Version of the Bible, in Philippians 1:1 and 1 Timothy 3:8–13, is the term *deacon*. Although the term *deacon* is found only twice, the Greek word from which it is taken, *diakonos*, is found thirty times. In most cases *diakonos* is translated "servant." A misunderstanding of the responsibilities of this new office may stem from the wording in Act 6:2: "Then the twelve summoned the multitude of the disciples and said, 'It is not desirable that we should leave the word of God and serve tables.'"

"Serve tables" to us now in this day brings forth an image of a waiter or waitress at your local restaurant. But the term is really a word play on the apostles' view of the current situation while taken in context. The complaint of the Hellenists was on the surface about food and essentials being withheld from the widows in their group, so in a sense the apostles were speaking out of frustration that such matters were even getting that far up the ladder. On the other hand, it was important enough to call a big meeting to sort things out. The urgency wasn't so much food as it was for the need of good administration. The phrase "leave the Word of God and serve tables" actually reveals the different levels of church ministry and administration. The apostles didn't mean they should stop teaching to put on an apron but rather that they didn't have the time or resources to do both teach and administrate at both levels. They needed help.

The best clue we see regarding the great responsibility and tasks set before them in administration duties for the growing church can be found in Acts 6:3: "Therefore, brethren, seek out from among you seven men of good reputation, full of the Holy Spirit and wisdom, whom we may appoint over this business." The requirements of this new office were strict and of the highest order. If one could equate the skill level needed to officiate these duties in today's terms, you would at the very least need a business degree with a strong emphasis on accounting and administration. The phrase "full of the Holy Spirit" implies a life in complete submission to the Holy Spirit's influence. The total person— spirit, soul, and body—is a hypersensitive vessel used to administer the gift of ministry. Both Stephen and Philip are mentioned in Scripture as high-level administrators, ministering to the needs of the people as they walked in the power of the supernatural.

Teaching

There are over forty some verses in the Bible about teachers and/ or teaching in both the Old and New Testaments. But the clearest and most dire admonition concerning teachers and their responsibilities can be found in James 3:1–2: "My brethren, let not many of you become teachers, knowing that we shall receive a stricter judgment. For we all stumble in many things. If anyone does not stumble in word, he is a perfect man, able also to bridle the whole body."

The serious nature of teaching can be best understood in view of the ripple effect it has on the lives of those influenced by it. Matthew 23 illustrates a stark contrast between the heart of the teaching and the intent of the heart of the teacher. When the gift of teaching is in operation, the ability to convey and apply deep spiritual truths is supplied by the supernatural and transcends man's ability to communicate divine truths. A clear understanding of these spiritual truths is granted to the hearers through a direct Spirit-to-spirit communication. That is, the Holy Spirit communicates to the spirit (the God-conscious part of man) through the mouth of the teacher. This kind of teaching presupposes the natural understanding that comes from study. It is revelatory by nature and often is the result of going through hardships and the valleys of life. The furnace of affliction is where dependence on God is revealed and the character of God is forged in us. Good teachers understand this principle, but great teachers are able to help others apply these life lessons to their own lives and circumstances in conjunction with the revealed truths in God's Word.

Exhortation

This one carries with it a double meaning, which is "to call near or far" and "to console." Someone who operates with the gift of exhortation is an encourager. His or her messages are able to inspire people into action in either averting danger or rising to a daunting task.

Giving

The basic meaning is to give out of a spirit of generosity. The Bible tells us that God loves a cheerful giver, but what is often overlooked in the context of that verse is that it's God Himself who is the supplier who allows the giver to give. If God is the One who supplies the provisions of life, how could we ever out-give God or find ourselves lacking out of what we give? The more we give, the more God will supply. This principle is one of the hardest for man to learn and enter into because giving is unnatural to the natural man—that is, the man of the flesh, whose spirit is asleep. The spirit of generosity comes from a complete and total trust in God. When we are able to share liberally and generously out of the one thing we as humans, governed by a monetary system, need the most (money), then we exit out of man's system and enter into the limitless economy of God, the kingdom.

Leadership

This gift refers to one who is in the forefront. Everybody wants to be the leader, but being a leader is more than barking orders and delegating duties to be carried out. Leadership is born out of the necessity to facilitate care and responsibility. A good leader anticipates the needs of his or her people and tries to meet those needs before they arise. But a great leader will invoke the desire to follow in those being led. When people know and understand that those in charge have a genuine care for their health, safety, and well-being, they will naturally look up to and follow that leader. Leading God's people is a tremendous responsibility and shouldn't be taken lightly. A leader must always remember that he or she too is subject to the leadership of the Godhead. Final authority and rule over life comes from the Word of God. A leader must apply this rule to his or her own life before trying to apply it to others. People will know whether your life aligns with the Scriptures, and any selfish ambitions will soon be exposed. But if you have this gift, then by all means exercise it and lead.

Mercy

It is worthy of mention that there are seven basic life gifts that come from the Father. Seven is the number of perfection. These seven gifts reflect the character of God. It is really cool to know that God is perfecting His character in us and perfecting His body through us as we partake of the divine nature and help facilitate the church. Like all actions in the universe, there is an opposite or equal reaction. Though the word *mercy* is a noun used to describe a certain state of compassion or forgiveness, when applied, it becomes an action. The best way to understand mercy is to view it in light of its opposite meaning. For our study, the antonym we will choose for *mercy* is "penalty" or "punishment." A judge may exercise mercy at sentencing by imposing a mitigated, presumptive, or minimum sentence, when a more severe punishment could be issued. Mercy is extended from the hand of the powerful to the undeserving and always seeks the highest level of good for the offending party. Mercy is an extension of forgiveness and the fruit of love. When it is within our power to grant mercy to those who have hurt or wronged us and we choose revenge over mercy, we doom ourselves to embitterment and judgment. God has called us to be forgiving and merciful just as He is toward us through Jesus's sacrifice.

In summary, mercy and justice go hand in hand. It is God who brings about correction where it is needed. We are to be His instruments of mercy and compassion during those times of correction. We will all stand before the judgment seat of Christ to receive our rewards, whether good or bad, so it is best to be found faithful. Second Corinthian 5:9–10 says, "Therefore we make it our aim, whether present or absent, to be well pleasing to Him. For we must all appear before the judgment seat of Christ, that each one may receive the things done in the body, according to what he has done, whether good or bad." James 1:12–13 says, "Blessed is the man who endures temptation; for when he has been approved, he will receive the crown of life which the Lord has promised to those who love Him. Let no one say when he is tempted, 'I am tempted by God'; for God cannot be tempted by evil, nor does He Himself tempt anyone." As for the administration of the gift of mercy, it is to be done with cheerfulness and not out of obligation. In its most general sense, it is the ability to sense the emotions of others and exhibit deep, meaningful empathy toward that person. It also includes those engaged in relief missions across the globe.

The second set of gifts we will address is the gifts of the Holy Spirit. These are not general giftings. They are specific and designed to illustrate God's sovereign power and willingness to share in the divine nature. Every single one of them is *supernatural* manifestations of the Holy Spirit. They are demonstrated throughout the book of Acts and Luke 10, especially verses 9 and 19. In John 14:11–13, Jesus said, "Believe Me that I am in the Father and the Father in Me, or else believe Me for the sake of the works themselves. Most assuredly, I say to you, he who believes in Me, the works that I do he will do also; and greater works than these he will do, because I go to My Father. And whatever you ask in My name, that I will do, that the Father may be glorified in the Son." Jesus connected the power of His name to great authority for the release of the Holy Spirit's supernatural power, the same power Jesus exhibited on earth.

Also, in Mark 16 we see a promise Jesus made to His disciples. Mark 16:16–18 says, "He who believes and is baptized will be saved; but he who does not believe will be condemned. And these signs will follow those who believe: In My name they will cast out demons; they will speak with new tongues: they will take up serpents; and if they drink anything deadly, it will by no means hurt them; they will lay hands on the sick, and they will recover." "These signs," Jesus said, would follow those who believe, but we must understand the context in which He spoke this promise.

Observe Mark 16:14–15: "Later He appeared to the eleven as they sat at the table; and He rebuked their unbelief and hardness of heart, because they did not believe those who had seen Him after He had risen. And He said to them, 'Go into all the world and preach the gospel to every creature.'" Belief was the doorway for the propagation of the gospel. "Go into all the world and *preach* the gospel to every creature" was the command, but they needed power to do it: power to witness, power to overcome the severe adversities ahead of them, power to convince and rebuke, heal, and deliver. That power came at Pentecost, fifty days after Jesus's ascension. The promise of the Father came upon the disciples and all humanity. (For a better understanding, please read Acts 1:1–8 and all of Acts 2.)

> When the Day of Pentecost had fully come, they were all with one accord in one place. And suddenly there came a sound from heaven, as of a rushing mighty wind, and it filled the whole house where they were sitting. Then there appeared to them divided tongues, as of fire, and one sat upon each of them. And they were all filled with the Holy Spirit and began to speak with other tongues, as the Spirit gave them utterance. And there were dwelling in Jerusalem Jews, devout men, from every nation under heaven. And when this sound occurred, the multitude came together, and were confused, because everyone heard them speak in his own language. Then they were all amazed and marveled, saying to one another, "Look, are not all these who speak Galileans? And how is it that we hear, each in our own language in which we were born? Parthians and Medes and Elamites, those dwelling in Mesopotamia, Judea and Cappadocia, Pontus and Asia, Phrygia and Pamphylia, Egypt and the parts of Libya adjoining Cyrene, visitors from Rome, both Jews and proselytes, Cretans and Arabs—we hear them speaking in our own tongues the wonderful works of God." (Acts 2:1–11)

The young church was now ready to take on the Great Commission. The book of Acts records exponential growth everywhere Jesus preached under the influence of the Holy Spirit. Those same gifts enjoyed by the early church are still in operation and available today for every believer. But unbelief, hardness of heart, and disobedience can stifle the full measure of God's plans and giftings in your life. We must be completely obedient and subject to Jesus and let the Word of God be our rule of faith and final authority for our conduct in life. When our lives align with the Word of God, He pours out His Spirit on us, and the miraculous takes place. Let's take a look at the gifts of the Holy Spirit, as revealed in 1 Corinthian 12:8–12, 28:

> For to one is given the word of wisdom through the Spirit, to another the word of knowledge through the same Spirit, to another faith by the same Spirit, to another gifts of healings by the same Spirit, to another the working of miracles, to another prophecy, to another discerning of spirits, to another different kinds of tongues, to another the interpretation of tongues. But one and the same Spirit works all these things, distributing to each one individually as He wills. For as the body is one and has many members, but all the members of that one body, being many, are one body, so also is Christ … And God has appointed these in the church: first apostles, second prophets, third teachers, after that miracles, then gifts of healings, helps, administrations, varieties of tongues.

Word of Wisdom

Wisdom is the application of knowledge and understanding. It is when and how to use knowledge and the understanding gained from it. For example, one learns what an umbrella is; when fully extended, it provides a protective shelter from rain or sun. Wisdom teaches that the best time to open our umbrella is not in the house but outside when the rain is pouring or the sun is at its hottest. That is normal human wisdom, but the gift of the word of wisdom is the supernatural ability to apply wisdom from knowledge not yet learned. It is God's ability to see the big picture of all life, all at once, from the perspective of eternity and transfer that knowledge, understanding, and wisdom to guide the recipient in the way he or she should go as God orchestrates any given circumstance. Simply put, it is divine direction that guides an action leading to a supernatural conclusion.

Word of Knowledge

Knowledge is the supernatural perception of what to do. It includes insight into any given situation or set of circumstances in which the recipient had no prior knowledge. It also pertains to the application of moral judgments and decision making. It also applies to a greater depth of understanding of the Word of God.

Faith

We all begin with a measure of faith in life. Reoccurring themes in our lives give birth to a certain confidence that things will continue on schedule as they always have, such as the sunrise and sunset or the seasons ushering in rain, snow, and color. But the Holy Spirit's gift of faith goes far beyond this learned confidence. This kind of faith rejects doubt on every level and believes in God to sustain someone through any circumstance and is directly tied to obedience.

Gifts of Healing

Primarily, this gift refers to deliverance from human sickness, diseases, broken bones, blindness, and such things by a supernatural intervention. One minute you're blind, and then—*poof*—in the name of Jesus, you're not. But it also translates to the hands of the surgeon as God skills those hands to perform an operation that may be at high risk. Not every person prayed for will be healed, but every God-ordained healing will occur. The signs and wonders God has allowed us to be witness to are a testimony of His existence and the willingness to be involved in the lives He created. The critical thing to remember is that God is sovereign and in control. Just because someone we pray for isn't healed instantly doesn't mean God doesn't care or doesn't exist. It's always up to Him, and He always knows what is best. Signs and wonders build our faith, but God doesn't need our faith to exist. He is the great "I am," having always been and always will be God and God alone. There is none other beside Him.

I have been witness to many deliverances and healings, and am not surprised when they happen. My first memorable healing took place in prison. A young man, healthy otherwise, one day fell ill in his feet. He experienced severe, crippling pain in his feet. He couldn't walk. I saw him emerge from the health unit door on crutches. He was in severe pain. He could barely touch his tiptoes on the ground while his full weight leaned on the crutches. He moved unbearably slow while in excruciating pain, a grimace plastered across his sweat-laden and furrowed brow.

I asked him what had happened, and he said he didn't know, that he had woken up that way, and he was very scared. I told him to come to the chapel so we could pray for him. I had never seen a healing before. I had no idea what would happen. All I did know was that something inside me knew I needed to get him to the chapel. We slowly made our way there, and once in, my spiritual father, whom I will introduce you to shortly, immediately knew something was wrong.

He said to the young man, "Do you believe Jesus can heal you?"
The man said, "Yes."

Then my father, whose name is Doyle, said, "Everybody who has little or weak faith, *out*!" He had me lay my hands on the young man's feet while he went to rebuking the Devil and exercising authority over the infirmity. By noon that day, the young man had thrown his crutches down and was running around like a child on the playground. Many years have passed since then, and many healings have taken place before my eyes: people who have had spine surgery and have lived in chronic pain for twenty-plus years were delivered, with all traces of pain removed. A woman with a terminal heart disease was given a clean bill of health, with no traces of the degenerative heart condition left. It was supposed to take her life but was just gone one day after seven years of faithful prayer. For seven years the doctors told her, "You're getting worse."

For seven years, she said, "I am believing in God to heal me." Then—*poof*—she was completely healed. The doctors were dumbfounded. They had no explanation. She didn't need one, and she knew why. One thing is for certain: it's God who does the healing in His time at His prescribed pace. Sometimes it's instant, and sometimes it takes a while, but it's always supernatural.

Workings of Miracles

This gift works closely with the gifts of faith and healing to bind and exercise authority over sin, sickness, and evil. It is a display of power that exceeds the natural realm and intercedes to overcome seemingly impossible situations. An example of a miracle that happened to me took place right after I got out prison. I had served all my DOC time, but they gave me probation on top of that. Getting probation on a class-two felony with a criminal history spanning twenty years was a miracle in itself. Probation is usually reserved for first-time offenders to try to keep them out of the system and redirect their lives. Some people look at probation as a "setup" to fail by the court. But that mind-set is obviously stemming from a heart and mind unwilling to change. I was more than willing to change. I was ready to do what it took to get my life together. There I was, being dragged back to court.

They came and got me from DOC to face more identity theft and fraudulent schemes charges. I knew they were going to do it, just not when, and of course there was the hope that it would just go away. I had stolen my own mother's bank card to support my drug habit. I had thought it was a credit card, but it was her debit card. I ran it up, and when she went to make her house payment, the money was gone.

She called me and said, "What did you do?"

I said, "It's just a credit card. Report it stolen, and insurance will cover it."

What a loser I was. Not only was that the twisted thinking of a junkie, but it wasn't a credit card; it was her debit card, and the actual amount of real cash in her checking account was wiped out. I felt so ashamed. I told her just to call the cops and report it stolen. "I'll do time, and you'll get your money back," I said. I was already doing time for the same charges, fraudulent schemes and identity theft, so the likelihood of their aggravating my sentence was very good, not to mention my long history. Yep, I was in deep doo-doo. God was dealing with me, all right, and things had just gone from bad to worse.

I didn't even see or know who my public defender was until I was in the court room. The aggravated sentence on that class two was staggering. I didn't even want to think about that. My attorney was rattling off this and that, and I said, "Whoa, slow down. Don't just rush me through my due process in fear like there's nothing you can do. Fight for me! Ask them for probation. I don't care how long it is. I can do it." She just blinked back at me in disbelief, mouth agape.

After a few long seconds, she composed herself and conceded to give it a try. I didn't know whether her efforts would be halfhearted or whether her words would meet resistance or fall on deaf ears altogether. But what I did know was that I wasn't going to just sign whatever she threw in front of me and say, "Thanks." This was my only opportunity to beg for mercy. I couldn't go back to my cell, thinking, *Why didn't I say something?* So I did. And she did. And the Lord showed up. They granted me probation!

Though be it, they probably did view it as an opportunity to do away with me forever should I fail. I knew—and more importantly, God knew—I wouldn't. Not only did I not fail, but I completed my probation sentence in half the time. It wasn't just unsupervised probation but intense probation, the strictest, hardest kind. That is a statistical miracle in itself, but that's not what I want to share.

So there I was, on intense probation, trying to get my life in order. I had made a pretty good mess of things. I had no money, no steady job, no car, no nothing … except my God and of course my dear mother, who had let me do parole to her house. Yep, I was on probation and parole at the same time. I was at the mercy of whoever had a car. I went to the MVD (motor vehicle division, this acronym varies from state to state), to get my driver's license, which had been suspended of course for my driving a car with suspended plates. Go figure.

Everything was going okay when suddenly, the clerk stopped and just stared at her terminal.

"Is something wrong?" I asked.

"Ummm, it appears that you have some other violations in another state that have not been satisfied," she said.

Another state? I thought. What was she talking about? Then she read them off.

"Oh yeah, I forgot about that," I said. I had a handful of driving infractions I had never paid and, worst of all, a failure to appear. I became very discouraged. I had just paid the state of Arizona in excess of $1,500, and now another state wanted over half again that much. I started wondering, *How bad do I really need a license anyway?* I went to the Lord with the matter.

"Father, I don't have the money," I said.

"I will provide a way," He said. And of course He did. But that wasn't the miracle. Once I had gotten all the money, I contacted the two different counties I owed money in. Everything was looking good until the clerk informed me that there wasn't a fine for the FTA (failure to appear). I would have to appear in person.

But I'm on intense probation, I thought. How in the world was I to leave the state when I couldn't even leave my own house? I went to my probation officer, who was the head guy and of course the strictest. I had only been out and on probation for a very short time. I was doing well on probation, but that didn't matter. When I pled my case and explained my situation, he got all flustered. "I don't care what your obligations are outside of this county. If you try to leave, you'll violate your probation and go to jail!" Of course I hadn't really expected any other response, but my situation had become quite humanly impossible.

I had a bright idea and called the public defender I'd had on one of my cases back there. He was real laid back and genuinely cared. He was the coolest, most honest, down-to-earth attorney I ever met. And I've met a bunch! But he was different. If anybody could help, it was he. So I placed a call, several calls actually, and finally got to talk with him in person. He said he would try his best and thought under the circumstances that it looked favorable. I was excited. *God came through again!* I thought. But after a few weeks of dialogue, the story changed, and he said, "I am sorry, but there appears that there is nothing I can do. My hands are tied. You'll have to appear."

I was completely deflated. "That's it. There's no way I am going to get my license back. Not until I am off probation anyway."

He said, "Call back next Friday at such and such a time in between court, and I'll make one last plea on your behalf." He hung up.

Now I was at a serious crossroads in my life. I was in a real moral and faith dilemma. I had the money to pay off all my fines, but what was the use of paying them all that money if I wasn't going to get my license back? The natural man in me, the man in the flesh, said, "Don't give them a dime. What's the point? You have a bunch of extra money now. You can pay them later when you get off probation." Yes, that indeed is what the "natural man" said.

But God had a totally different perspective. The Holy Spirit told me, "Send the money. I will make a way. I want you debt free." Well, let me tell you, that was one serious struggle in the flesh. It was so hard to trust when I couldn't see any way at all for me to go out of state. But finally I gave in and did what God had told me to do. I sent the money to address the different fines in the different counties, none of which had anything to do with the appearance charge. I just couldn't see any relationship, but I did it anyway.

The Friday came when I was supposed to call. I was at work, but I took my lunch break early to make the call. I went outside, dialed, and waited. "Public defender's office. How can I help you?" I made my request, and she put me on hold. I was on hold for over twenty minutes. My lunch break was just about over. This whole thing had been going on for four weeks. Phone call after phone call. High hopes, no hope. It was a roller coaster of emotions, and now I had used up my lunch break without talking to anyone and wasted twenty-plus minutes on my cell phone. It was unbearable.

Then the phone picked up. "Hello, are you still there?" the voice said.

"Yes, of course," I said.

"I am sorry to keep you on hold so long, but I have been down in records for the past two hours, and the strangest thing has happened," the public defender said.

"Oh, what do you mean? What happened?" I asked.

As I listened intently, he told me that he had gone to pull my records for viewing to try to figure something out but couldn't find a single trace of any record. Nothing, not electronic, not paper, nothing. It was like it had never existed.

I received in the mail copies of all the fines I had paid. I marched myself down to MVD and got in line. *Here we go, God,* I thought. *This is all You.* My number came up. I went to the window.

"How are you doing today, sir?" the clerk asked.

"I'll let you know in a minute," I retorted.

She began computing information, and after a while she looked up and said, "Oh, that will be twenty dollars please."

The power of God completely amazed me. He had performed a miracle on my behalf. I walked out of there with a valid driver's license and a *huge* smile on my face. My God cared for me. He wanted me to succeed, and He'd shown up to help me in an otherwise-impossible situation. It was a miracle.

Now we are talking about the gift or workings of miracles. Though this account didn't involve a single person raising his arms to part the Red Sea, it illustrates an impossible situation becoming possible through the supernatural intervention of the divine. Mark 10:27 says, "But Jesus looked at them and said, 'With men it is impossible, but not with God; for with God all things are possible.'"

Prophecy

Here the gift of prophecy, as the Holy Spirit granted, is a specific, divinely inspired, supernatural utterance that is separate from intellect of any prior knowledge of a given situation. It will declare the heart and mind of God through a known spoken language. It is supernatural insight into and of an event that hasn't yet come to pass, but most certainly will. The three tests a prophetic utterance must pass to be considered genuine are the following:

1. It must align with God's Word.
2. It always magnifies Jesus.
3. It must come to pass.

Anyone filled with the Holy Spirit could at any time break forth in prophetic utterance. That is to say that all believers who have been filled with the Holy Spirit are vessels at the disposal of the Holy Spirit for a prophetic word.

Discerning of Spirits

This is the supernatural ability to see into the spiritual realm and detect, avoid, and confront, when prudent, the spiritual forces of wickedness. It also allows the one operating in this gift to detect false teaching and doctrines.

Different Types of Tongues

This is the supernatural ability to speak in a language unknown to the speaker, whether it be a known foreign language or an unknown heavenly language. The known languages always convey the gospel message and prove to convince the hearer of God's call unto salvation. The unknown heavenly languages are meant to edify (build up) both the individual and/or corporate body of Christ. In either case, the Holy Spirit speaks through the individual. Acts 2:1–12 says,

> When the Day of Pentecost had fully come, they were all with one accord in one place. And suddenly there came a sound from heaven, as of a rushing mighty wind, and it filled the whole house where they were sitting. Then there appeared to them divided tongues, as of fire, and one sat upon each of them. And they were all filled with the Holy Spirit and began to speak

with other tongues, as the Spirit gave them utterance. And there were dwelling in Jerusalem Jews, devout men, from every nation under heaven. And when this sound occurred, the multitude came together, and were confused, because everyone heard them speak in his own language. Then they were all amazed and marveled, saying to one another, "Look, are not all these who speak Galileans? And how is it that we hear, each in our own language in which we were born? Parthians and Medes and Elamites, those dwelling in Mesopotamia, Judea and Cappadocia, Pontus and Asia, Phrygia and Pamphylia, Egypt and the parts of Libya adjoining Cyrene, visitors from Rome, both Jews and proselytes, Cretans and Arabs—we hear them speaking in our own tongues the wonderful works of God." So they were all amazed and perplexed, saying to one another, "Whatever could this mean?"

To better understand tongues and their purpose, please read on your own the following Scripture verses I have provided for you: Isaiah 28:11; Mark 16:17; Acts 2:4; 10:44–48; 19:1–7; 1 Corinthians 12:10, 28–31; 13:1–3; 14:2, 4–22, 26–32.

Interpretation of Tongues

This gift can best be understood in its relationship to prophecy. In both instances, the gift operates apart from human intellect—that is, it transcends the intellect into the supernatural. In both instances, a manifestation of the spirit provides a revelatory message, whether it be of warning, rebuke, correction, or edification. The interpreter never claims to understand the tongue that is being spoken but rather gives its meaning but not a literal word-for-word translation. The Scriptures place the gifts of tongues and their interpretation at the same level of prominence as prophecy because the body is thereby edified through interpretation. It is important to note that prophecy or the interpretation of tongues should never replace the written Word as a rule of faith or code of conduct. The Word of God is final authority for all humanity, and the gifts of the Godhead are meant to facilitate the body of Christ. They are literally a manifestation of "Thy Kingdom come, Thy will be done in earth, as it is in heaven." (Matthew 6:10). The gifts or manifestations are given to us for the perpetuation of the gospel during the dispensation of grace (the church age or last days).

Next we move on to the gifts of the Son (the equipping of the saints). God has called all humanity into service. It is up to us to answer that call. Whatever degree of service we are called into, whether a mother, chef, plumber, or minister, God gives us the talent we need to accomplish the task set before us. God would not, will not, does not, and cannot send us into battle without our weaponry. The time of the great awakening is at hand. Arise all you who sleep, for the time has come to do your part in the battle with an ancient enemy. God, our God, the one, true, and living God, has ordained victory and appointed us to bear His image. Do not be afraid but go forth in courage and smite the Enemy in his own camp. Amen.

> For though we walk in the flesh, we do not war according to the flesh. For the weapons of our warfare are not carnal but mighty in God for pulling down strongholds, casting down arguments and every high thing that exalts itself against the knowledge of God, bringing every thought into captivity to the obedience of Christ, and being ready to punish all disobedience when your obedience is fulfilled. (2 Cor. 10:3–6)

> Finally, my brethren, be strong in the Lord and in the power of His might. Put on the whole armor of God, that you may be able to stand against the wiles of the devil. For we do not wrestle against flesh and blood, but against principalities, against powers, against the rulers of the darkness of this age, against spiritual hosts of

wickedness in the heavenly places. Therefore take up the whole armor of God, that you may be able to withstand in the evil day, and having done all, to stand. Stand therefore, having girded your waist with truth, having put on the breastplate of righteousness, and having shod your feet with the preparation of the gospel of peace; above all, taking the shield of faith with which you will be able to quench all the fiery darts of the wicked one. And take the helmet of salvation, and the sword of the Spirit, which is the word of God; praying always with all prayer and supplication in the Spirit, being watchful to this end with all perseverance and supplication for all the saints—and for me, that utterance may be given to me, that I may open my mouth boldly to make known the mystery of the gospel, for which I am an ambassador in chains; that in it I may speak boldly, as I ought to speak. (Eph. 6:10–20)

The Gifts of the Son

Ephesians 4:11 says, "And He Himself gave some to be apostles, some prophets, some evangelists, and some pastors and teachers."

Apostles

The term *apostle* means "one who is sent out or commissioned." The term focuses back the attention on the One who sends, Jesus Christ. The term also carries with it the full authority of the sender like an ambassador who, being a spokesperson, fully represents the government from which he came. In a historical context, an apostle was one who had actually walked with Jesus and was assigned a role in completing the closed canon of Scripture (what we call the Holy Bible). It also refers to the task of propagating the gospel into new and faraway places, establishing a strong foothold for Jesus, and overseeing the facilitation of that church growth in large sections.

Prophets

Again we see another manifestation of prophecy as Jesus administered it. This is an authoritative voice speaking a message of divine direction for the body and all humanity concerning future events. Two examples I would like to share are John the Baptist and John the Apostle. Saint John the Apostle penned both accounts. They follow:

> The next day John saw Jesus coming toward him, and said, "Behold! The Lamb of God who takes away the sin of the world! This is He of whom I said, 'After me comes a Man who is preferred before me, for He was before me.' I did not know Him; but that He should be revealed to Israel, therefore I came baptizing with water." And John bore witness, saying, "I saw the Spirit descending from heaven like a dove, and He remained upon Him. I did not know Him, but He who sent me to baptize with water said to me, 'Upon whom you see the Spirit descending, and remaining on Him, this is He who baptizes with the Holy Spirit.' And I have seen and testified that this is the Son of God." (John 1:29–34)

Here we see John the Baptist operating in the office of prophet. His main message is that the Lamb of God takes away the sin of the world. This phrase is purely prophetic, as Jesus is still quite alive, but it alludes to His sacrificial death and the consequent result of that sacrifice, man's salvation. The second part of this passage is prophetic as well and alludes to the coming of the Holy Spirit and Jesus as the baptizer with the Holy Spirit. We will discuss the subject of the baptism with the Holy Spirit in detail in a later chapter.

The second example is found in Revelation 22:6–21.

> Then he said to me, "These words are faithful and true." And the Lord God of the holy prophets sent His angel to show His servants the things which must shortly take

place. "Behold, I am coming quickly! Blessed is he who keeps the words of the prophecy of this book." Now I, John, saw and heard these things. And when I heard and saw, I fell down to worship before the feet of the angel who showed me these things. Then he said to me, "See that you do not do that. For I am your fellow servant, and of your brethren the prophets, and of those who keep the words of this book. Worship God." And he said to me, "Do not seal the words of the prophecy of this book, for the time is at hand. He who is unjust, let him be unjust still; he who is filthy, let him be filthy still; he who is righteous, let him be righteous still; he who is holy, let him be holy still." "And behold, I am coming quickly, and My reward is with Me, to give to every one according to his work. I am the Alpha and the Omega, the Beginning and the End, the First and the Last." Blessed are those who do His commandments, that they may have the right to the tree of life, and may enter through the gates into the city. But outside are dogs and sorcerers and sexually immoral and murderers and idolaters, and whoever loves and practices a lie. "I, Jesus, have sent My angel to testify to you these things in the churches. I am the Root and the Offspring of David, the Bright and Morning Star." And the Spirit and the bride say, "Come!" And let him who hears say, "Come!" And let him who thirsts come. Whoever desires, let him take the water of life freely. For I testify to everyone who hears the words of the prophecy of this book: If anyone adds to these things, God will add to him the plagues that are written in this book; and if anyone takes away from the words of the book of this prophecy, God shall take away his part from the Book of Life, from the holy city, and from the things which are written in this book. He who testifies to these things says, "Surely I am coming quickly." Amen. Even so, come, Lord Jesus! The grace of our Lord Jesus Christ be with you all. Amen.

This is the closing passage of Scripture. There are no more stories, no more history. Nothing further is to follow or be removed from the closed canon of Scripture. Saint John is sitting in a cave on the desolate Isle of Patmos operating in the office of prophet to its fullest measure. The result is the final warning of a most-certain event that will take place sometime in the future. The most astonishing thing for you as a reader is that some of you will be reading this book after the event has taken place. Those of you who have been left behind, who refused to believe, are now confronted with an undeniable truth that Jesus was and is who He says He is, the Son of God, the Messiah, the Holy One of Israel, the Risen Christ, the King of Kings and Lord of Lords. Blessed be His name forever. Amen.

Evangelists

From now on we will refer to the gifts of the Son as the offices. Though Scripture clearly says that Jesus gave gifts to men (Eph. 4:7 says, "But to each one of us grace was given according to the measure of Christ's gift."), Ephesians 4:11–16 also clearly shows that these gifts operate in an official capacity to facilitate and oversee growth and shepherd the flock of God. The office of evangelists is similar to that of the pastor/teacher but much broader in scope. It refers to the especially effective way the salvation message is preached or witnessed. The evangelist is able to convey the message in a way that draws the hearer to a place of deep personal understanding, a place where repentance is invoked and the total dependence on God is realized. The evangelist's stage is usually set before a huge audience, where as many people can be reached at one time. An evangelist will come into new territory to preach the message, and hundreds (if not thousands) will be converted from death unto life. It is then the job of the local pastors to nurture those who have just given their lives to Jesus. The evangelist will then move on to the next stage. The gift of healing and/or miracles often accompanies the evangelist.

Mark 16:15–18 says, "And He said to them, 'Go into all the world and preach the gospel to every creature. He who believes and is baptized will be saved; but he who does not believe will be condemned. And these signs will follow those who believe: In My name they will cast out demons; they will speak with new tongues; they will take up serpents; and if they drink anything deadly, it will by no means hurt them; they will lay hands on the sick, and they will recover.'"

Pastors/Teachers

The word *pastor* in Greek, *poimen*, means "shepherd." According to *Strong's Concordance, poimen* (#4166) is properly translated "a shepherd." Its figurative translation is someone whom the Lord raises up to care for the total well-being of His flock (the people of the Lord). The pastor/teacher picks up where the evangelist leaves off. You will find the pastor deeply involved in the individual lives of the people of his congregation. It is his job to rightly divide the Word of Truth, give the whole counsel of God—expounding on the Scriptures, whether contextual, topical, or analytical—and bring to the surface the deep spiritual meanings that can be applied here in the physical world. The pastor has a deep love for his congregation, God's people, and is by his very nature a protector.

Missionaries

Some see the missionary as apostolic or evangelistic in similarity, but it is the author's view that though there may be similarities, the office of missionary is unique unto itself. The missionary, like the evangelist, is driven by an inner force that he must share the gospel of salvation in both approach and longevity. Once the evangelist has given his message and invitation, he or she leaves the area and moves on. The missionary actually takes up residence among the people to which he preaches and helps to set up an autonomous, indigenous, self-governing body. The time the missionary stays with the indigenous people is much longer than that of the evangelist. He or she will eventually move on to start another body of believers, starting the process all over again, and will not leave until his or her growth is self-sustaining and maturing in leadership. Unlike the evangelist, the missionary will return to the beginning of his or her circuit to strengthen and make sure doctrinal purity is being enforced. The apostle Paul was a perfect example of a missionary. The missionary also has a hub he or she will return to, as Paul did at Antioch. Also the missionary is totally dependent on God for supply and support both monetarily and for the ability to communicate the gospel message to a people whose language he or she doesn't know.

Lastly, concerning the twenty-one documented gifts of the Godhead, we add three special graces also mentioned in Scripture:

Hospitality

This word literally means "to love," "to do," or "to do with pleasure." It is the practical application of ministry, no matter how mundane the task is done with the attitude of joy for joy's sake.

> As each one has received a gift, minister it to one another, as good stewards of the manifold grace of God. If anyone speaks, let him speak as the oracles of God. If anyone ministers, let him do it as with the ability which God supplies, that in all things God may be glorified through Jesus Christ, to whom belong the glory and the dominion forever and ever. Amen. (1 Peter 4:10–11)

> For I was hungry and you gave Me food; I was thirsty and you gave Me drink; I was a stranger and you took Me in; I was naked and you clothed Me; I was sick and you visited Me; I was in prison and you came to Me. (Matt. 25:35–36)

Celibacy

Since marriage is considered honorable and ordained by God, celibacy is a special grace that frees the individual of marital distractions and allows that person to dedicate himself or herself totally to God.

> For I wish that all men were even as I myself. But each one has his own gift from God, one in this manner and another in that. But I say to the unmarried and to the widows: It is good for them if they remain even as I am … But I want you to be without care. He who is unmarried cares for the things of the Lord— how he may please the Lord. But he who is married cares about the things of the world—how he may please his wife. There is a difference between a wife and a virgin. The unmarried woman cares about the things of the Lord, that she may be holy both in body and in spirit. But she who is married cares about the things of the world—how she may please her husband. And this I say for your own profit, not that I may put a leash on you, but for what is proper, and that you may serve the Lord without distraction. (1 Cor. 7:7–8, 32–35)

Martyrdom

A martyr is someone killed for his or her beliefs, like Stephen in Acts 7:59–60: "And they stoned Stephen as he was calling on God and saying, 'Lord Jesus, receive my spirit.' Then he knelt down and cried out with a loud voice, 'Lord, do not charge them with this sin.' And when he had said this, he fell asleep."

Martyrdom is also foreshadowed in 2 Timothy 4:6–8: "For I am already being poured out as a drink offering, and the time of my departure is at hand. I have fought the good fight, I have finished the race, I have kept the faith. Finally, there is laid up for me the crown of righteousness, which the Lord, the righteous Judge, will give to me on that Day, and not to me only but also to all who have loved His appearing."

The Scripture admonishes us and gives us strength and warning in 1 Peter 4:12–19.

> Beloved, do not think it strange concerning the fiery trial which is to try you, as though some strange thing happened to you; but rejoice to the extent that you partake of Christ's sufferings, that when His glory is revealed, you may also be glad with exceeding joy. If you are reproached for the name of Christ, blessed are you, for the Spirit of glory and of God rests upon you. On their part He is blasphemed, but on your part He is glorified. But let none of you suffer as a murderer, a thief, an evildoer, or as a busybody in other people's matters. Yet if anyone suffers as a Christian, let him not be ashamed, but let him glorify God in this matter. For the time has come for judgment to begin at the house of God; and if it begins with us first, what will be the end of those who do not obey the gospel of God? Now "If the righteous one is scarcely saved, where will the ungodly and the sinner appear?" Therefore let those who suffer according to the will of God commit their souls to Him in doing good, as to a faithful Creator.

CHAPTER 26

RESTORATION AND THE SIXTY-FOLD HARVEST

We have extensively covered a lot of ground together, you and I. Mainly, this book is a guide, one man's journey to an awakening. The truth of the Scriptures stands on its own merit as the inspired Word of God and needs no human interpretation. My story is how those words, God's Word, became alive to me. My understanding deepens as my desire to know God increases. Just when I think I know something, God takes me to another level.

At the time of the writing of this book, I have been out of prison for seven-plus years. On January 20, 2015, the Arizona District Council Credentials Committee approved my pastoral license. The recommendation has gone on to the final phase before the General Council of the Assemblies of God for approval. Each day I check the mail with great anticipation. I have been studying through the Berean School of the Bible since 2010. I had failed miserably in school, always thinking I was too dumb to pass any class. And though I do have a disability in math, I know now that my self-esteem played the largest role in my life's failures. How did I get so far from God? How did I become to feel so unloved and unlovable?

Earthly circumstances obviously affect the emotions of any human being, but the spiritual world is where the real war is being waged. Each of us comes into this world to be tested and refined, and circumstances play their role in the shaping of our character. But when we realize our origin—that all life comes from one source—then we are led on a journey of discovery. We either seek the Creator or the created. The ancient people of the Middle East, what is referred to as the "cradle of civilization," were torn between these two choices. It was by their meddling into things that they shouldn't have that spiritual hosts of wickedness gained entrance into this world, and a foothold into the hearts and minds of the children of the earth was established after the flood. These belief systems were passed down from civilization to civilization, culture to culture, continent to continent, empire to empire. They all worship the serpent and claim the same exact thing: that the gods of wisdom came down from the stars and merged with man to become god kings to be worshipped.

There are over 270 accounts across the globe of an ancient flood that covered the earth. All of them tell the same story, even down to the number of people who were saved in a boat from the flood. That boat came to rest on the mountains of Ararat. In Noah's day, prior to the flood, the earth was covered in lush vegetation. Its atmosphere supported huge beasts, as found in the fossil record. But after the flood, the atmosphere and vegetation changed. They became weaker and couldn't support the mammoth beasts any longer. When Noah exited the boat, the Scripture says that Noah planted a vineyard. Today Mount Ararat is a seventy-five-square-mile area. Much of it is inaccessible because of snow and ice, some places as thick as a ten-story building!

The archeological work Ronald E Wyatt did at the Durupinar site in Turkey, just eighteen miles south of Ararat itself but still within the range, may provide the most compelling evidence of Noah's ark. In addition, the base of Mount Ararat is covered in wild vineyards and is the home of the world's oldest winery. Noah had three sons: Shem, Ham, and Japheth. The Bible tells us that out of these three men came the whole multitude of the earth. The Bible gives an account in Genesis 6:1–7 that speaks of the entrance of fallen angels and the subsequent evil that emerged as a by-product. The Lord destroyed the earth and all that was in it, but the seed of the serpent found its way into one of the sons of Noah. The Bible gives an account in Genesis 9:18–27 of an act by Ham that had sexual connotations against his father, Noah. The Bible then records the first human curse placed on another human. Historically, Canaan did become the servant of Shem as Israel conquered the land of Canaan, but the act gave entrance to the serpent. Ham had children and grandchildren, one of whom was a man called Nimrod. It was through Nimrod that the occult empires, such as Babylon and Egypt, emerged.

All the ancient megalithic cultures, such as the Egyptians, Cambodians, and those found in South America (though separated by thousands of miles of water), share the same worship of the serpent and mimic the tower of Babel through their pyramid building. They were built for one purpose: to invite the interdimensional beings into this realm. The earth began to fill once again with the violence and the twisted insanity of a prideful and jealous fallen race of angels. So man came to the crossroads of faith and obedience. The side of Noah that chose the path of righteousness came through Shem. This is the lineage of the Messiah. Every son of righteousness that followed Shem right down to Jesus Himself chose to worship and serve the one true God and to be obedient even unto the death of the cross. I too came to this crossroads. Many times I—and yes, you—have strayed and gone my own way. We drag the Holy Spirit into every rotten, stinking place we chase our lusts into, but He doesn't give up on us because of Jesus's sacrifice.

Even if you've done horrible things you think you can never be forgiven for, there is room for you at the foot of the cross. The blood of Jesus is able to cover your sins and grant you forgiveness. He is able to give you a new heart, a new mind, and awaken the spirit within you that yearns to know God, to know your Creator, our Father. There is no ancient, secret wisdom or knowledge apart from Jesus. There is no mystery religion that can save or impart grace. Only Jesus's sacrifice can cover the iniquity of every single sin that was ever committed or will be committed. His sacrifice is more than enough. The knowledge of Him is what brought me to my knees before a holy God, and in His shadow I am hidden from all the powers of darkness. In Him I make my choice to live, love, and be loved. All my past failures melt away, and in my weakness His strength is made perfect. Each of us has a choice to make and a test to pass ... or fail, but God is gracious enough to leave that choice up to us. He would never force us to love Him, yet He remains faithful and loves us anyway.

> For when we were still without strength, in due time Christ died for the ungodly. For scarcely for a righteous man will one die; yet perhaps for a good man someone would even dare to die. But God demonstrates His own love toward us, in that while we were still sinners, Christ died for us. Much more then, having now been justified by His blood, we shall be saved from wrath through Him. For if when we were enemies we were reconciled to God through the death of His Son, much more, having been reconciled, we shall be saved by His life. And not only that, but we also rejoice in God through our Lord Jesus Christ, through whom we have now received the reconciliation. (Rom. 5:6–11)

> But, beloved, do not forget this one thing, that with the Lord one day is as a thousand years, and a thousand years as one day. The Lord is not slack concerning His promise, as some count slackness, but is longsuffering toward us, not willing that any should perish but that all should come to repentance. (2 Peter 3:8–9)

Today my self-esteem, not to be confused with pride, is high. It is high because I know who I am, a son of righteousness, a son of the Most High. Using drugs or alcohol never enters my mind; even their memory has faded into obscurity. I have been far removed—yes, even delivered—from their grasp, because "greater is he that is in you, than he who is in the world". (1 John 4:4) I know I can succeed, and I'm not afraid to try, nor do I shun the responsibility that comes with success. Today I'm willing and able to sacrifice and put others before myself so Jesus may live through me. I'm not perfect, but I'm being perfected. I have come a long way from that scared little boy behind the wall of shame. Only God can remove our shame and pain, and clothe us with love. Today I walk in a confidence that can come only from knowing

God. What I mean is that there's no place the born-again believer will go where God hasn't already been before us, preparing our way. God is orchestrating our lives and prepares our path before us so we enter into the exact place at the exact time we're supposed to always make sure we have provision and anointing to carry out each task.

> The steps of a good man are ordered by the Lord, and He delights in his way. (Ps. 37:23)

> A man's heart plans his way, but the Lord directs his steps. (Prov. 16:9

> Trust in the Lord, and do good; Dwell in the land, and feed on His faithfulness. Delight yourself also in the Lord, and He shall give you the desires of your heart. Commit your way to the Lord, Trust also in Him, and He shall bring it to pass … Rest in the Lord, and wait patiently for Him; Do not fret because of him who prospers in his way, Because of the man who brings wicked schemes to pass. (Ps. 37:3–5, 7)

> Trust in the Lord with all your heart, And lean not on your own understanding; In all your ways acknowledge Him, And He shall direct your paths. (Prov. 3:5–6)

> Be strong and of good courage, do not fear nor be afraid of them; for the Lord your God, He is the One who goes with you. He will not leave you nor forsake you … And the Lord, He is the One who goes before you. He will be with you, He will not leave you nor forsake you; do not fear nor be dismayed. (Deut. 31:6, 8)

> I will go before you and make the crooked places straight; I will break in pieces the gates of bronze and cut the bars of iron. (Isa. 45:2)

Yes, the Lord will give what is good; And our land will yield its increase. Righteousness will go before Him, and shall make His footsteps our pathway. (Ps. 85:12–13)

And my God shall supply all your need according to His riches in glory by Christ Jesus. (Phil. 4:19)

Upon being released, God made sure I had a place to go. Then He made a way for me to get my driver's license. Then He provided a car. Soon I was working. I landed a job working at a large grocery store. I started out bagging groceries. Let me tell you, that was very humbling to see many of the people I had gone to school with purchasing their groceries. There they were at one end of the register with mounds of food, and I was at the other, waiting to bag them. They had all become successful and obviously well off. And there I was, broke as a joke, a forty-year-old man doing the job that should belong to a high school teenager. Yep, that was pretty humbling indeed.

But God put me there for a reason. It wasn't just to grant me gainful employment because I barely made enough to pay for gas. It wasn't to keep my probation officer off my back, though it did. It was to teach me to be content and to trust in God while He worked things out on my behalf. Also, it gave me a tremendous opportunity to witness and pray for people. I always had to ask the customer, "Would you like help carrying this out to your car?" The Lord gave me insight when people needed prayer, like when a mother came through with two or three unruly toddlers and was at her wits' end. You could see she was at the breaking point and needed to be gently reminded of God's love and constant presence and how God had chosen her out of millions of people to be the mother and protector of those little faces. And you could physically see the frustration melt away and be replaced with peace and a new sense of dedication. Or there were old people who were so alone, because their spouses had died. You could see the sadness that overwhelmed them. They needed a hug and kind word, and for you to listen for a time. After prayer their eyes would well up, and they couldn't stop thanking you.

What a feeling it is to be a servant of the Most High. Of course, talking about politics or religion was strictly forbidden, and the checkers used to get so mad at me for saying, "God bless." But that never stopped me because I knew God had put me there for just such a time as that, to be His comforting voice. I was promoted to a department (the deli) where I continued my holy antics, only now I was praying for people right there in the middle of the store, even holding their hand over the meat and cheese counter. LOL.

Eventually the economy forced my hours down. My last check was sixty-six cents! I had to get another job. I started the painful process of filling out applications and job hunting again. It can be really hard when you don't have much work history, and there are long gaps between jobs. Then there's that pesky question that always appears on any application: "Have you ever been convicted of a felony?" It's enough to break a "brutha" all the way down, but I filled them out nonetheless and pressed on. One day, while driving down a road, I saw a small-engine repair shop. I slowed and wondered whether I should even bother.

I said, "What good would that do, Lord? I don't know anything about small-engine repair."

And He said, "I know you don't, but I do. Go and apply."

So I did. The owner of the place had just moved from Chicago. He was pretty well off and decided to purchase the saw shop and make a go of it. He had everything he needed: plenty of inventory and a good mechanic. But his inventory was a mess and needed to be categorized. The first thing I told him was my situation. To my astonishment, he was unphased. He was a Christian man with God's heart beating in him. He said, "Everyone makes mistakes. Can you start tomorrow?"

I couldn't believe it! Of course, the Lord led me there at just the right time. I worked there for a short time and was in need of getting my own place. I was too old to be living with my mother. There was a piece of equipment that had been repaired, but the owner hadn't come back for it for a long time. There were several items like that lying around. It was my job to call the people and inform them to either come and get their equipment or forfeit it for sale. One of the people called back and informed us that he or she had been away and had just returned and that he or she would be coming down to get it.

Once the customer arrived, he paid, and right as he was leaving, he said, "Do you know of anyone who would like to work on our ranch for free room and board plus a certain amount in cash per month with all utilities paid?"

My eyebrows went up, and so did my hand. I said, "I do!" Now I had two jobs and a place to live.

This ended up being a good thing because close to a year after I started at the saw shop, the owner passed away. The business was downsized, then sold. Of course, I was the first to be let go. Only the mechanic remained to try to bring in some sort of revenue while waiting for the business to sell. The whole thing was a big mess and left everyone hurting and uncertain about their futures. Fortunately for me I had the other job to fall back on. But that season too came to an end. I ended up having to move into my dad's house and keep it in order while he was doing his own time for DUI. He had drunk and driven all his adult life and had never gotten caught—that is, until he was in his late sixties and early seventies. Prison is no place for an old man; it's no place for anyone, but there he was, and there I was, staying at his house.

Though my circumstances had changed, my faith in God hadn't. I knew God was working out my future, and all I had to do was remain faithful and wait. That doesn't mean I just sat there on the couch, waiting for money to fall out of the sky. I continued my job search and my studies, and of course I continued praising God. One day I was behind a plumbing van, its name and phone number in bold black type. I said, "Lord, I used to work in the plumbing industry. Should I call and see if they need help?"

He said, "Yes, call."

So I did. The guy said, "Not now but maybe soon. I am not sure. Call back." I kept calling and calling and calling. Finally the guy was like "This guy isn't gonna quit calling until I hire him." So he set up an appointment to meet with me. During our meeting the whole thing came out. He and I both had stories to tell, and both of us needed each other's help. The new construction aspect of plumbing had come to a grinding halt, save a few lucky or rather prudent builders. But the service end of plumbing was still a necessity. What he wanted to do was hire someone to become his service manager and try to keep the business afloat while he relocated elsewhere. He already had two very capable plumbers working for him, who were way more qualified than I was. But for him the choice wasn't as much about skill or experience as it was about trust.

Here I was, a year and a half or so out of prison, on probation for fraud, and this man was putting all his trust in me! This is a testimony to the workings of God. First, God had transformed my entire being into a useful vessel. I could now be trusted for the first time in my life. It wasn't my actions or words that persuaded this man but Jesus shining through me. He hired me right there, on the spot, our first meeting, to be his service manager without any qualifying experience save what little I had in the plumbing industry. Let me show you what the Word of God says. Romans 8:28 says, "And we know that all things work together for good to those who love God, to those who are the called according to His purpose." You see, even though this man's business was in trouble and coming to an end, God used the circumstance to benefit us both. Genesis 50:19–20 says, "Joseph said to them, 'Do not be afraid, for am I in the place of God? But as for you, you meant evil against me; but God meant it for good, in order to bring it about as it is this day.'"

What I want you folks to understand is that it wasn't so much that the owner could trust me as much as it was that God could now trust me. God gives us more responsibility as we mature. God knew it was my trustworthiness and Christian witness, as expressed in my walk, that this man needed most. He needed someone who could give him some peace of mind while he sorted things out. Also, I ministered to him as often as possible, shining the light of Jesus on his circumstances. He believed in God and was reminded through the life of another person that God was still in charge. It's been close to five years now since we parted ways, and just recently I made contact with him, and he informed me that his life was now back in order and prospering again;

moreover his relationship with God, his wife, and his family was too. God is in the restoration business, and He knows what He's doing.

The circumstances of life continued, and so did the orchestration of God's providence in my life. The plumbing company finally closed, as the man finished his move to another part of the state. I was living in a 1969 camper shell up on blocks on a piece of property for which I was working as caretaker. The winter that year was particularly hard and cold. My mother had a friend who lived in the suburbs and would be traveling back east to stay with family for a while. He didn't want to leave his home and property unattended and asked my mother whether I would be interested in house-sitting. Of course my mother was concerned about my current situation in the camper shell with no heat. I was fine, but my poor dog shivered most of the time. I agreed.

It was December of 2010, and I was reeling from a really bad relationship filled with nothing but lies and betrayal. I had been given a DVD box set of a pastor by the name of Ron Carpenter. He has a big church called RWOC (Redemption World Outreach Center) out of Southern Carolina. The box set was titled *Why Everyone Needs an Enemy*. It was just what I needed at the time. It was all about betrayal and how an enemy is used to announce the closing of an old era and the birthing of a new one. Ironically, it had come through the very person who betrayed me. That is how God administers His love, mercy, and justice. So I took up residence at the man's house. My dog was all too happy. He really enjoyed the crackling fireplace.

It was there where I contemplated social networks to try to make connections with other human beings. I got on the two big ones of the day and created my profile in hopes that my children, whom I hadn't seen in fifteen years, might get curious and search my name. And guess what? They did! The situation was pretty rocky at first. Finally, things got better, a lot better. During that time, I also checked out some of those online dating sites. That was pretty stressful, let me tell you: posting pictures, creating profiles, answering a myriad of personal questions, and the worst part ... waiting for a response. I found that a lot of people on there were just like me: hurt and alone. Unfortunately, hurt people carry a lot of baggage with them. Sifting through the mountains of damaged women and being sifted became a monumental task.

On too many of these sites, the women were just looking for sexual encounters. I became very discouraged. After all, my profile said I was a man of God looking for a godly woman who was looking for a lasting relationship with a godly man. So why were they dissin' me by trying to just hook up? I was poor and barely making enough money for gas by doing plumbing jobs. I know, kind of a loser profile, right? Yeah, that's what I thought too. I was just about to give up when I saw an ad for a site. At first I rejected it because of the name, but I had found that the so-called Christian sites were just as full of nonsense as any other.

So I started the arduous chore of creating a profile. It was December 26, 2010, the day after Christmas. I guess you could say Santa came late that year, but in truth it wasn't Santa but God who was moving the chess pieces of my life around at just the right moments. I found a brand-new profile of someone who had just posted her picture and information. She lived right there in town, loved the outdoors, and was looking for a long-term meaningful relationship. Oh, you know, I sent her a witty message. I waited all day for a response, with only the beauty of the silently falling snow to stem the ebbing tide of anxiety welling up within me. Alas, nightfall arrived, and so did my bedtime, with no response. My dog passed me an indignant look, let out a deep sigh, rested his head on his crossed paws, and closed his eyes. *I feel ya*, I thought. I turned off the computer and lights, and tossed myself to sleep.

By morning the fire had reduced itself to a single ember with a soft orange glow. I forced myself from my warm cocoon to face the day. I turned on the computer to boot up. I started a pot of coffee and removed the ashes from the fireplace but left the ember to rekindle the fire. Soon the sound of my efforts crackled and popped, with smoke rising and disappearing into the flue to mingle with the cold frosty air outside. The warmth of the fire felt good on my face and gave me hope. I filled my cup and made my way apprehensively to the computer. I signed into the site and blankly stared for a second at the blinking heart icon: It read, "You have a message from ...." At first it didn't register, but then my heart began to pound.

She responded, I thought. Then I became nervous. What if she doesn't like me? What if she's just being courteous and saying, "Thanks for the interest but …"? *Oh, for goodness' sake, quit being a dork and open it. See what she said already! Oh, okay,* I thought.

She not only responded in kind but was going to be able to chat with me all day. We talked and talked and shared dreams and poured our hearts out to each other. We fell in love instantly. We had the same dreams and values and goals. She didn't mind that I was studying to be a minister. She was totally open and ready to being in a relationship with Jesus and me. We began dating, and one day while riding our bikes down a trail that had once been a railroad track, she accepted Jesus as her Lord and Savior. On February 25, 2011, just a few short weeks after meeting online, we were married. What an honor it was and is to have been the one to lead my wife to Jesus. That was four years ago.

Since then our lives together have been challenged and tested. My mother got cancer, and the chemo proved to be too much. She passed away on July 17, 2012, and asked my wife and me to take her grandson, my nephew, whom she'd adopted and was raising, as our own. We agreed and adopted him, and now he is our son. We have three children still living with us at the time of this writing. Our oldest son is still at home and graduated in 2015. Our daughter just turned fourteen; she plays as many sports as she possibly can and is pretty much an A student in advanced classes. Our other children are grown and making their own way in life.

The fact that God allowed me to share in raising these kids is a miracle in itself. My wife, on the other hand, has never been in trouble, broken the law, or used drugs. For the judge to consider her as an adopting parent, it was clear she was a good candidate. I'll never forget that day or those words he spoke. "After reviewing the application and upon hearing the evidence, I do hereby find you both fit and proper persons to adopt." Did you hear that? Me, a fit and proper person! My wife, yeah, sure, of course, but me? That was just another example of how we can be used when God can trust us.

We moved into a brand-new house in a walled community in 2011. God is faithful, but He is also a God of abundance. The more trustworthy we became, the more He trusted us with. Just think, I got out penniless, was living in a camper shell on blocks, and now I live in a brand-new home! For three years, the Lord tested me after I got out to see whether I would remain faithful or just be another poser with jailhouse religion. You know the type, the one who spouts off all about God and how he or she is going to go straight and serve God while he or she is locked up, but as soon as the person gets out, he or she goes right to the dope house.

After three years of testing, I was still standing tall in Jesus, and God rewarded me with a beautiful, loving wife; three great children; a new home to live in; and a good job—but not just any ol' job. Remember that saw shop I worked in? Well, some local business people bought it. They kept the mechanic and started to rebuild. The business moved two doors down from the old location, giving it a storefront with main road access. It really started to grow fast, and they needed another person, so they called me. At first it was working part time, doing customer service and the front counter, and cleaning toilets and such. But I was being tested again. *Just remain faithful and praise God,* I kept reminding myself.

One day I was talking to the mechanic, with whom I'd become friends, and he told me they were going to hire again. He also said a position was available in the shop. I was toying with the idea of transferring to the shop, but I didn't know anything at all about being a mechanic. Then the still, small voice said, "I know you don't, but I do. Ask for the transfer."

Being encouraged by the Holy Spirit, I blurted out, "What about me?"

The mechanic said, "You'd want to work back here?"

I said, "Yes." The problem was, I didn't know anything, and the position was for a skilled mechanic who could meet the needs of a fast-growing company, and its busy season was just days away from starting. I had to think quickly if I was going to land this position and make my family proud. I said, "I know I don't know anything about being a mechanic but give me one week to learn. If I don't come up to speed, then I'll go back to the front desk, and I'll work for free while you train me."

He and the owners agreed. This was a huge gamble on my part. I was offering to work for free and come out of pocket to pay for fuel to drive the thirty-plus-mile daily commute. My wife probably thought I was crazy, but she went along with it and trusted me. That was three years ago. God anointed my mind and skilled my hands to be able to fill the position. After only one week of training, they gave me a raise and a salaried position. That meant full-time, year-round work with twelve days of paid vacation, company picnics, Christmas dinner, bonuses—the whole nine yards. God had most definitely showed up right on time again. But we must remember than it's God's timing that is perfect, not ours. God had shown up and positioned me all those years before when I was driving down the street that day, looking for work. Had I not been tuned into the voice of the Holy Spirit, I would have totally missed that opportunity. I'm where I am today because I listened to God's voice when it didn't make any sense to me.

"But Lord, I don't know anything about working in a saw shop."

"I know you don't, but I do. Go and apply."

I had come full circle, from poverty to plenty through God's providence and positioning. My employers are wonderful, caring, prudent people who genuinely care about their employees. The chief mechanic and I have grown to be good friends. I had been elevated in God's economy from just enough to more than enough, from the thirty-fold harvest to the sixty-fold harvest. all because when we are faithful to God, He is faithful to us. Don't misunderstand; I don't serve God just to get something from Him. I serve Him because He died for me. He remains faithful no matter what, but the more trustworthy we become, the more we are entrusted with. The more we are entrusted with, the greater are the responsibilities; the greater the responsibilities, the greater the rewards. It's that simple. Please take some time now, go to your Bible, and read Luke 12:35–48. Pray and ask the Holy Spirit to give you understanding and wisdom to apply this principle to your daily lives.

CHAPTER 27

FULFILL YOUR MINISTRY

I shared this story to show you from my life's experiences how God is interested and in constant orchestration of our lives. God is always setting things before us to draw us into a relationship with Him. Once we are in that relationship, obedient and humbly seeking to do His will and know Him, great things begin to happen. Romans 2:4 says, "Or do you despise the riches of His goodness, forbearance, and longsuffering, not knowing that the goodness of God leads you to repentance?" Repentance is the gateway to relationship. Here are a few Scripture verses to encourage you.

> May the Lord answer you in the day of trouble; May the name of the God of Jacob defend you; May He send you help from the sanctuary, And strengthen you out of Zion: May He remember all your offerings, And accept your burnt sacrifice. Selah. May He grant you according to your heart's desire, And fulfill all your purpose. We will rejoice in your salvation, And in the name of our God we will set up our banners! May the Lord fulfill all your petitions. (Ps. 20:1–5)

> Trust in the Lord, and do good; Dwell in the land, and feed on His faithfulness. Delight yourself also in the Lord, And He shall give you the desires of your

heart. Commit your way to the Lord, Trust also in Him, And He shall bring it to pass. (Ps. 37:3–5)

For a day in Your courts is better than a thousand. I would rather be a doorkeeper in the house of my God Than dwell in the tents of wickedness. For the Lord God is a sun and shield; The Lord will give grace and glory; No good thing will He withhold from those who walk uprightly. O Lord of hosts, blessed is the man who trusts in You! (Ps. 84:10–12)

And my God shall supply all your need according to His riches in glory by Christ Jesus. (Phil. 4:19)

The economy of God is limitless, but that doesn't necessarily mean you will walk out your front door and find the jackpot lottery ticket. What it does mean is that you can stop worrying about tomorrow. God begins to restore us from the inside out. Monetary provision and blessings will come as our trustworthiness, maturity, and needs increase. Matthew 6:31–33 says, "Therefore do not worry, saying, 'What shall we eat?' or 'What shall we drink?' or 'What shall we wear?' For after all these things the Gentiles seek. For your heavenly Father knows that you need all these things. But seek first the kingdom of God and His righteousness, and all these things shall be added to you."

I would like to take a second to share some great news. I just received confirmation of my approval by the Assemblies of God for my ministerial credentials. I am now a license minister. Yeah! That's right, seven years, folks—that's how long I have been working toward my credentials. This brings to remembrance one particular cellie who doubted the authenticity of my new birth. He said, "We'll see where you are when you get out, how long this God stuff lasts." It wasn't that he didn't believe in God; it was just that he, like so many other people, had seen too many fake Christians. But as they say, the proof is in the pudding. I'm living proof that a person who has lost everything because of his or her poor choices can be completely restored—not just restored but abundantly restored. When you turn your life over to Jesus, the possibilities are endless. And the exciting thing is that God is the One preparing your future. That doesn't mean we don't make plans and such, but rather that along the way, God directs our paths for the very best.

I will give you an example of my plans versus God's plans and timing. One day while in a holding cell, awaiting sentencing, God spoke to me and said, "I am sending you back to your generation." Historically and statistically, returning to your old stomping grounds is a recipe for disaster. According to rehabilitation principles, the recovering user should at all costs abstain from any old behaviors, relationships, or both that may trigger a relapse. Of course, this logic makes perfect sense, so why would God send me right back into the thick of it? I didn't know it yet, as my sentencing was about an hour away, but I would be put on intense probation for five years on top of being on parole when I got out. That meant I would be subject to both state agencies and their requirements and conditions of release. I would have two different state agencies breathing down my neck, telling me when and where to report, where I should and shouldn't be and when. And most daunting of all, I would have two different times when I would have to drop a U/A (urinalysis). Daunting, that is, for someone who didn't have Jesus, but I did have Him, and God the Father knew I did. He knew that by the time I got out I would be firmly established. He didn't have one little concern about sending me into battle because He Himself had fully armed me and was my shield. Up until then I had *never* passed a U/A outside of prison. I had always stayed clean in there because I wanted out, but as soon as I was released, I always went right back to drugs and alcohol, and the lifestyle that came with them.

So when God said, "I am sending you back to your generation," I wasn't worried at all, but I knew the challenges ahead of me. He was sending me back to be a voice from the past, a voice of victory proclaiming a message of hope, deliverance, and restoration. The vision that came with the command was for me to establish a discipleship. It would serve both categories of offenders: those who were being released from prison and as an alternative sentencing structure for prison. Once established, it would work hand in hand with the court and probation departments to keep people out of prison.

There are some states that embrace disciplineships and see their spiritual value in curbing bad behaviors and choices. Arizona has yet to fully commit to such programming. My vision is so huge that it will take God Himself to establish it. The politics and bureaucracy involved in allowing a so-called religious entity to play a role in what the state defines as its territory are seemingly insurmountable. It will take an act of God to overcome this obstacle, but that's what makes this so exciting. I know there's nothing I can do or say to change the state's mind or attitude toward the concept of church and state merging, but God can and will. I have already been met with opposition and distrust by local authorities. The jail chaplain and program's director had been open and hopeful. Seeing that there was great benefit to having someone who had been there and done that, they urged me to apply as a jail volunteer, which I did. I even met the sheriff and gave him my vision, but ultimately my application was rejected. I don't view this as defeat because the greater the opposition, the greater the victory when God establishes His plan and vision. Amen. So we don't get discouraged, but we praise God for His wisdom and timing as we press on.

Don't get me wrong. There is a great value and wisdom for those in "recovery" to stay clear of old hangouts and old behavior patterns. Twelve-step programs have their place, and all courts accept them as fundamental and even mandated programming. But without Jesus at the core of any program, your potential can never be reached. As I've stated before, I'm not in recovery; I'm delivered! *Deliverance* is a word that eludes the recovery community. It seems they would rather see you chained in recovery than completely freed by Jesus Christ.

I am *not* bashing recovery programming, and the principles they employ have a great many truths and values psychologically, but they don't do anything for the spirit of man. The closest they get to God is step three, which says, "Made a decision to turn our will and our lives over to the care of God as we understood Him." This leaves the understanding of God open to the interpretation of the individual. That means that you can have any ol' God you want. He can be anything or anyone. By leaving the interpretation up to individuals, there is no absolute moral authority outside the individuals to answer to. They become their own god and interpret their own morality as circumstances change. I can surrender my will and life to the care of a rock or door knob and receive no instruction or awakening. It's an empty lie.

What I find most disturbing is how Satan has infiltrated these twelve-step programs by excluding Jesus. Twelve-step programs open their meetings by reciting the "serenity prayer" but omit its actual and entire ending. There are many variations of this prayer, and its author throughout times has been disputed. It is generally accepted that Dr. Reinhold Niebuhr is the original author. Where the dispute truly lies is in the context of the prayer, as these truths have been around as long as man has, but our good doctor penned the actual prayer as it is read today in association with a sermon he wrote on practical Christianity. That's right folks: the prayer is a Christian prayer disclosing the one true God as Jesus Christ. It reads as follows: "God, grant me the serenity to accept the things I cannot change, the courage to change the things I can, and he wisdom to know the difference. Living one day at a time, enjoying one moment at a time; accepting hardship as a pathway to peace; taking, as Jesus did this sinful world as it is; not as I would have it. Trusting that You will make all things right if I surrender to Your will; so that I may be reasonably happy in this life and supremely happy with You forever in the next. Amen."

Thankfully, not all twelve-step programs remove Jesus from the prayer, and, in fact, there are many good, solid, Christ-centered programs available to you. Check with your attorney, public defender, or even probation personnel for availability and participation options in your area.

So God sent me back to be His voice in the face of hopelessness. If God can take my life and turn it around, He can do the same for you. Nothing is impossible with God, but we have to let Him into our lives if we expect anything to change. Continuing to do the same old things will always yield the same results. There is a whole new world waiting for you out there. I know change can be scary, and yielding your life to God can seem like an unnatural idea, but I assure you that it's the most natural thing one can do once the spirit is awake. When God takes control, life takes on a whole new meaning. We now dance to a different tune. The more you surrender to the Holy Spirit, the less you will find the things that once captivated you so appealing. As a matter of fact, you will see them for what they are, a form of slavery. We are enslaved to the things we let control us. I would rather be Christ's slave and share in eternal life in unspeakable glory than continue to live a lie while enslaved to the Devil and bound for hell with a needle in my arm.

When God sends us back to our generation, it's always to speak of His love and the freedom that comes from knowing Jesus. You will truly know whether you are sent into a set of circumstances that are yet governed by past experience (old behaviors and haunts) by two unshakable truths:

1. You will have no desire to relive or share in any of those behaviors. You will actually feel sorry to see those trapped by their destructive self-wills.

2. The people from the old gang will automatically see something drastically different in you. They will physically see a difference and voice it out loud. "You've changed," they'll say. They will automatically know that any attempt to get you back in the game is fruitless. They will actually be physically afraid to even attempt it, and as soon as you start speaking truth in their presence, they will flee. It's not really them but the evil spirits oppressing them that instantly recognize Jesus in you; they are paralyzed with fear and don't want to lose their captive to Jesus. So they force the person out of your presence.

Now, there will remain those who thirst for the truth and deliverance. It is these to whom you are called to present Jesus, both by word and deed (your Christian walk). Not everyone is called to be a minister, but everyone is called into ministry. By simply sharing our testimony (our life experience) and presenting Jesus as the focus and source of a transformed life, we thereby minister to others. Their needs and questions begin to get answered, and life starts to make sense and become hopeful. There is a light at the end of the tunnel, and His name is Jesus.

> Then Jesus spoke to them again, saying, "I am the light of the world. He who follows Me shall not walk in darkness, but have the light of life." (John 8:12)

> In Him was life, and the life was the light of men. (John 1:4)

> As long as I am in the world, I am the light of the world. (John 9:5)

> Then Jesus said to them, "A little while longer the light is with you. Walk while you have the light, lest darkness overtake you; he who walks in darkness does not know where he is going. While you have the light, believe in the light, that you may become sons of light." These things Jesus spoke, and departed, and was hidden from them … "I have come as a light into the world, that whoever believes in Me should not abide in darkness." (John 12:35–36, 46)

> If we say that we have fellowship with Him, and walk in darkness, we lie and do not practice the truth. (1 John 1:6)

> The people who walked in darkness have seen a great light; those who dwelt in the land of the shadow of death, upon them a light has shined. (Isa. 9:2)

God will present you with many opportunities to minister to people, so make sure and be ready to step through the open door of opportunity and meet those needs. When you are engaging in one of these times, make sure to be a good listener. This connection does two things: (1) it allows the person to whom you are ministering to vent and see that you genuinely care about his or her concerns; and (2) it gives you a perfect setting to present Jesus through your own experience. Be careful not to interrupt but let him or her fully vent.

Men, when you are ministering to women, make certain you take a careful inventory of your own motives. A woman who is hurting is extremely vulnerable. If her spirit isn't awake, she could misconstrue your sympathetic ear for something more. So be careful to always present Jesus as the answer and focus of your conversation. Always, always, when ministering to a woman who isn't your spouse or close relative, do so in the presence of another Christian witness so no one can bring reproach on your ministry by gossiping or speculating as to what you were doing alone. Husbands, if you are ministering to a woman, always without fail do so with your wife present, period.

Also, it is very important for men to understand that women aren't always seeking a definitive solution to their concerns, even if they express them through countless tears and sobs. Many, many times they want only someone to listen and share some empathy. So don't get all uppity and know it all like you got all the answers and then get mad when she rejects your carefully and masterfully presented solution. This move will leave you both very frustrated. This is a pitfall men cannot help falling into because we are wired *totally* different. It is in our nature to fix what is broken or, in this case, what we *think* is broken and then receive some praise for our problem-solving skills. Women don't want to be fixed any more than we want to be fixed. This would imply that there is something wrong with us. This mind-set is presumptuous at best. Just be a good listener with either gender.

Women, the same goes for you as far as being alone with a man, especially if he is married. If you aren't married, then his wife must be present or a mature Christian witness his wife agrees with if she can't be there. And men are looking for answers and solutions, even if they won't admit it. Just present a workable solution to him, and eventually it will become his idea, and all will be well. Make very sure you make that same moral motive and inventory check. Men may or may not be as emotionally vulnerable in the same ways, but men are subject to praise. The right words or a touch on the arm can convey a powerful message to him that says something you aren't really trying to say. You say, "You're a hard worker." He hears, "She thinks I'll be a good provider for her." Be very careful to keep Jesus as the focus and don't praise the man, just encourage him. When encouraging him, you can say, "You can do it" but don't say "You can do it. You're smart." See the difference? Lead them to Jesus and the Word of God, where all their answers can be found.

There will be times when a situation arises, and you are presented with an opportunity to pray for a stranger, like at the grocery store where I worked. Lots of times I have prayed for both genders right there in the parking lot. I think that as long as the exchange is in public, though no one else can hear what you're saying, it's okay to minister in that situation without a chaperone. Say your prayer, present Jesus, and move on quickly. What we want to avoid is the chance to form an undesirable relationship with the other gender and give people a chance to bad-talk Christianity. All things must be done in holiness and purity. You can and should invite people to your church assembly, but again, make your motive known that it's Jesus you're presenting, not yourself.

To be effective in ministry, we need to get over our shyness. This can be one of the most daunting tasks you'll ever do because it's new and, let's face it, unnatural to the natural man (one whose spirit is barely awake or yet sleeping). But you will get better and more confident with practice and lots of Bible reading under your belt. It will be very beneficial for you to memorize some Scripture verses. Start with the verses that pop out and apply to your personal circumstances. Soon you will have an arsenal of God's Word at your disposal to encourage other people and defeat the enemy, just like Jesus did. Some of us are more shy or entrenched in fear than others, or their calling is more specific and demanding. In these cases, God will orchestrate circumstances to help you overcome your fears and build confidence. These tests and trials are for your growth and benefit all to the glory of God. It will be very stressful and scary at times but don't resist the Holy Spirit. God is trying to teach you how to totally trust and depend on Him. You'll know it's a

God-growth moment when you don't want to do it. Every fiber in your being will say, "No way, Jose!" But it's during these insurmountable moments when God shines in your life and shows up right on time.

Let me share one of my God-growth moments with you. It was the time when I had just arrived at the good yard I told you about, where God had changed my destination. I was on the lookout for a certain man I knew preached the gospel. He was doing life, so I figured he was still there from the first time I was there ten years earlier. This guy was, and still is at the time of this writing, doing time for a crime he didn't commit. I know, I know—they all say that, but in his case it's true. He couldn't have done it because he was already in jail on an unrelated charge of DUI at the time of the murder. The murdered guy was his friend.

So a case was made against him, and it stuck. He is still fighting for a fair trial. The evidence that could exonerate him has been unfortunately lost. Anyway, my point is that if there is anyone who would have the motive to be mad at God for unjustly being incarcerated, it's him. He has been in prison for forty-one years, and he hasn't turned his back on God; rather he has grown stronger in faith and wisdom. If he was guilty, why would he still be preaching Jesus after all these years? So I knew by that evidence and the prompting of the Holy Spirit that his Christian walk was genuine. I needed to seek this man out, sit at his feet, and be instructed in the Way. Jesus said in John 14:6, "I am the way, the truth, and the life. No one comes to the Father except through Me." I knew I needed to go to this man and learn about Jesus. He had what I needed, the Word of God living inside and through him.

There was just one little problem. He's a black man, and I'm a half-breed who had chosen a side to be identified with. This status posed a serious and seemingly insurmountable obstacle politically. Everyone knows how the race game is played. You are allowed to talk to other races and play sports and cards with them so long as one of your own race is with you. You are *not* allowed to sit and eat with another race, especially in the dining area. Each race has its own section. Violating any race rules is a big no-no and can bring unwanted attention upon yourself. God was most definitely dealing with multiple issues with me: fear, prejudices, fear, trust, and more fear.

I had a serious dilemma. There I was, on the best yard in the system. All I had to do was lie low and do my time, just conduct myself like all the other convicts, and all would be well. By then, I had put in eight or so years altogether here and there, so I knew the rules and had always followed them. It is to your best interest, of course. Of all the things I could have picked to get unwanted attention, race violations was probably the most volatile. It tends to have a ripple effect. The problem was that I was getting out soon, and I needed as much of God as I could get. Besides, God Himself had orchestrated the whole thing. He had placed me there for a reason. If I ran from God again, it would be a very bad thing. He had taken me to a place in life where the futility of my self-will was made crystal clear. I understood without a doubt that I deserved everything I had gone through, but more over that, God was waiting for me on the other side with arms wide open.

Would I choose to embrace the One who died for me and delivered me or the political idealism of prison politics? My mind was racing and my heart pounding. Why would God rescue me from my fears and send me to the best possible place, only to make me make a choice that could seriously endanger me? Therein lies the paradox. When God pulls the veil back and allows you to see glimpses of His providential mercy and power, and then places you right in the middle of something so controversial and potentially dangerous, it is without a doubt a disturbing, scary, and most blessed thing. God was taking me to school, and class was in. The bell had rung. The teacher stood at the head of the class with a stone-faced strictness and said, "There will be a test."

Oh great! What am I going to do now? I dropped out of school. So there I was, confronted with one of the most difficult decisions of my life. This wasn't going to be easy by any means, but I really didn't have a choice. That's how God does us sometimes. He makes us confront our own fears and weaknesses to show us how His strength is made perfect through our weakness. It's all about trust!

So one day soon after my arrival, I was walking by the chaplain's office, and there he was, cleaning and sweeping. The chaplain was inside, busy at his desk, but he heard our conversation. The man acknowledged remembering me ten years earlier, but he seemed disinterested in me. He was outright brushing me off. He acted annoyed with my questions. At first I thought the problem was the race thing, but that was furthest thing from the truth. And the more I pressed him, the more annoyed and dismissive he got. *Sheesh!* I thought. *Could I have this whole thing wrong?*

But then finally he said in his most gruff and dismissive voice, "All right, we'll see if you're serious or not. We meet at the chapel every morning after breakfast. Now get. I'm busy." I walked away, half smiling and half frowning. I couldn't figure out why he was so grumpy. I mean, he'd really tried to make me turn away, but I hadn't.

That night I was restless and excited with anticipation and full of apprehension at the same time. What was going to happen? Who would be there? It was a tense and fitful night's sleep. When dawn broke, I got dressed and tried to act normal, but inside I was all fired up and nervous. Something inside told me I had to go. There was something on the horizon that would change my life forever. Breakfast came and went, and hurried footfalls found me at the chapel more quickly than I wanted to get there. There they were, all lined up against the building outside, waiting for the CO (Corrections Officer) to come and open the building. I was relieved to see that there were other races there too, mostly black guys. I approached the group, trying to act cool and not be nervous, but my tight clutch on my Bible probably betrayed me. And my apprehension wasn't ill founded.

As soon as I was close enough for conversation, he said, "What you got?"

"Huh?" I said.

"What you got?" he repeated irritably.

"Just my Bible," I said sheepishly.

"No man, what you got to tell us about Jesus. Tell us what you got."

I was dumbfounded. I had never in my life been put on the spot like that. There they all stood or sat, intently staring at me and waiting for me to usher forth a dissertation on the divine mysteries. An inaudible and extremely embarrassed chortle is all that surfaced. I was quickly beginning to feel that I had made a serious mistake. I finally just threw up my arms in surrender and said, "I don't know anything. That's why I am here. All I do know is that God sent me here."

He said, "You mean to tell me, you're walking around with that Bible in your hands and you got nothing to speak on for Jesus?"

At that point my defensive nature kicked in to try to save whatever self-respect I had left, and I said, "I already told you I didn't. That's why I am here. Are you going to teach me or not?"

There was a long pause of silence, and then everyone broke out laughing except him. We kept eye contact, but I felt much better now that the mood had lightened up some. He stood up, walked over to me, and said, "Sorry I had to be so rough on you, but I had to make sure you were serious. Too many jokers around here are playing with God."

A huge sigh of relief flooded over me, and the Holy Spirit assured me that I was in the right place. I said, "I am dead serious about serving God and giving my life to Him."

He said, "I can see that, son. Let's go inside."

Once the chapel was opened, we all started to move inside. Everyone grabbed a chair and formed a circle on either side of him. I could see by the obedient ritual that everyone was as excited as I was. We were in store for something great. How marvelous and ironic that the very best in life, which we all had received thus far, was being granted behind the razor wire, a symbol of complete forfeiter and a constant reminder of that loss.

Everyone settled in and grew silent. "Join hands," he said. As one of the guys led us in prayer, Doyle went around the circle and anointed each man with a special prayer and the laying on of hands.

He made his way back around and sat at the head of the circle. He began to expound on "the spirit man" and presented Jesus and the Word of God in a powerful, dynamic, and living way. I had never heard anybody preach like that before. He was speaking right to me, and it wasn't just me. We all felt like that. I knew I was in the right place and that God had most certainly sent me there not only to learn but also to see with my own eyes how the power and love of God could penetrate the darkest and most hopeless places through the life of a convict. How could any man or woman be wrongfully imprisoned for forty-plus years and not be insane, institutionalized, or angry beyond measure, let alone happy, content, and filled with praise and purpose? How indeed?

There is only one way: because God has assigned that person and anointed him or her to endure while filled with the Holy Spirit. Jesus was and is his or her main focus. There's no telling how many men and lives he has touched by his Christian witness all these years, changed forever by that one man's willingness to be obedient to God and faithfully preach and teach Jesus. Doyle, you are my father in Christ, who has begotten me by the gospel of salvation. You were hard on me because you love me and know the challenges of life. You pressed me hard because I needed pressing. You never relented because life doesn't. And you made me study hard and challenged me because you saw potential. You are worthy of the title "father and faithful servant" of the Most High, Jesus Christ. Amen.

When the siren sounded for count, I couldn't believe that hours had gone by. I was so satisfied yet thirsting for more. It was going to take forever for the next day to come. I went away astonished and hopeful. I felt a new me rising from the ashes of my past. No, it was the real me awakening from a long, long sleep. The knowledge I had received was beyond intellectual. It was spiritual. My mind was having trouble processing the truths my spirit already knew.

Things were going to be different from now on. I could feel the power of God resurrecting my spirit and making sense of all things. God was most certainly alive and well and very interested in the affairs of man. Each morning was better than the one before it. The group changed daily in number and race, but there was always a core number of men who attended daily. These men were all black. This wasn't really an issue because (1) mostly there were multiple races present daily and because (2) it was in the chapel, kind of neutral ground. But I noticed that many of our topics and discussions were seemingly extensions of previous teachings taught elsewhere. When I had made mention my suspicion, Doyle said they were going over the previous night's Bible study.

Then came the serious test of faith and trust in God. As a matter of fact, everything that had happened up until then was only a precursor for that moment. He said, "Yeah, we have Bible study every night, in depth, down at my housing unit. You are welcome to join." Now Doyle knew full well the consequences of such a move on my part. To willfully join an activity that was predominantly a race not of your own was asking for it. By inviting me, he removed any wiggle room I might have had. I either loved and needed Jesus as much as I claimed to, or I didn't. I either trusted God to deliver me from sure retribution, or I walked in fear. He knew my thirst for God was going to compel me to attend, and he left it up to God to protect me.

Perhaps in retrospect it was a test for both of us to see the hand of God at work. I was conflicted, to say the least. He had what I needed most, the Word of God, raw and undiluted. I had pretty much talked myself out of going, reciting many valid reasons why I shouldn't attend, but strangely enough, during my walk back from dinner, I stopped only briefly to pick up my Bible and then press on. I kept my head down, watching my feet fall one after the other, and suddenly there I was. They had just sat down at a table outside for the entire world to see. All the races were going to notice me, for sure. It wouldn't take long for this juicy morsel of gossip to circulate.

They all turned and looked at me, wide eyed, like I was crazy—everyone except Doyle. He had a proud papa look and just nodded his approval and said, "Well, don't just stand there, lame. Sit down."

There was no turning back now. I sat down where there was a seat, pale as can be, looking like the last Oreo cookie in a package. I was a nervous wreck and could feel the eyes of passersby staring at me. I can only imagine what they thought. I know what I was thinking: *How long before I get it?* I pushed the fear aside and remembered the words of that cellie I had before. *"God wants to use you, but you're too afraid."* I resolved that whatever they could do to me couldn't compare to another moment without Jesus. I needed Jesus. I needed to really know the Son of God, God incarnate, who laid down His life for mine. I owed Him my faith and my trust. It was the hardest thing I ever had to do.

The study was over, and I was trying to figure out how to stand up and leave an all-black table without being seen, but by then prying eyes were firmly fixed on me. I walked away the same way I'd come in, with my head down, watching my feet, and looking up only briefly to see who was watching. It felt like everyone was glaring at me with disagreement, but I'm sure I was just being paranoid. I made it back to my unit without incident. That night was fitful as well. Our morning session came, and it felt less heavy, of course, being on neutral ground with other races present. Then, before I knew it, it was night Bible study time again. I tried to get there as fast as I could to get an outside seat but failed. God was sure dealing with my fears all right.

This went on for a few days, and then it happened. One of my race approached me, asking me what was up with me and the all-black table. I said, "It's a Bible study. Is there something wrong with going to a Bible study and trying to make myself better so I can stop going to prison?"

He said, "No, but why don't you go to a study with your own race?"

I said, "I do, but they aren't preaching Jesus like he is. I'm not getting the same in-depth Spirit-filled growth." He walked off. That was warning number one.

Two more warnings followed shortly after the last one by a high-up. I told him, "I understand your position, the whole race thing. I get it, but I am not choosing one race over the other. I am seeking God, not man. And the meat of God's Word is being presented there, and they don't care what color I am. We are all one in Christ. If I am to be a real Christian, then I can't be walking in fear and hold the color of a man's skin as a reason to reject the gospel. That would go against everything God stands for, and I would be living an empty lie. My whole life has been an empty lie. I have to make a stand for Jesus." He walked away, unphased.

I knew I was in real trouble, but it was too late. I was a serious nervous wreck and anticipated a beatdown at any moment. Many of my race were looking at me as all crazy. I could feel the tension in the air. Then that night at diner, I was sitting next to the guy who was the race rep in our unit. We got along fine. He was an older guy doing a lot of time. Suddenly he began to choke on his food. I had never seen anyone choking to death before. It was gruesome and sad. I looked around, and everyone just sat there, staring at him. No one even moved or asked whether he was okay; some even just kept eating. I was astonished and mortified. I couldn't just sit there and watch this man die a horrible death, even though I knew that if he was given the order to beat me down, he would see to it. I had to try to save him.

I jumped up, got behind him, and carefully placed my hands the way I had learned in my first-aid class twenty years before. I placed my thumb just so directly beneath his rib cage and gave a mighty squeeze, pulling back and up … Nothing. Again! Nothing. Time seemed to stand still. I kept position and looked around the dining hall for some kind of hope, but they all just sat there, expressionless. I gave another tremendous heave, and a big whole chunk of food popped out of his throat and fell onto his plate. He began to breathe painfully.

I said, "Are you okay?"

Through teary eyes, he rasped, "Yes." And that was it.

They resumed their eating, picking up conversations where they had left off, not missing a beat. I thought, *What a hard place and hardened people.* Not another word was spoken or mentioned later about the incident. But God's hand was in it. He had by design, all the way from eternity past, positioned me to be there to save that man's life.

That night I didn't sleep. I stayed awake, fully expecting a mob to rush in and do their dirty work, but morning came instead. After lunch count, I was on my knees, praying. I had been fasting and asking God to be merciful. I asked Him, "Why would You send me here to this place to learn about Jesus only to get beat up and run off?" Then my name was called from the doorway. I looked up, and it was the head guy.

This is it! He's going to say, "Come to the showers. We want to have a word with you."

I gathered my courage and just came to terms that I was going to get it. When I got to the door and came face-to-face with him, the most unbelievable thing happened. He stuck his hand out to shake mine and said, "I don't have the right to tell you how to worship God. I was wrong. You have permission to keep attending your Bible studies. Just attend some of ours too to share it!"

My jaw dropped. God had torn down the barriers, kept me safe, softened the heart of my people, and granted me favor in the sight of all men. The Bible says in Proverbs 16:7, "When a man's ways please the Lord, he makes even his enemies to be at peace with him." Now, my people, my race, were certainly not my enemy. They saw that my walk and talk were genuine, that my efforts to know and serve God weren't just a front I was putting on. I proved that by taking a stand for Jesus when it could have cost me everything. And I'm not certain, but I think that saving one of the head guy's life, even while knowing he would carry out orders against me, may have had some influence. God had orchestrated everything perfectly; moreover, He taught me trust—that is, that I could trust Him completely.

When I married my wife, I told her all about Doyle, and she was excited to meet him. She applied for visitation, as I had a year before, and my mother did too. We finally all got approved and went to visit him together. My mother passed away on July 17, 2012, but we still got to visit on food visit days. Our relationship with this man of God continues to this very day. I thank my God and my people for allowing me to attend those Bible studies, as they were the foundation of my spiritual growth and a key factor in my continued success and ministry.

Friday nights and Sunday mornings were worship services. I especially loved Friday nights because the chaplain might bring in a preacher from the street or a whole group, such as the guys from California who had all been down and were now serving Jesus through Living Waters. But regardless of whoever came and was bringing the message, it was always a Holy Ghost–filled good time in the Lord. Service would last until the yard closed at ten o'clock at night. We would start with music, and to hear all those men lift their voices to the Lord was a treasure to my heart. There were so many men whose lives had been turned upside down and whose hearts had been as hard as stone, but the love of Christ had now touched them. Filthy mouths, once spitting hate and contempt, were now transformed into holy vessels of praise. It was absolutely amazing. No one held back, but all gave their whole heart to Jesus in song and worship. Those men were truly grateful for having been found and rescued by their Savior, Jesus Christ. Many fell to their knees in humble adoration and total submission to God in the presence of the Holy Spirit. Never have I seen so many imprisoned souls be set free.

Services on the outside seem to be diluted by contrast. Everyone has such busy lives that he or she wants to give God only thirty minutes of his or her busy schedule. People's attention spans for God seem to drift after that thirty-minute mark. They start to yawn and fidget, and they look at their watches or drift away in thought. It seems that no one is hungry for more and more God. They are consumed by their preoccupations. What we need is revival, a full-blown Holy Ghost encounter, just like the first day of Pentecost, complete with signs and wonders and speaking with new tongues. People just don't realize how good they have it until it's all taken away.

Those of us who have trodden a life of sorrow and loss have a different sense of appreciation for the restored order of things. Of course, there are those who live inside the prison of their own minds, suffering from depression or some horrible physical affliction, which entombs their souls and spirits in a broken body of decay. These, I think, are the ones who suffer the most, who long to be set free but are chained through no fault of their own. But I'm talking about the masses of people who take life for granted and are too busy to seek a deep, meaningful, and dynamic relationship with their Creator.

But there, where *you* are right now, *you* can sit still; *you* can begin to cultivate that relationship with God that will enrich your life and feed your spirit man. You can choose from this moment on to give your life to Jesus and let Him turn your life completely around. You had already begun your journey when you picked up this book, and by the very virtue that you have made it this far is evidence of your willingness to do whatever it takes to change your circumstances from the prison to the palace, from jail to jubilee, and from poor to plenty. Trust in Jesus to meet your needs. Don't leave the same way you came in. Cry out to God for deliverance. He is abundant in mercy and gracious to answer. He will pour out His love on you and be there when all else fails. When everyone you have trusted and cared for abandons you, God is there. Jesus is there, the Holy Spirit is there, and the Word of God is there, beckoning you into a relationship. Christianity is *not* a religion. It *is* a relationship with the living God through His Son, Jesus, the Christ, and the Spirit of holiness.

This is your divine appointment. It was no mistake that you picked up this book. Your heart needs mending. Your spirit strives to awaken. Your soul longs for knowledge, and your body seeks to be set free. There is One who holds the key, and what door He opens, no man can close; and what door He closes no man can open. Let Jesus open the door to your future and close the door to your past. Freedom is only a breath away. You know you need to do something differently. You know your way hasn't worked. You know you cannot do it by yourself. You know there's something out there greater than you. You know you were destined for something better, and you got trapped in a revolving door by an unseen power trying to keep you from your destiny and reaching your full potential. You know it's time to surrender to God and let Him rule your life. Your heart wants to believe, needs to believe. Brothers and sisters, your time has come. Second Corinthians 6:2 says, "For He says: 'In an acceptable time I have heard you, and in the day of salvation I have helped you.'" Jesus said in Revelation 3:19–21, "As many as I love, I rebuke and chasten. Therefore be zealous and repent. Behold, I stand at the door and knock. If anyone hears My voice and opens the door, I will come in to him and dine with him, and he with Me. To him who overcomes I will grant to sit with Me on My throne, as I also overcame and sat down with My Father on His throne."

Don't put it off another second. Join our hands and step into eternity with us. Stop holding onto the failures of the past and give them back. Your future is bright and full of hope and victory. You are a child of the Most High.

If you're ready to do what it takes to commit your life to Christ, repeat this prayer aloud:

> Father God, I am a sinner. I admit and confess my sins and need of a savior. I have lived my own life apart from You. I have hurt everyone around me, but most importantly, I hurt You. I am ready to repent and turn

back to You. Please accept my plea and forgive me. I believe Jesus is the Son of God and God incarnate. I believe He came to earth in human form to die for me. I accept His sacrifice on the cross on my behalf. I believe He died and rose again on the third day and is now seated at the right hand of power, interceding as our great High Priest. Lord Jesus, I accept You as my personal Lord and Savior. Come inside and cleanse me of all unrighteousness and make me fit for kingdom service. From now on my life is Yours. May Your will be done. I resist sin, Satan, and temptation on every level and renounce the works of the Devil, in Jesus's Name. Amen.

Congratulations! I'm so proud of you. You've decided to do what it takes to get yourselves back on track and give your life to Jesus. Your greatest days await you. From now on, as you follow in the footsteps of Jesus, you can be sure your future is secure. Not only have you stepped into eternity, but your current circumstances are being worked out as well. Some of you are going to see the miraculous happen immediately. Some of you will see charges reduced or dropped altogether. Do not forget that the Lord is the One who has done this and granted you a second chance. When you walk out those gates or that door, don't leave Jesus back inside. Take Him with you wherever you go. The street doesn't care about Jesus and the things of God, and it will certainly try to drag you back down to its gutters. But you now have weapons at your disposal: the name of Jesus, the blood of Jesus, and the Word of God.

For some of you, miracles have already begun. Some of you have started to receive mail again, some visits, some phones turned back on. All these things have come from the hands of the One who loves you and were pierced on your behalf. Never forget what He has done and continues to do in your daily life. James 1:16–18 says, "Do not be deceived, my beloved brethren. Every good gift and every perfect gift is from above, and comes down from the Father of lights, with whom there is no variation or shadow of turning. Of His own will He brought us forth by the word of truth, that we might be a kind of firstfruits of His creatures."

God loves to give—and give graciously. Don't take His love for granted. You know very well that those relationships and trust that is being restored right now is an act of God's mercy and kindness. Your family and loved ones see a change in you. They are hopeful and encouraged that this change is permanent. Be on guard for the Devil and his tricks and lies. You know his tactics now, so be vigilant and expose them by name when they surface and try to lead you backward, where only misery and hopelessness await. There are only three little tactics, but they are very powerful: (1) the lust of the flesh, (2) the lust of the eyes, and (3) the pride of life.

Be careful not to fall into an attitude of entitlement—you know, like "I deserve a cold beer. I worked hard all day." That is a trap. Be very careful about going back to old hangouts and seeing the old crowd. There's nothing there for you right now except temptation. Concentrate on feeding your spirit man. The spirit man's food is the Word of God. Period. *Do not* try to feed the spirit man with junk food, such as new age philosophies or any movement that claims spiritual enlightenment apart from Jesus. Jesus is the One God the Father has chosen to reveal and express Himself through. There is *no* other way. You will only confuse yourself by mixing belief systems with the Word of God. The Word of God rejects all counterfeits, so to mix is to reject God's revelation of Himself. Taking a little of this and a little of that and applying it here and there aren't pleasing steps to God. Philosophical mixing and applications are only our own efforts to achieve some special level of wisdom or enlightenment. It is self-willed and is rejecting of God and the truths He has set in place for humanity. This is the same autonomous trap and conduct that caused Eve to partake of the forbidden fruit. All religions and belief systems apart from Christ fall into this category. It is the Devil's intent and desire to pull as much worship away from God as he can. Any and all worship that is not given to God the Father through Jesus, His Christ, is either directly or inadvertently given to Satan. Remember what the Devil said in Isaiah 14:12–14:

How you are fallen from heaven,
O Lucifer son of the morning!
How you are cut down to the ground,
You who weakened the nations!
For you have said in your heart:
"I will ascend into heaven,
I will exalt my throne above the stars of God;
I will also sit on the mount of the congregation
On the farthest sides of the north;
I will ascend above the heights of the clouds,
I will be like the Most High."

Every single occult belief system ever created is of the Devil. If we start with Nimrod and the Tower of Babel (the first great pyramid) and every subsequent megalithic occult religion that spread across the globe afterward, you will find two things in common: First, they all claim that a serpent god came down from the stars and gave man "secret knowledge." That is what *occult* means. And second, they all not only read the stars but also brought the stars down to earth by building exact zodiac replicas on earth exactly aligned with the movement of the constellations. Star worship and serpent worship are devil worship any way you slice it. Just remain faithful and hold fast to these words.

For I want you to know what a great conflict I have for you and those in Laodicea, and for as many as have not seen my face in the flesh, that their hearts may be encouraged, being knit together in love, and attaining to all riches of the full assurance of understanding, to the knowledge of the mystery of God, both of the Father and of Christ, in whom are hidden all the treasures of wisdom and knowledge. Now this I say lest anyone should deceive you with persuasive words. For though I am absent in the flesh, yet I am with you in spirit, rejoicing to see your good order and the steadfastness of your faith in Christ. As you therefore have received

Christ Jesus the Lord, so walk in Him, rooted and built up in Him and established in the faith, as you have been taught, abounding in it with thanksgiving. Beware lest anyone cheat you through philosophy and empty deceit, according to the tradition of men, according to the basic principles of the world, and not according to Christ. *For in Him dwells all the fullness of the Godhead bodily; and you are complete in Him, who is the head of all principality and power.* (Col. 2:1–10 emphasis added).

We are adding some word definitions and topic commentaries in the back for your benefit. My wife and I thank you for taking this journey with us. We hope and pray that this shared experience will help you grow in Christ. You are *not* alone. There are other people out there like you who have made it. Your future is bright and secure.

There are two last things we would like to add to encourage you. During the rough draft writing of this book, I was waiting for the governing body of my denomination to approve my application for a general ministerial license. On March 12, 2015, the General Council of the Assemblies of God issued an official document approving my application. After seven years of training, waiting, jumping through hoops, and later schooling, I finally made it. On April 22, 2015, everyone in my cycle appeared for a special commissioning ceremony in Phoenix. If I can do it, so can you!

The second item we went to share is an opportunity to trust God for us that came up while waiting for our credentials. I'm referring to my wife when I say "our credentials." Though she has never applied or gone to school for ministry, we are nonetheless one, hence my reference to "our" credentials. Anyway, during the process there is, of course, a background and credit check. That's right, a credit check. Having a criminal history or bad credit doesn't immediately exclude you from the ministry. They just want to make sure your debts are satisfied both to society and any financial institutions. So as a result of my inquiry, a very old debt surfaced. I had taken out a student loan roughly fifteen years ago and never paid it back. I had pretty much dismissed it because it was so old, and I hadn't heard anything about it for a very long time. Well ... God wants us out of debt. I'm not referring to mortgages or loans in good standing. I'm talking about bad debt.

So anyway, my original principle was only a couple thousand dollars, but the interest had accrued to a whopping $10,000. When I opened the letter, I was sick to my stomach. How was I going to tell my wife? So I did what any normal guy would do ... I *freaked out*! I put the letter in my Bible and hoped it would disappear, but it didn't. Instead, a second notice appeared and then a third. I knew God was working out my debit situation by shoving it in my face. It wasn't going to go away. He wanted me to deal with it. He wanted me to trust Him.

So I told my wife, and of course she was very unhappy. I had blindsided her with a debt she didn't have anything to do with. All her life she had been prudent and was very careful not to overspend and to save. Now here I was, asking her to accept this debt as her own. I can't tell you how ashamed and embarrassed I was. It was my entire fault. There was no excuse. But because she is a woman of God, she tried her best to understand. We took the matter to the Lord in prayer. "Father God, I brought this debt into our marriage at no fault of my wife's. It is too much to bear in its entirety. Ten thousand dollars is too much. We cast our cares upon You because You care for us. We commit our finances to You, Lord. Thank You for helping us, in Jesus's name, amen."

I contacted an attorney to see whether the debit was forgivable, but because it was a federal loan, it wasn't. But as God often does, He didn't allow help to come from man. He wanted us to trust Him. So I called the collection agency and pled my case. I was expecting a payment plan at a reduced rate of perhaps eight thousand, but the Lord showed up and reduced it by $5,000. He could have wiped it out entirely, sure. But it was proper that I learn a lesson about debt, so He allowed there to remain some interest. My wife still wasn't very happy with me, and understandably so, but cutting the debt in half, I would say, is favor from the Lord. We are mailing the payment off today.

I want to thank all of you friends out there for allowing me to share so much of our lives with you. It has been an honor to walk this journey with you. It is our sincere desire to see you all set free and walking in victory. It is also our desire to see the establishment of a discipleship where people who are incarcerated can go after serving out their sentences to receive instruction. Also, we hope to be able to form a working relationship with the courts and probation departments as an alternative sentencing structure to jail or prison. God willing, by the time this book is published, He will have made a way for that to happen. Amen.

TOPICAL STUDY GUIDE

ANOINTING

This word means to authorize, commission, or set apart. In this regard, it is closely related to the term *sanctify*. But anointing is both the physical and, more importantly, the spiritual outflow of authoritative power from its source. It is the anointing "authority" that makes the person or object sanctified. In the Old Testament kings, priests, prophets, and the articles of the sanctuary were anointed with oil. The oil signified the invisible presence of the Holy Spirit, who brought, gave, and maintained the anointing. Once an object or person is anointed, he or she becomes holy unto the Lord, set apart for God's special purpose, and authorized to act and speak and perform functions on His behalf.

Jesus is the Anointed One, as described by His title Messiah or Christ. Jesus is the One God the Father chose to carry His full authority in every respect. There isn't one single aspect, atom, or particle in all of creation, whether it be in this physical world or the spirit realm in this dimension or any other, that isn't subject to Christ's authority.

Transference of the anointing:

1. Jesus received His anointing for earthly ministry. See Matthew 3:13–17; Mark 1:9–11; Luke 3:21–22; and John 1:29–34.
2. Jesus commissioned all believers and transferred His anointing or authority. See Matthew 28:16–20; Mark 16:14–18; Luke 24:36–49; John 20:19–23; and Acts 1:4–8.
3. Jesus's anointing was effectually transferred into the earthly realm. See Luke 10:17–20 and Acts 2:1–39.

4. What was the purpose of the anointing?
   a. Discernment of the truth (1 John 2:24–27)
   b. Practical life application, prophecy, glorification of Jesus, and revelation of knowledge (John 16:13–15)
   c. Teaching and recollection of Scripture (John 14:26)
   d. Evangelism and discipleship (Matt. 28:18–20; Mark 16:15; Luke 24:48–49; John 20:21–22; Acts 1:8)
5. Second meaning: In the New Testament, anointing is associated with healing. A medicinal salve and/or oil is applied to the sick. In Mark 6:13, we see the results of the Twelve acting under Jesus's authority. James 5:13–18 brings even more clarity to this medicinal type of anointing. There are some elements added that reinforce the spiritual principle behind the anointing.
   a. Verse 14 says, "Let him [*the sick*] call for the elders of the church". Why the elders? Because the elders are spiritually mature Christians who are "prayed up." That is, they have given themselves over to a prayer curriculum. They are "prayer warriors" who bombard heaven with prayers of all types and are open and sensitive to the Holy Spirit.
   b. Verse 14: Here, "anointing him with oil" is tied directly to its power source "in the Name of the Lord." The oil represents the "power" of the Holy Spirit. But it's the name of the Lord Jesus who grants authority to use that power.
   c. Verses 15 and 16: Here "the prayer of faith" and "the effective, fervent prayer" denote the relationship between the person praying and God, who supplies the answer. It underscores the total dependence on God for provision. It reveals the nature of prayer that is "effective." And it shows the urgent, determined purpose of the one praying as "fervent."

BAPTISM

There are three types: water baptism, baptism of the Holy Spirit, and baptism in the Holy Spirit. First, let's look at the word in Greek, *baptizo* (Strong's Greek #907): it comes from the prime root word *bapto* (Strong's Greek #911), which means "to dip" or "to dye." *Baptizo* means "to immerse, submerge," literally "to dip under water." The world is specific to ceremonial consecration. It stands in contrast to *antexoma* (Strong's Greek #472), which means "to sprinkle, hold fast to, hold firmly to." There are seven occurrences in the New Testament of using the word *baptize*, and every single one uses the Greek word *baptize*, "to submerge." Jesus Himself was baptized by John his cousin (John the Baptist). The Scripture says in both Matthew 3:16 and Mark 1:10 that Jesus "came up out of the water." He was totally and completely submerged.

(Note: Jesus wasn't baptized because He needed to repent of sin. The Scripture says in Matthew 3:13–17 that the reason for Jesus's baptism was to "fulfill all righteousness." By Jesus's obedience to the ordinance, He (1) confirmed John's ministry, (2) led by example the model for humility and obedience, (3) fulfilled the Father's will, and (4) received the Holy Spirit's anointing to empower His coming ministry.)

Another overlooked clue into John the Baptist's ministry is found in John 1:29–34, especially verse 31. "But that He [*Jesus*] should be revealed to Israel, therefore I came baptizing with water". To better understand Jesus's baptism, let's go back in time and take it step by step.

1. Genesis 1:26; 2:7 (Man is created in God's image.)

2. Genesis 3:1–24 (The image fell.)

3. Isaiah 60:1–11 (The Word of salvation was spoken into the earthly realm in pre-incarnate form.)

4. John 1:1, 14 (The Word, "Jesus," is sent to earth.)

5. Matthew 3:16 (Jesus received His anointing and was commissioned. He was baptized.)

6. Luke 4:18 (Jesus embodied the word of salvation in incarnate form.)

7. John 28:19–30 (Jesus fulfilled the prophetic Word.)

Just as the Holy Spirit empowered the word of creation to uphold all things (in other words, mass, atomic structure, and the law of physics), so did Jesus need the empowerment of the Holy Spirit. Jesus is the living, eternal Word in bodily form, and He must be one with the Holy Spirit to perform the functions of His office. In summary, Jesus's baptism was the Word of God in flesh form receiving its power.

Again, the Greek word *baptize* means "to immerse or submerge." Jesus's model for us is total and complete immersion, all the way underwater. For us, water baptism is a commandment from Jesus. It's one of the two ordinances for the New Testament church, the other being Holy Communion (Matt. 28:19; Mark 16:15–16).

Our reason for water baptism:

1. It is a commandment (Matt. 28:19; Mark 16:15–16).

2. It shows the relationship and workings of the Holy Spirit under the new covenant (Col. 2:11–12).

3. It is faith in action as we enter into the salvation that came through Christ's death, burial, and resurrection. Our conscience is clear toward God, knowing that He has provided atonement for our sins through Jesus's sacrifice. It is not baptism that saves, but it's the finished works of the cross the baptism represents that saves (1 Peter 3:18–21).

4. It's our public announcement of our allegiance to Christ. It is an outward sign of an inward work of the Holy Spirit and God's Word made alive to us. And finally it identifies us with Christ

in totality: His death (sacrifice for sin), burial (our putting to death our old ways and character), and resurrection (the promise of eternal life in the coming age and newness of life in this age victoriously led by the Holy Spirit). See Romans 6:4–6.

In summary, water baptism is a commandment from Jesus Himself. The formula is found in Matthew 28:19. "In the Name of the Father, the Son, and the Holy Spirit." By definition, it is total and complete submergence in water. And it's our public duty as a Christian and an announcement to the world that we now fly the banner of Jesus Christ, the King of Kings and Lord of Lords, over our lives. Amen.

The second type is the baptism *of* the Holy Spirit. This is commonly mistaken for the third type, which is the baptism *in* or *with* the Holy Spirit. Let us examine 1 Corinthians 12:13: "For by one Spirit we were all baptized into one body—whether Jews or Greeks, whether slaves or free—and have all been made to drink into one Spirit." Here, clearly the Holy Spirit is the subject doing the action of baptizing believers into the body, the spiritual kingdom of Christ. We are immersed into an invisible family unit supplied by the storehouses of heaven for every need, including spiritual, emotional, and physical needs.

The third type of baptism is the baptism *in* or *with* the Holy Spirit. First, we must understand that it's Jesus who is doing the baptizing (Matt. 3:11; Mark 1:6–8; Luke 3:15–16; John 1:32–33). Note: After Jesus's water baptism, immediately coming up out of the water, He too received the baptism in or with the Holy Spirit. The Scriptures reveal that upon receiving the Holy Spirit, Jesus began His earthly ministry. He healed the sick, cast out devils, and performed miracle after miracle. If Jesus Himself needed the power of the Holy Spirit, how much more so do we?

Observe: The account in Luke 24:44–49 is fulfilled in Acts, the whole book. But in chapters 1 and 2, we see it all unfolding just as Jesus said it would. The need for Holy Spirit–empowered ministry is manifested in the resulting propagation of the gospel. Acts 1:5 records about 120 people present, praying, and waiting. Then in Acts 2:1–4, the Holy Spirit was poured out on the 120. They began to speak in other tongues (other known languages of the world that were unknown to them) the wonderful works of God. They began preaching under the power, influence, and authority of the Holy Spirit, and the result was exponential. Acts 2:40–47 records that the 120 Spirit-filled believers turned into three thousand, and then more were added daily, as we see in verse 47. Acts 4:4 records yet another whopping five thousand, and so the church grew and multiplied until this present hour. That is why we need the baptism *in* the Holy Spirit. Everyone receives the baptism *of* the Holy Spirit at conversion, when the Holy Spirit baptizes us into the family of God, the body of Christ, and seals us unto salvation. But for empowered ministry and growth to take place, we must have all the fullness of the Holy Spirit.

The baptism *in* or *with* the Holy Spirit is for *everyone today*! Observe Luke 24:49: "Behold, I send the Promise of My Father upon you; but tarry in the city of Jerusalem until you are endued with power from on high." Also see Acts 2:39: "For the promise is to you and to your children, and to all who are afar off, as many as the Lord our God will call." Did you see that? The promise is for *everyone*! *Today*! So how do we get it? Good question.

1. Present yourself (covered in the blood of Jesus). See Hebrews 4:16.

2. Through faith (be thirsty, hungry). See Isaiah 55:12; John 4:13–15; 7:37–38; and Revelation 22:16–17.

3. Ask. Luke 11:9–13 says, "So I say to you, ask, and it will be given to you; seek, and you will find; knock, and it will be opened to you. For everyone who asks receives, and he who seeks finds, and to him who knocks it will be opened. If a son asks for bread from any father among you, will he give him a stone? Or if he asks for a fish, will he give him a serpent instead of a fish? Or if he asks for an egg, will he offer him a scorpion? If you then, being evil, know how to give good gifts to your children, how

much more will your heavenly Father give the Holy Spirit to those who ask Him!"

In summary, the baptism in or with the Holy Spirit is our being totally immersed or submerged in the Holy Spirit. Jesus is the One doing the baptizing, and it is for empowered ministry and victorious living for everyone today.

CIVIL GOVERNMENT

We added this section for obvious reasons. Where you are right now illustrates that civil government means little or nothing to you. Your poor choices have caused grief and have affected not only you but also all who care about you. Observe Proverbs 14:11–13:

> The house of the wicked will be overthrown,
> But the tent of the upright will flourish.
> There is a way that seems right to a man,
> But its end is the way of death.
> Even in laughter the heart may sorrow,
> And the end of mirth may be grief.

So the way to circumvent unwanted grief is to be submissive to rule—first to God's rule, then that of the civil authority. You are at the point now that you not only understand you've done wrong but also are ready to accept responsibility and start moving forward in life. The rules our governments establish are for the best interest of society as a whole. Where you are right now, you have rules set in place both by the institutions you're in and by your own race. These rules set boundaries and help keep order.

But the most important truth to understand is that God Himself puts authority in place. If those in positions of authority abuse that authority, they will ultimately have to answer to God. So don't go to fretting or using a grumpy CO or DO (Correction and Detention

Officer) or corrupt official to make a case for your own selfish ambitions. If you see an injustice or are subject to one, just take it to God and let Him deal with it. Pray for those in authority, even if they are being mean or are mistreating you. God sees your plight, and He will work it out if you are serving Him. Unless a civil authority asks you to break the law or deny Jesus, obey the law (Rom. 13:1–7; 1 Peter 2:13–17).

HOLY COMMUNION (OR THE LORD'S SUPPER)

This and baptism form the ordinances of the church. They are both done publicly as declarations and as memorials to the death, burial, and resurrection of Jesus, the Christ. The promise of eternal life that comes with His sacrificial atonement is celebrated and commemorated. The Scriptures show that it was during the Passover meal that Jesus instituted the ordinance (Matt. 26:17–29; Mark 14:12–25; Luke 22:7–22; and 1 Corinthians 11:23–26). In the author's opinion, the meaning of the Lord's Supper has been distorted and hijacked. The focus has been taken off Christ and placed on the elements: the bread and the fruit of the vine. Jesus is the central figure in all things, including the ordinance of Holy Communion.

Jesus's Last Supper, the Passover meal, was as intimate and personal as it could get. The main point in sharing the meal, both for them and for us, is fellowship in anticipation of the Lord's return. What does it mean to have fellowship? Ultimately Jesus said it best (John 17:20–26). How beautiful these words are; how full and complete this prayer is that we should have unity and the provision and comfort of being one with God. It truly is beyond our understanding to fully grasp all that means for humanity. To explore and exhaust this study topic would be too great in volume for this book. But search the Scriptures yourself and discover the beauty and simplicity of this ordinance, and then examine yourself (prove, test) daily and boldly, graciously partake of Holy Communion, and be filled with the joy and power of Christ.

FASTING

First, let's look at the nature of fasting. There is only one fast God demanded, which is recorded in the Law of Moses. It is related to the Day of Atonement. *Atonement* means to pardon or forgive. Thus, the Day of Atonement was the most solemn holy day of all the feasts and festivals. It was the day when the High Priest would once a year enter the Holy of Holies and make a sacrifice for himself of a bullock and be ceremonially clean and properly dressed in holy garments. Then and *only* then could he enter into the Holy of Holies, where God's presence enthroned the mercy seat and God would pardon the sins of the people for the year.

The sacrifices came from the flocks of the people. In ancient times, one's wealth and livelihood was determined and provided for by the animals he or she owned. It was costly to give up an animal, even just one. So the weight and burden of atonement were cause for serious reflection. Ultimately, the price for humanity's atonement would cost God the price of the life of His only begotten Son, Jesus, the Christ. So God required a fast for that day by law so the people could acknowledge that they couldn't provide atonement on their own for themselves. The clearest example of this is when Adam and Eve tried to cover their sin with fig leaves, but God made them tunics of skin. That meant that an innocent animal had to die to cover (make atonement for) their sin.

So respectively, fasting is the humbling of oneself for the purpose of reflection and God's provision. But elsewhere throughout the Bible we find the theme of fasting. Apart from the Day of Atonement, fasting was practiced as a means of urgency for God to address a distressful situation. Whether it was impending war or the death of someone, many of the Bible's biggest characters prayed and fasted for God's intervention or answers.

Second, let's look at the formula for fasting. Generally speaking, fasting is the abstinence of food or water or both, but it is not limited to either. One can fast from anything that has become a priority in life that takes one's focus off God. For instance, sports, whether playing or watching—one can spend time engaged in either as a participant.

So if one abstains from any activity that puts its focus on God, one is technically fasting. But traditional fasting is abstaining from food or water or both. The concept behind fasting is to remove the flesh from the equation and humble oneself before God.

Fasting can be an individual practice or a corporate one. Moses fasted forty days and nights. The result was an audience with God Himself and the writing and receiving of the Ten Commandments. He also received many other instructions concerning moral and ceremonial laws and governmental instruction (Exodus 20—40).

Corporate fasting is where a leader calls for the whole assembly to fast. These are extreme instances of an urgent need for God to respond to a situation. King Jehoshaphat called for a fast in all of Judah when he was faced with three opposing enemies, who had joined forces against him (2 Chron. 20:1–30).

Two examples of fasting, given to us in the New Testament, are found in Acts 13:1–3 and Acts 14:21–23. In both instances we find that fasting and praying were directly tied to evangelization and church leadership. The understanding of the great need for instruction and direction from the Holy Spirit was manifest through the fast and prayer.

When answering His disciples on why they had failed to cast out a demon from a boy, Jesus said, "This kind come out by nothing but prayer and fasting" (Mark 9:29). There was apparently an element of unbelief in both the boy's father and Jesus's disciples, but it's not clear whom Jesus was addressing. Perhaps both. But whatever the case may have been, the unbelief was tied to a misunderstanding of one's power and provision as it flows from the source in accordance with the will of God. Jesus knew that it takes extra spiritual exercise to walk this earth and meet every challenge. Olympic athletes don't just do a few pushups and say, "Okay, I'm ready to compete." They spend their whole lives training for that one moment of competition. Jesus's extracurricular prayer life exemplified his faith, which included fasting.

The last example of corporate prayer we will examine is taken from the Old Testament. We chose to include this example to demonstrate God's involvement in this fast. It comes from the book of the prophet Jonah. You remember Jonah, don't you? He's the guy the big fish swallowed; he was in his belly for three days. We won't explore that aspect of the story but rather focus on Jonah's mission. Jonah was given instructions to go to Ninevah, "that great city," and cry out against it. Ninevah has huge spiritual significance. Nimrod, Noah's great-grandson, built the city.

In Jonah's day, roughly 770 BC, Ninevah had already been a great city for thousands of years. But as great as the city was, its wickedness was even greater. God told Jonah to go and "cry out," proclaim against, or warn the people of the city that judgment was coming. Jonah, of course, as the story goes, disobeyed and tried running from God and His mission. That's how he ended up in the belly of the fish. But that's not our study point. God told Jonah to go because He saw the great need of humanity in the midst of its rebellion.

Jonah 4:11 reveals that there were more than one hundred and twenty thousand persons lost and dying in their sins. They had no direction, no instruction, and they were perishing. Jonah didn't want to go because they were pagan Gentiles. They were a noncovenant people and long-standing enemies of Israel. But God wanted to extend His mercy, grace, and message of salvation to all humanity. God's objective was to invoke a heart of repentance so He could relent and stay the coming judgment.

So Jonah did as he was instructed. We see the result in Jonah 3:5–10. The people believed God. The king proclaimed a fast for the whole city, both man and beast. Talk about a corporate fast! The result in verse 10 was that "God saw their works that they turned from their evil way; and God relented."

In summary, fasting is seeking God by acknowledging our total dependence on Him. Abstaining from food or water or both stands in contrast to our first parents' partaking of the forbidden fruit. We choose either autonomy or dependence. When we remove the flesh out of the way to seek God, He honors that effort.

1. Choose a subject for your fast (in other words, ministry, your pastor, family or friends to come to Christ, direction).

2. Proclaim the fast. How many days as well as food, water, or both?

3. Commit yourself spiritually, emotionally, and physically. Have the resolve to finish what you start.

4. Set time aside for prayer during your fast and stick to the schedule.

5. Choose Scripture verses that pertain to your need and speak them aloud to God during your fast, especially during your scheduled prayer time. Remember, God is watching over His Word to perform it. Jeremiah 1:12, says, "Then the Lord said to me, 'You have seen well, for I am ready to perform My word.'" Isaiah 55:11 says, "So shall My word be that goes forth from My mouth; it shall not return to Me void, but it shall accomplish what I please, and it shall prosper in the thing for which I sent it." When we speak the Word of God in faith, over and into our circumstances, especially when fasting and praying, God brings that word to pass. Amazing! Remember that fasting is intensely personal and doesn't force God to act out our will but rather aligns us with His. May you find joy and a deeper relationship with God as you dedicate your fast. Amen.

FITTING IN

Now that you've given your life to Jesus, you may find there is some difficulty fitting in. The people you once entertained and the places you hung out in won't have the same appeal they once did. It's time to reflect on new life-giving principles. Don't get discouraged if your family or friends reject, scoff, or even downright laugh at you. They are going to find it hard to believe that you aren't the same old you. Some of them will actually get mad, ridicule, and challenge your faith. They don't want a new you. They like the old you. They will do everything they can to make you fall and go back to hopelessness because that is where they are. Some will actually hate you for your newfound faith in Jesus. But don't be discouraged. It isn't really you they hate but the Jesus inside you. Here are some Scripture verses to comfort you during these times. And take heart because God will honor you, begin to rebuild your life, and surround you with like-minded believers to minister to you and strengthen you (Matthew 5:11; 10:24-26; Mark 10:29-30; John 15:18-21; 1 Peter 4:12-16)

SABBATH

This can be a very complex and hotly debated topic, but by definition the word means "rest" or "cessation." Genesis 2:1–3 records the institution of the Sabbath, though it's not mentioned by name, until Exodus 16. The Sabbath is more than a day of rest. It's a day to reflect on the provision of God. But it's more than that—much more. It's a day on which God's presence is brought down to meet His people. The Ten Commandments record the Sabbath day as the fourth commandment, but the Sabbath precedes the Law of Moses. It's the law of a Sabbath rest from creation that inexorably ties creation, redemption, rest, man, God, time, and space all together.

When you read verses like Exodus 31:13–16 and Isaiah 66:22–23 side by side, you could surmise that the Sabbath observance is perpetual. And also consider that Genesis 2:1–7 (the end of the creation account) doesn't record an evening at the end of the seventh day. Once could conclude that the Sabbath observance stands forever. But we must also view this in light of New Testament Scripture concerning the Sabbath.

Hebrews 4:1–10 is the most concise description of the Sabbath and its meaning. "Rest" is the central theme, while faith and disobedience are contrasting bookends on the subject. The Greek word used for "rest" in verse 9 is *sabbatismos*, which literally means "Sabbath rest." It is used only once in the entire New Testament. The idea the author of Hebrews is trying to convey is that the fulfillment of the Sabbath rest is found in Jesus. Jesus said, "Do not think that I have come to abolish the law. . . but to fulfill it." (Mathew 5:17 NIV) When we move from merely hearing about Jesus to actually believing in Him, we enter into that rest. All attempts to earn our way into heaven through works are futile. The Scriptures plainly tell us that. Ephesian 2:8–9 (KJV) says, "For by grace are ye saved through faith; and that not of yourselves: it is the gift of God Not of works, lest any man should boast."

It is worthy to note one Scripture verse here for clarification. Philippians 2:12 says, "Therefore, my beloved, as you have always obeyed, not as in my presence only, but now much more in my absence, work out your own salvation with fear and trembling." This verse doesn't mean that we through works earn salvation. It must be read in the context of verses 12–16. Our good works are a product of our salvation, not a means of achieving it. Therefore, when we come to Christ, we find that rest or enter into it, and our lives become a product of God's love for us.

Let us conclude this topic with two more Scripture verses. Colossians 2:16–17 says, "So let no one judge you in food or in drink, or regarding a festival or a new moon or sabbaths, which are a shadow of things to come, but the substance is of Christ." The New Testament is clear that all methods of worship, sacrifices, and observances foreshadowed Jesus who is the image who makes the shadow. Just like a person walking with the rising sun to his or her back casts a long shadow before him or her, so did Christ cast His shadow on the earth and the hearts of man in the revelation of Himself through the Holy Scriptures. Jesus is the substance of Sabbath rest. He is our Sabbath rest.

Now that all being said, let's take a look at one final Scripture verse. Romans 14:4–6 says, "Who are you to judge another's servant? To his own master he stands or falls. Indeed, he will be made to stand, for God is able to make him stand. One person esteems one day above another; another esteems every day alike. Let each be fully convinced in his own mind. He who observes the day, observes it to the Lord; and he who does not observe the day, to the Lord he does not observe it."

It is not the author's intention to impose a restriction or sway the reader one way or the other. It is his intention for the reader to search the Scriptures and draw his or her own conclusion while cultivating a dynamic relationship with Jesus Christ. Whether you choose to observe the true Sabbath day, the seventh day, or observe Sunday, the first day of the week, as a day of rest, it's up to you. Contemporary times observe the first day of the week, Sunday, because Jesus rose from the dead on that day. A new week of life begins in Him. Let the Holy Spirit fully convince you on this matter and be content in your own heart, letting others do the same, that there be no contention on this matter among the body of Christ.

STEWARDSHIP

This means care, distribution, conservation, financial soundness. In a nutshell, it means management. As human beings we are entrusted with life. All life on earth is subject to man who, in turn, is subject to God. God has entrusted men with all life on earth. God is the source of all life. As God's image bearer, we must do our very best to conserve and manage the things God has given us. The most precious resource we have been entrusted with is our children. Many of us have failed miserably as parents, but it's not too late. God, the God of restoration, is able to raise us up and become the parents God called us to be.

For more on stewardship and Christian duty, please read the following: Matthew 25:14–46; Luke 12:35–48; Acts 4:32–37; Romans 1:14–17; 12:1–8; Colossians 1:24–28; and 1 Peter 4:10–11.

TITHING

Basically the tithe is a percent of one's income that one gives back to the Lord from which all wealth comes (Deut. 8:17–18; Prov. 10:22; 1 Chron. 29:12). The principle of tithing isn't about the money. It is about acknowledging the Lord as the source of all things.

The reason for the tithe is found in Numbers 18:21–32. It was the portion allotted to the Levitical priesthood, those who served God day and night. All the other tribes of Israel received portions of land as an inheritance as they entered Canaan but not the Levites. God was their inheritance, and the tithe was their portion of food and money. So the tithe served two purposes: (1) it helped support the priests and their families, and (2) it paid for repairs and articles for the sanctuary and later temples.

There is only one place in the Bible where God tells man to test Him. Malachi 3:9–11 says,

> "You are cursed with a curse,
> For you have robbed Me,
> Even this whole nation.
> Bring all the tithes into the storehouse,
> That there may be food in My house,
> And try Me now in this,"
> Says the Lord of hosts,
> "If I will not open for you the windows of heaven
> And pour out for you such blessing
> That there will not be room enough to receive it.
> And I will rebuke the devourer for your sakes,
> So that he will not destroy the fruit of your ground,
> Nor shall the vine fail to bear fruit for you in the field,"
> Says the Lord of hosts.

In this verse, God implores His people to keep up their end of the bargain so God's corrective posture can be removed and a blessing can issue forth. God is a God of mercy and justice. His priests weren't being taken care of, and repairs weren't being done because people weren't tithing or were holding back some for themselves. They were greedy and not trusting God to meet their needs. He responded by saying, "I will open the windows of heaven and pour out a blessing that you cannot contain!" What a promise if we will only trust Him and be obedient.

Some folks today say, "The tithe was only for the Israelites at that time. There is no mention of a tithe in the New Testament." Well, they are partly correct. There is no mention of a "tithe" in the New Testament in relation to Christian giving. But the tithing principle precedes the Law of Moses. We first see the tithe appear in Genesis 14:18–20, and again we see Jacob, Abraham's grandson, reinforce it in Genesis 28:20–22. Here we see the tithe directly tied to a vow. Jacob prophetically acknowledged God's provision, and in so doing it, he vowed to return a tenth (that is, 10 percent) of all his earnings to God.

God honored Jacob's vow to the point that it became a statute and governing principle for Israel. God made it a law in Leviticus 27:30–32 because of Jacob's vow in Genesis 28:20–22. There is no record of God's requiring a tithe from either Abraham or Jacob. They both gave of their own free will as an acknowledgment of God's provision. It didn't become a requirement for Israel until after Jacob's vow. Remember that God changed Jacob's name to Israel in Genesis 35:9–11, so Jacob's vow carried over to an entire nation called by his new name Israel.

There are several New Testament and contemporary applications: although, no doubt, for many of the Jews in Jesus's day, their tithe continued as the Pharisees would have seen to that, but what about the newly birthed church? Jews and Gentiles alike formed the church. To the unbelieving Jews, the converted Jews would have been in apostasy and considered unfit to receive any help from the temple treasury. The new church would have been filled to the brim with widows and orphans, and with people in great need of daily supplies, as mentioned in Acts 6:1.

To meet this need and as a result of their new faith in Jesus, the rich sold all they had and threw it into one purse, then redistributed it so none lacked anything (Acts 4:32–25). But Christianity was growing fast—so fast, in fact, that within three hundred years Christianity overtook four thousand years of paganism and forced the Roman Emperor Constantine to make Christianity the official religion of Rome (but that's another story). Growth like that demanded supply and support. Today's missionaries are provided for in the exact same way. Our churches today collect tithes and offerings to help support every aspect of ministry from the local pastor and his family to the missionary and his family in a far and distant country. The tithe pays the bills to keep the church doors open. It puts food in the food banks. It keeps the soup kitchens open. Orphanages are built and staffed. Church property is bought, and buildings are erected. The list goes on and on.

When we by faith enter into Jacob's vow, we also enter into Jacob's blessings. Doing God's work is the greatest honor and privilege any human being can do. We should do it with a glad and generous heart, knowing we cannot out-give God. Here are some Scripture verses supporting our giving and its results. May our Lord Jesus Christ, who gave it all for us, grant you a generous and giving spirit. Amen (Luke 6:38; 1 Cor. 9:7–14; 16:1–3; 2 Cor. 8–9; Gal. 6:6–10; Phil. 2:4; 4:14–20.)

TRUST

This means absolute confidence, unequivocal hope, and unwavering faith. Aside from the message of salvation itself, trust is one of the main themes in the Bible. We should put our trust and confidence in God alone and not in man or any created thing. With man's quest to be autonomous and self-sufficient comes the never-ending concerns and worries that he or she is never doing well enough. The only way to escape this nagging feeling of impending failure is to stop trusting in ourselves and hand over our lives to God.

Trust and faith go hand in hand, but trust is born out of faith. Faith is a gift from God (Eph. 2:8–10). By His will, God has placed in us a measure of faith. It is our jobs and privilege to exercise our faith through a living and abiding trust. Trust is the action of faith.

The King James Version records 191 variations of the word *trust*. Forty-four are found in Psalms alone. When God brought me to my knees so He could begin restoring me, He took me to the place called "trust." That is the name I gave to the set of circumstances that drew me into a relationship with God the Father, God the Son, and God the Holy Spirit. In that time, God removed everything, all external support of any kind from my life. I was totally indigent and completely dependent on God for any provision. He lovingly and faithfully did this to reveal my condition, my spiritual condition. We as humans tend to measure success by the things we have. God had to strip all that away from me so I could see my true self and my desperate need for Him. It was in that place,(the place of trust,) where I confessed not only my sins and my need of a savior but also my complete dependence on God for all things. If I could trust God enough for my salvation, then I could certainly trust Him enough to supply all my needs.

Where you all are right now may or may not be your place of trust. But please don't miss the opportunity if it is. If you have found yourself at the end of your rope, with no place else to look but up, then God has found you. Reach out to Him and take His hand. He will not lead you astray. Your time of running is over. It's time to rest and be refreshed and restored. God is able to turn your life around. All you have to do is let Him. If you are ready for a new life filled with God's holy fire, let the love of Christ transform your heart. Cry out to God and say, "I am ready, Lord. *Do whatever it takes!*" Amen.

NOTES

[1] Ginger Allen, "From Dust to Dust," February 15, 2012, https://answersingenesis.org/human-body/from-dust-to-dust/.

[2] Lehman Strauss, "Man a Trinity (Spirit, Soul Body)" from the series *Death and Afterward,* https://bible.org/seriespage/2-man-trinity-spirit-soul-body, and Watchman Nee, *The Spiritual Man* (New York: Christian Fellowship, 1968), 25-35.

[3] *Nelson's New Illustrated Bible Dictionary,* rev. ed., s.vv. "Jesus," "Messiah," and Herbert Lockyer, *All the Men of the Bible* (Grand Rapids: Zondervan, 1967), 363-369.

[4] Peter W. Stoner and Robert C. Newman, *Science Speaks: scientific proof of the accuracy of prophecy and the bible* (Chicago: Moody, 1969), 106.

[5] Philip Schaff, *History of the Christin Church,* vol. 2, Ante-Nicene Christianity, A.D. 100-325, 3rd ed. rev. (Grand Rapids, MI: Christian Classics Ethereal Library, 1882), CD_ROM, created 2002.

[6] *Nelson's New Illustrated Bible Dictionary,* rev. ed., s.v. "Hebrew."

[7] Ibid., s.v. "Nero," and commentary notes on Matt. 24:15, *New Spirit-Filled Life Bible* (Nashville: Thomas Nelson, 2002), 1335.

[8] See articles entitled "82nd Airborne Division: 'All American'/'America's Guard of Honor'" at http://globalsecurity.org/military/agency/army/82ndabn.htm, and "82nd Airborne History" at http://www.bragg.army.mil.

[9] Commentary notes on Gen. 2:0, *New Spirit-Filled Life Bible* (Nashville: Thomas Nelson, 2002), 7.

[10] *Nelson's New Illustrated Bible Dictionary,* rev. ed., s.v. "Helper."

[11] "Kingdom Dymnamics on Prov. 12:4, The Wife: A Crown to Her Husband," in the Dynamic "Women in God's Design," *New Spirit-Filled Life Bible* (Nashville: Thomas Nelson, 2002).

[12] Commentary on Prov. 31:10-31, *New Spirit-Filled Life Bible* (Nashville: Thomas Nelson), 840, and Strong's #2428 #2342b, NAS Exhaustive Concordance, http://www.biblehub.com.

[13] *Nelson's New Illustrated Bible Dictionary,* rev. ed., s.v. "Holy."

[14] Word study on Strong's #5087, #3056, #2643, and #243 taken from *Strong's Concordance, NAS Exhaustive Concordance,* and the NASB translations found on http://www.biblehub.com.

[15] Word study on Strong's #3004, #1610, #1537, and #4492 taken from *Strong's Concordance* and *HELPS Word-studies,* 1987, on http://biblehub.com.

[16] Nelson's New Illustrated Bible Dictionary, rev, ed., s.v. "consecration."

[17] Word study on Strong's # 4336, #4314, and #2172 taken from *Strong's Concordance* and *HELPS Word-studies,* 1987 on http://www.biblehub.com.

[18] Word study on Strong's #266 taken from *Strong's Concordance* and *HELPS Word-studies,* 1987, on http://www.biblehub.com.

[19] *Nelsons New Illustrated Bible Dictionary,* s.v. "Doxology,"

[20] The title "The Gifts of the Godhead, its outline, and its general theme were expounded on and taken from the *New Spirit Filled Life Bible* (Nashville: Thomas Nelson, 2002).

CPSIA information can be obtained at www.ICGtesting.com
Printed in the USA
BVOW05s0010310516

449879BV00001B/1/P